6,000+
ESSENTIAL SPANISH WORDS

Expand Your Vocabulary!

LIVING LANGUAGE®

6,000+
ESSENTIAL
SPANISH WORDS

Expand Your Vocabulary!

**SPANISH TRANSLATION, EXERCISES,
SITUATIONS, AND GUIDE TO PREFIXES BY**
Enrique Montes

Published in the United States by Living Language, A Random House Company

www.livinglanguage.com

Editor: Suzanne McQuade
Production Editor: John Whitman
Production Managers: Helen Kilcullen and Heather Lanigan
Interior Design: Sophie Ye Chin

First Edition

ISBN 1-4000-2090-5

Library of Congress Cataloging-in-Publication Data available upon request.

This book is available for special discounts for bulk purchases for sales promotions or premiums. Special editions, including personalized covers, excerpts of existing books, and corporate imprints, can be created in large quantities for special needs. For more information, write to Special Markets/Premium Sales, 1745 Broadway, MD 6-2, New York, NY, 10019 or e-mail specialmarkets@randomhouse.com.

PRINTED IN THE UNITED STATES OF AMERICA

10 9 8 7 6 5 4 3 2 1

ACKNOWLEDGMENTS

Thanks to the Living Language team: Tom Russell, Elizabeth Bennett, Christopher Warnasch, Zviezdana Verzich, Suzanne McQuade, Amelia Muqaddam, Denise De Gennaro, Linda Schmidt, John Whitman, Alison Skrabek, Helen Kilcullen, Heather Lanigan, Fabrizio La Rocca, Guido Caroti, and Sophie Chin. Special thanks to Marisa Cid.

CONTENTS

How to Use the Book

Welcome to *6,000+ Essential Spanish Words* – the perfect vocabulary-building tool. Whether you're a beginner, intermediate, or advanced student of Spanish, you've most likely chosen this book because you wish to expand your vocabulary, both generally and in specific areas. This program is the ideal supplement for you. A cross between a language course and a reference book, *6,000+ Essential Spanish Words* is a great companion to any Spanish program, and a simple and effective way to improve your vocabulary in Spanish.

This is not a dictionary. You won't need to pick random words out of thin air to build your vocabulary. Instead, be your own guide through thematic categories that matter to you—sports, nature, work, or school. You'll improve your vocabulary theme by theme at your own pace, in the order that works for you. Here's how it works. Perhaps you wanted to write an e-mail to a pen-pal in Mexico, and tell her about what you're studying in school. If you had a dictionary, you'd have to look up each individual word. With *6,000+ Essential Spanish Words*, simply flip to the School category, where you'll find a slew of words for everything from lockers, to mathematics, to extracurricular activities. Or maybe you enjoy reading a Spanish daily newspaper, and find yourself struggling over certain words related to politics, or the economy. Build up your comprehension of these themes by reviewing the Politics & Government and Money & The Economy categories of the book, doing the exercises, and even creating some exercises of your own. Or let's say you're writing an essay on planning a safari. Simply flip to The Natural World: Wild Animals to describe the various animals you might see on safari, or to Human Society: Continents and Countries of the World to find a list of African countries you might visit.

However you choose to use this book, the best part about it is that you don't have to start at page 1; the structure allows you to pick the categories where you feel you need improvement, start from there, and move on wherever and whenever you choose.

Here's how this book is broken down:

Categories and Sub-Categories

There are 23 categories in this book such as General Descriptive Words & Phrases, Sports & Leisure, and Work, and each divided into several sub-categories. The categories and sub-categories should help you narrow your search when looking for particular themes of words, but keep in mind that words may overlap. Some categories and sub-categories are also cross-referenced, indicating other sections where you may find more words of the same nature.

The word lists in each category will usually appear in a logical, thematic order, but occasionally will be alphabetized. Nouns, adjectives, and verbs are grouped together for convenience.

Words in Use

At the end of each sub-category, you will see a set of examples, showing some of the vocabulary words in use. Use this section to understand better how the vocabulary words are used in context, as well as noting any changes to the words (in gender, person, and number) when used in a sentence.

Exercises

Helpful review exercises appear at the end of every category. They are meant to serve as a brief review of some of the words you learned in each category and a chance for you to begin to use your new words right away. The answer keys appear at the end of each exercise.

Situations (Part II)

The Situations section of the book contains longer examples using vocabulary words from various categories and sub-categories in a realistic form. They range in level from beginner to advanced. Use them to improve your comprehension of vocabulary when used in context.

Spanish Prefixes (Part III)

This brief reference section offers a list of the most important Spanish prefixes to help you expand your vocabulary comprehension. Each prefix is followed by examples of words in Spanish with similar prefixes, as well as some examples of these words in use.

Customize This Book

Open-Ended Exercises and Tasks—Make a shopping list in Spanish, write a letter to a friend in Spanish, or even make a list of places you'd like to visit and the sites you'd like to see there. When you've finished, look in the book to check your translations and spellings.

Reading Exercises—Go online or to an international newsstand and find a Spanish newspaper or magazine. Look for vocabulary words you know, and make a list of the ones you don't. Constant reading practice will greatly improve your vocabulary comprehension, not to mention your Spanish in general.

Transparent Language® CD-ROM—The enclosed Transparent Language® CD-ROM contains over 500 Spanish words in 51 categories, as well as English translations for each word. With the help of flash cards, audio clips with adjustable playback speed, and progress reports detailing the areas that need improvement, you will quickly acquire and retain vocabulary in basic lists. Finally, you can create your own advanced and specialized lists, customized for your specific needs. You can even record your own audio clips to help you customize this course even further.

Now it's time to get started! Go anywhere you want: start off with Plants if you wish, maybe even learn some terms for Office Supplies, Crime and Justice, or Tennis and Ping-Pong. It's entirely up to you!

Part I

General Descriptive Words & Phrases

Palabras y frases descriptivas

COMMON ADJECTIVES*

Adjetivos comunes

bueno	*good*
malo	*bad*
grande	*big*
pequeño	*small*
caliente	*hot*
frío	*cold*
bonito	*beautiful*
feo	*ugly*
alto	*tall*
bajo	*short*
largo	*long*
corto	*short*
fuerte	*strong*
débil	*weak*
oscuro	*dark*
claro	*light*
inteligente	*intelligent*
tonto	*stupid*
caro	*expensive*
barato	*cheap*
gordo	*fat*
delgado	*thin*

* Spanish adjectives change in gender and number. Spanish adjectives ending in "o" form the feminine by changing the "o" into "a." Add an "s" to form the plural. Adjectives ending in a consonant or the vowel "e" have only one form for both the masculine and the feminine. Most adjectives that denote nationality and end in a consonant, add an "a" to form the feminine.

El vaso está vacío. *The glass is empty.*
La playa está vacía. *The beach is empty.*
El niño es débil. *The boy is weak.*
La niña es débil. *The girl is weak.*
Él es español. *He is Spanish.*
Ella es española. *She is Spanish.*

ancho	*wide*
estrecho	*narrow*
derecho	*straight*
torcido	*crooked*
cerca	*near*
lejos	*far*
alto	*high*
bajo	*low*
amistoso	*friendly*
antipático	*unfriendly*
feliz	*happy*
triste	*sad*
joven	*young*
viejo	*old*
nuevo	*new*
alto	*loud*
silencioso	*quiet*
mojado	*wet*
seco	*dry*
duro	*hard*
suave	*soft*
profundo	*deep*
llano	*shallow*
difícil	*difficult*
fácil	*easy*
pesado	*heavy*
ligero	*light*
saludable	*healthy*
enfermo	*ill*
perezoso	*lazy*
diligente	*diligent*
áspero	*rough*
liso	*smooth*
vacío	*empty*
lleno	*full*
sucio	*dirty*
limpio	*clean*
enérgico	*energetic*

cansado	*tired*
bueno	*good*
malvado	*evil*

NOTE: More specific descriptive words can be found in other categories in this book, such as the Food & Cooking or People categories.

Words In Use

El carro es **nuevo**. *The car is new.*

La muchacha es muy **inteligente**. *The girl is very intelligent.*

El café está muy **caliente**. *The coffee is very hot.*

El vaso está **lleno**. *The glass is full.*

Los diamantes son **caros**. *Diamonds are expensive.*

El examen fue muy **difícil**. *The test was very difficult.*

Es un edificio **alto**. *It's a tall building.*

La cocina está **sucia**. *The kitchen is dirty.*

POSITIVE ADJECTIVES
Adjetivos positivos

agradable	*pleasant*
asombroso	*astounding*
beneficioso	*beneficial*
de buen gusto	*tasteful*
deleitable	*enjoyable*
divertido	*fun*
emocionante	*exciting*
estimulante	*stimulating*
estupendo	*great*
excelente	*excellent*
gracioso	*funny*
imaginativo	*imaginative*
increíble	*incredible*
inspirante	*inspirational*
interesante	*interesting*
magnífico	*terrific*
maravilloso	*amazing, wonderful*
original	*original*
placentero	*pleasurable*
que merece la pena	*worthwhile*

relajante	*relaxing*
rentable	*profitable*
simpático	*funny*
único	*unique*
valioso	*valuable*

NOTE: More specific descriptive words can be found in other categories in this book, such as the Food & Cooking or People categories.

Words In Use

Es un negocio **rentable**. *It's a profitable business.*

Tuvimos una conversación **estimulante**. *We had a stimulating conversation.*

La decoración es **de buen gusto**. *The decoration is tasteful.*

Fue un fin de semana **magnífico**. *It was a terrific weekend.*

Ella tiene una personalidad **única**. *She has a unique personality.*

La lección fue **interesante**. *The lesson was interesting.*

Fue un viaje **estupendo**. *It was a great trip.*

NEGATIVE ADJECTIVES

Adjetivos negativos

absurdo	*absurd*
aburrido	*boring*
abusivo	*abusive*
arriesgado	*hazardous, risky*
asqueroso	*filthy*
atroz	*awful*
blasfemo	*blasphemous*
de mal gusto	*distasteful, tasteless*
desastroso	*disastrous*
destructivo	*destructive*
doloroso	*painful*
fatal	*fatal*
grosero	*rude*
horrible	*horrible*
imprudente	*reckless*
indiscreto	*tactless*
insultante	*insulting*
loco	*crazy*
maleducado	*rude*

Common
Adjectives

Positive
Adjectives/
Negative
Adjectives

Numbers

Calendar and
Time

Colors

Adverbs of Time

Adverbs of
Manner and
Degree

Weights,
Measurements,
and Describing
Quantity

malvado	evil
molesto	annoying
monótono	dull
ofensivo	offensive
opresivo	oppressive
peligroso	dangerous, hazardous
perjudicial	harmful
precipitado	reckless
provocativo	provocative
ridículo	ridiculous
soso	dull
terrible	terrible

NOTE: More specific descriptive words can be found in other categories in this book, such as the Food & Cooking or People categories.

Words In Use

Es un proceso **doloroso**. *It's a painful process.*

El discurso fue **ofensivo**. *The speech was offensive.*

Es un régimen **opresivo**. *It's an oppressive regime.*

El plan es **malvado**. *It's an evil plan.*

Él está en una relación **abusiva**. *He's in an abusive relationship.*

Es una carretera **peligrosa**. *It's a dangerous road.*

La película es **aburrida**. *The movie is boring.*

NUMBERS

Números

CARDINAL

cero	zero
uno	one
dos	two
tres	three
cuatro	four
cinco	five
seis	six
siete	seven
ocho	eight
nueve	nine
diez	ten
once	eleven

doce	*twelve*
trece	*thirteen*
catorce	*fourteen*
quince	*fifteen*
dieciséis (diez y seis)	*sixteen*
diecisiete (diez y siete)	*seventeen*
dieciocho (diez y ocho)	*eighteen*
diecinueve (diez y nueve)	*nineteen*
veinte	*twenty*
veintiuno (veinte y uno)	*twenty-one*
veintidós (veinte y dos)	*twenty-two*
veintitrés (veinte y tres)	*twenty-three*
veinticuatro (veinte y cuatro)	*twenty-four*
veinticinco (veinte y cinco)	*twenty-five*
veintiséis (veinte y seis)	*twenty-six*
veintisiete (veinte y siete)	*twenty-seven*
veintiocho (veinte y ocho)	*twenty-eight*
veintinueve (veinte y nueve)	*twenty-nine*
treinta	*thirty**
treinta y uno	*thirty-one*
treinta y dos	*thirty-two*
treinta y tres	*thirty-three*
treinta y cuatro	*thirty-four*
treinta y cinco	*thirty-five*
treinta y seis	*thirty-six*
treinta y siete	*thirty-seven*
treinta y ocho	*thirty-eight*
treinta y nueve	*thirty-nine*
cuarenta	*forty*
cincuenta	*fifty*
sesenta	*sixty*
setenta	*seventy*
ochenta	*eighty*
noventa	*ninety*
cien (ciento)	*one hundred***
ciento uno	*one hundred one*
ciento dos	*one hundred two*
doscientos	*two hundred*
trescientos	*three hundred*

* *The numbers above 30 are in the form* "tens y units" (y *means* "and"). *For example, forty-two is* cuarenta y dos.
** *One hundred is a special case. One hundred itself is* cien, *but to form any number 101-199 it becomes* ciento. *Take the stem* ciento *and follow it with the relevant number from one to ninety-nine. So for example one hundred and fifty-two is written* ciento cincuenta y dos. *Note that* ciento *is not merged with the number following it.*

mil	one thousand
dos mil	two thousand
un millón	million
mil millones	billion
un billón	trillion

ORDINAL

primero (primer*)	first
segundo	second
tercero (tercer*)	third
cuarto	fourth
quinto	fifth
sexto	sixth
séptimo	seventh
octavo	eighth
noveno	ninth
décimo	tenth
undécimo	eleventh
duodécimo	twelfth
decimotercero (decimotercer*)	thirteenth
decimocuarto	fourteenth
decimoquinto	fifteenth
decimosexto	sixteenth
decimoséptimo	seventeenth
decimoctavo	eighteenth
decimonoveno	nineteenth
vigésimo	twentieth
vigésimo primero	twenty-first
vigésimo segundo	twenty-second
vigésimo tercero (vigésimo tercer*)	twenty-third

FRACTIONS

un medio	one-half
la mitad	half
un tercio	one-third
una tercera parte	a third
un cuarto	one-quarter
una cuarta parte	a quarter
un octavo	one-eighth
una octava parte	an eighth

* The ordinal numbers primer(o) and tercer(o) drop the final -o before any masculine singular nouns. Juan es mi primer hijo—Juan is my first son.

Words In Use

Hay **cincuenta** estados en los Estados Unidos de América. *There are fifty states in the United States of America.*

Es una botella de **dieciocho** onzas. *It's an eighteen ounce bottle.*

Mi número favorito es el **ochenta y cinco**. *My favorite number is eighty-five.*

Yo soy la **tercera** persona en la fila. *I'm the third person on line.*

La mitad de **un medio** es **un cuarto**. *Half of one-half is one-quarter.*

Ciento veinticinco menos **veinte** es **ciento cinco**. *One hundred twenty-five minus twenty is one hundred and five.*

CALENDAR AND TIME

Calendario y Hora y tiempo

GENERAL

el día	day
la mañana	morning
el mediodía	noon
la tarde	afternoon
la noche	evening, night
el alba	dawn
el amanecer	dawn
la madrugada	dawn
la salida del sol	sunrise
la puesta del sol	sunset
el anochecer	dusk
la medianoche	midnight
el fin de semana	weekend
la semana	week
el mes	month
el año	year
la década	decade
el siglo	century
el milenio	millenium
la fecha	date

NAMES OF DAYS

lunes**	Monday
martes	Tuesday
miércoles	Wednesday
jueves	Thursday
viernes	Friday
sábado	Saturday
domingo	Sunday

** *In Spanish, the names of the months and days of the weeks are not capitalized unless they are at the beginning of a sentence.*

Common Adjectives

Positive Adjectives

Negative Adjectives

Numbers

Calendar and Time

Colors

Adverbs of Time

Adverbs of Manner and Degree

Weights, Measurements, and Describing Quantity

MONTHS

el calendario	*calendar*
enero**	*January*
febrero	*February*
marzo	*March*
abril	*April*
mayo	*May*
junio	*June*
julio	*July*
agosto	*August*
septiembre	*September*
octubre	*October*
noviembre	*November*
diciembre	*December*

SEASONS

la estación	*season*
la primavera	*spring*
el verano	*summer*
el otoño	*fall/autumn*
el invierno	*winter*
el tiempo	*time*
la hora***	*time, hour*
el segundo	*second*
el minuto	*minute*
el cuarto de hora	*quarter hour*
la media hora	*half hour*

Words In Use

¿Qué **día** es hoy? *What day is today?*

Hoy es **martes**. *Today is Tuesday.*

¿Cuál es la **fecha** de hoy? *What is today's date?*

Hoy es el quince de **agosto**. *Today is August 15th.*

¿Cuál es tu **estación** favorita? *What's your favorite season?*

Mi estación favorita es el **verano**. *My favorite season is summer.*

Son las ocho y veinticinco de la **noche**. *It's 8:25 p.m.*

** *In Spanish, the names of the months and days of the weeks are not capitalized unless they are at the beginning of a sentence.*
*** *When asking the time you use the expression:* ¿Qué hora es?

COLORS

Colores

BASIC COLORS

rojo	*red*
naranja	*orange*
amarillo	*yellow*
verde	*green*
azul	*blue*
púrpura	*purple*
morado	*purple*
marrón	*brown*
beige	*beige*
rosado	*pink*
negro	*black*
blanco	*white*
gris	*gray*
dorado	*gold*
plateado	*silver*

ADJECTIVES DESCRIBING COLOR

claro	*light*
oscuro	*dark*
azul claro	*light blue*
verde oscuro	*dark green*
de un solo color	*solid, monochromatic*
sólido	*solid*
multicolor	*multicolored*
vivo	*brilliant*
pálido	*pale*
mate	*flat/matte*
reluciente	*shiny*
brillante	*shiny*
vibrante	*vibrant*
neón	*neon*

Words In Use

El carro es **rojo vivo**. *The car is brilliant red.*

La pared es **beige mate**. *The wall is flat beige.*

Ella prefiere la camisa **de un solo color**. *She prefers the solid shirt.*

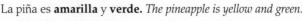

La piña es **amarilla** y **verde.** *The pineapple is yellow and green.*

Prefiero las manzanas **rojas**. *I prefer red apples.*

La bicicleta **azul clara** es más bonita que la **oscura**. *The light blue bicycle is prettier than the dark one.*

ADVERBS OF TIME

Adverbios de frecuencia y de tiempo

siempre	*always*
a menudo	*often*
frecuentemente	*frequently*
usualmente	*usually*
a veces	*sometimes*
rara vez	*rarely*
nunca	*never*
jamás	*never*
todos los días	*every day*
todas las semanas	*every week*
todos los meses	*every month*
dos veces al año	*twice a year*
cada dos semanas	*every other week*
por la mañana*	*in the morning*
por la tarde	*in the afternoon*
por la noche	*in the evening, at night*
al mediodía	*at noon*
a medianoche	*at midnight*
en el pasado	*in the past*
en el presente	*in the present*
en el futuro	*in the future*

Words In Use

Nosotros vamos al cine **a menudo**. *We go to the movies often.*

El tren **siempre** llega a tiempo. *The train always arrives on time.*

Ella **rara vez** mira la televisión. *She rarely watches television.*

Yo leo el periódico **todos los días**. *I read the newspaper every day.*

¿Visitas a tus padres **todas las semanas**? *Do you visit your parents every week?*

Anoche me acosté **a medianoche**. *I went to bed at midnight last night.*

*Mañana *also means "tomorrow."*

ADVERBS OF MANNER AND DEGREE
Adverbios de modo

no	*not*
bien	*well*
mal	*poorly*
muy	*very, terribly*
extremadamente	*extremely*
apenas	*hardly*
algo	*somewhat*
un tanto	*somewhat*
perfectamente	*perfectly*
completamente	*perfectly, completely*
terriblemente	*terribly*

Words In Use

Quedamos **algo** escandalizados. *We were somewhat shocked.*

Me fue **muy mal** en el examen. *I did very poorly on the test.*

¡Eso **no** es bueno! *That is not good!*

Escalar el Everest es **extremadamente** difícil. *Climbing Everest is extremely difficult.*

Apenas la conozco. *I hardly know her.*

WEIGHTS, MEASUREMENTS, AND DESCRIBING QUANTITY
Pesos, medidas y describiendo cantidades

GENERAL

un poco	*a little, a few*
pocos	*a little, a few*
mucho	*a lot, much/many*
muchos	*much/many*
algo	*some*
ninguno	*none*
ningún	*none*
algún	*any*

DISTANCE

la medida	*measurement*
la pulgada	*inch*
el pie	*foot*

la yarda	yard
la milla	mile
el milímetro	millimeter
el centímetro	centimeter
el metro	meter
el kilómetro	kilometer

WEIGHT

el peso	weight
la onza	ounce
la libra	pound
la tonelada	ton
el gramo	gram
el kilogramo	kilogram

VOLUME

la cucharada	teaspoon
la cucharadita	tablespoon
la taza	cup
la pinta	pint
el cuarto de galón	quart
el galón	gallon
el centilitro	centiliter
el litro	liter

Words In Use

Me siento **un poco** cansado hoy. *I feel a little tired today.*

Tengo **mucho** que hacer. *I have a lot to do.*

Hay **muchas** tiendas allí. *There are many stores there.*

¿Cuántos **pies** hay en un **metro**? *How many feet are there in one meter?*

Dos **cucharaditas** de azúcar, por favor. *Two teaspoons of sugar, please.*

¿Cuánto cuesta el **galón** de gasolina? *How much does one gallon of gas cost?*

EXERCISES

I. Match the Spanish word on the left with the English word on the right.

1. feo	A. *month*
2. enfermo	B. *eight*
3. seco	C. *well*
4. aburrido	D. *Monday*
5. ocho	E. *always*
6. ochenta	F. *ugly*
7. mes	G. *eighty*
8. lunes	H. *boring*
9. siempre	I. *ill*
10. bien	J. *dry*

II. Fill in the blanks with the appropriate Spanish word.

1. *The opposite of* sucio *is* _____.

2. *The opposite of* blanco *is* _____.

3. La manzana es _____ (*red*).

4. Hay siete _____ (*days*) en una _____(*week*).

5. La muchacha es _____ (*pretty*).

ANSWERS: I. 1. F, 2. I, 3. J, 4. H, 5. B, 6. G, 7. A, 8. D, 9. E, 10. C
II. 1. *THE OPPOSITE OF* SUCIO *IS* **LIMPIO**. 2. *THE OPPOSITE OF* BLANCO
IS **NEGRO**. 3. LA MANZANA ES **ROJA**. 4. HAY SIETE **DÍAS** EN UNA **SEMANA**.
5. LA MUCHACHA ES **BONITA**.

1

Common
Adjectives

Positive
Adjectives

Negative
Adjectives

Numbers

Calendar and
Time

Colors

Adverbs of Time

Adverbs of
Manner and
Degree

Weights,
Measurements,
and Describing
Quantity

2 People

Gente

GENERAL TERMS AND TITLES FOR PEOPLE

Términos y títulos generales

GENERAL TERMS FOR PEOPLE

la persona	*person*
la gente	*people*
el ser humano	*human being*
el hombre	*man*
la mujer	*woman*
el niño	*child (male)*
la niña	*child (female)*
el chico	*boy*
la chica	*girl*
el adulto	*adult*
el individuo	*individual*
el anciano	*old man*
la anciana	*old woman*
el viejo	*old man (can be offensive)*
la vieja	*old woman (can be offensive)*
el/la bebé	*baby*
el/la niño/a que empieza a andar	*toddler*
el/la adolescente	*teenager, adolescent*

TITLES

Señor (Sr.)	*Mr., Sir*
don	*Mr.*
Señora (Sra.)	*Mrs., Ma'am*
doña	*Mrs.*
Señorita (Srta.)	*Miss.*
Señora (Sra.)	*Ms.*
doctor/a	*Dr.*
reverendo/a	*Rev.*

padre	*Father*
hermano	*Brother*
hermana	*Sister*
madre	*Mother*
Honorable	*Honorable*
capitán	*Captain*
oficial	*Officer*
almirante	*Admiral*
sargento	*Sergeant*

NOTE: More words related to People can be found in other categories in this book, such as the section on Professions.

Words In Use

Es un **ser humano** increíble. *He's an incredible human being.*

Tengo una cita con el **doctor** Matos. *I have an appointment with Dr. Matos.*

Hay dos **capitanes** en este vuelo. *There are two captains on this flight.*

El **bebé** tiene dos meses. *The baby is two months old.*

¿Cómo se llama la **mujer**? *What's the woman's name?*

Los **niños** están jugando en el parque. *The children are playing in the park.*

PHYSICAL DESCRIPTIONS OF PEOPLE
Descripciones físicas de una persona

alto	*tall*
bajo	*short*
bello	*beautiful*
bonito	*pretty*
bronceado	*tan*
calvo	*bald*
de edad media	*middle-aged*
delgado	*thin*
feo	*ugly*
gordo	*fat*
joven	*young*
mayor	*elderly*
moreno	*brunette*
musculoso	*muscular*
obeso	*obese*
pálido	*pale*
pelirrojo	*red-headed*
promedio	*average*

rubio	*blond*
simple	*plain*

NOTE: More specific descriptive words can be found in other categories in this book, such as the General Descriptive Words & Phrases category.

Words In Use

¡Él es un hombre muy **musculoso**! *He is a very muscular guy!*

Me gustaría estar más **bronceado.** *I would like to be more tanned.*

Es un chico muy **alto**. *He's a tall boy.*

Quisiera estar más **delgado**. *I'd like to be thinner.*

Eres más **bajo** que yo. *You are shorter than I am.*

Es una muchacha muy **bella**. *She's a beautiful girl.*

OTHER DESCRIPTIONS OF PEOPLE

Otras formas de describir a una persona

aburrido	*dull/uninteresting*
agradable	*pleasant*
agresivo	*aggressive*
amable	*friendly, kind*
arrogante	*arrogant*
astuto	*sly, cunning*
bullicioso	*boisterous*
cálido	*warm*
cínico	*cynical*
comprensivo	*understanding*
correcto	*proper*
cortés	*polite*
crédulo	*gullible*
crítico	*judgmental*
de última moda	*stylish, fashionable*
disciplinado	*disciplined*
dócil	*docile*
dulce	*sweet*
encantador	*charming*
espontáneo	*spontaneous*
extrovertido	*outgoing*
gracioso	*funny*
grosero	*rude*
hablador	*talkative*

humilde	*humble*
lacónico	*laconic*
listo	*smart*
loco	*crazy*
maleducado	*rude*
mezquino	*mean*
mundano	*worldly*
odioso	*obnoxious*
optimista	*optimistic*
pesimista	*pessimistic*
precavido	*cautious*
repugnante	*nasty*
sentimental	*sentimental*
simpático	*funny*
terco	*stubborn*
tímido	*shy*
tosco	*coarse*
único	*unique*

2

General Terms
and Titles for
People

Physical
Descriptions of
People

**Other
Descriptions
of People/The
Life Cycle**

Parts of the Body

Anatomy

NOTE: More words for describing People can be found in other categories in this book, such as Human Society, Work, or School.

Words In Use

Tus niños son muy **dulces**. *Your children are so sweet.*

¡No seas tan **terco**! *Don't be so stubborn!*

Ella tiene una personalidad **encantadora**. *She's got a charming personality.*

Él solía ser una persona muy **cálida**. *He used to be a warm person.*

Los gatos son animales **precavidos**. *Cats are very cautious animals.*

No me gusta la gente **arrogante.** *I don't like arrogant people.*

THE LIFE CYCLE
El ciclo de la vida

LIFE CYCLE NOUNS

el nacimiento	*birth*
la vida	*life*
la niñez	*childhood*
la adolescencia	*adolescence*
la edad adulta	*adulthood*
la edad madura	*old age*
la muerte	*death*

LIFE CYCLE VERBS

nacer	*to be born*
vivir	*to live*
crecer	*to grow up*
envejecer	*to grow old*
morir	*to die*

Words In Use

La **adolescencia** es la etapa más difícil. *Adolescence is the most difficult period.*

Él no tuvo una **niñez** feliz. *He didn't have a happy childhood.*

¿**Naciste** el primero de enero? *Were you born on January 1st?*

¿Quién quiere **vivir** cien años? *Who wants to live one hundred years?*

Murió de una manera tranquila. *She died peacefully.*

PARTS OF THE BODY

Partes del cuerpo

la cabeza	*head*
el cabello	*hair (on head)*
el pelo	*hair (on head)*
la frente	*forehead*
la sien	*temple*
el ojo	*eye*
la ceja	*eyebrow*
la pestaña	*eyelash*
el párpado	*eyelid*
la nariz	*nose*
la fosa nasal	*nostril*
la oreja	*ear*
el lóbulo de la oreja	*earlobe*
la mejilla	*cheek*
la boca	*mouth*
el labio	*lip*
la lengua	*tongue*
el diente	*tooth*
la barbilla	*chin*
la mandíbula	*jaw*
la barba	*beard*
el bigote	*moustache*
las patillas	*sideburns*

el pelo de la barba	*whisker*
el cuello	*neck*
la garganta	*throat*
el hombro	*shoulder*
la articulación	*joint*
el brazo	*arm*
la axila	*armpit*
el codo	*elbow*
el antebrazo	*forearm*
la muñeca	*wrist*
la mano	*hand*
la palma de la mano	*palm*
el dedo	*finger*
el pulgar	*thumb*
el dedo índice	*index finger*
el dedo cordial	*middle finger*
el dedo anular	*ring finger*
el dedo auricular	*little finger, pinky*
el dedo meñique	*little finger, pinky*
el nudillo	*knuckle*
el pecho	*chest*
el pecho	*breast*
el pezón	*nipple*
el estómago	*stomach*
el abdomen	*abdomen*
la cintura	*waist*
la cadera	*hip*
la pierna	*leg*
el muslo	*thigh*
la rodilla	*knee*
la espinilla	*shin*
el tobillo	*ankle*
el pie	*foot*
el dedo del pie	*toe*
el vello	*body hair*
la uña	*nail*
la piel	*skin*
el pene	*penis*
la vagina	*vagina*

2

General Terms
and Titles for
People

Physical
Descriptions
of People

Other
Descriptions of
People

The Life Cycle

**Parts of the
Body**

Anatomy

las nalgas	buttocks

NOTE: More words related to Parts of the Body can be found in the Health, Hygiene, and Safety category of this book.

Words In Use

En el accidente él se fracturó la **cadera**. *He fractured his hip in the accident.*

Debes protegerte la **piel** contra el sol. *You should protect your skin against the sun.*

Tengo un dolor de **hombros** muy fuerte. *I have a strong shoulder pain.*

El futbolista tiene unas **piernas** muy rápidas. *The soccer player has very fast legs.*

La **muñeca**, el **antebraz**o y el **codo** son partes del **brazo**. *The wrist, the forearms, and the elbow are parts of the arm.*

ANATOMY
Anatomía

ANATOMICAL NOUNS

la célula	cell
el cerebro	brain
el nervio	nerve
la médula espinal	spinal cord
el corazón	heart
la sangre	blood
la arteria	artery
la vena	vein
el vaso capilar	capillary
el hueso	bone
el cráneo	skull
la costilla	rib
la médula	marrow
el tuétano	marrow
la espina dorsal	spine
el pulmón	lung
la tráquea	trachea
la laringe	larynx
el esófago	esophagus
el estómago	stomach
los intestinos	intestines
el colon	colon
el ano	anus

el riñón	kidney
el hígado	liver
el páncreas	pancreas
el músculo	muscle
la grasa	fat
el tendón	tendon
la enzima	enzyme
la hormona	hormone
la glándula	gland

ANATOMICAL VERBS

respirar	to breathe
aspirar	to inhale
inspirar	to inhale
espirar	to exhale
circular	to circulate
ingerir	to ingest
digerir	to digest
vaciar	to pump
flexionar	to flex
relajar	to relax
funcionar	to function
sudar	to perspire, sweat
sangrar	to bleed
producir	to produce
secretar	to discharge, to secrete
absorber	to absorb
regular	to regulate
apoyar	to support

NOTE: More words related to Anatomy can be found in the Health, Hygiene, and Safety category of this book.

Words In Use

Es importante que aprendas a **relajarte**. *It's important that you learn how to relax.*

El cuerpo **produce hormonas** importantes. *The body produces important hormones.*

Come despacio para que **digieras** bien. *Eat slowly so that you digest well.*

Gracias al **cerebro** podemos pensar. *Thanks to the brain we're able to think.*

El **corazón** hace que la **sangre circule**. *The heart makes blood circulate.*

2

General Terms and Titles for People

Physical Descriptions of People

Other Descriptions of People

The Life Cycle

Parts of the Body

Anatomy

EXERCISES

I. Match the Spanish word on the left with the English word on the right.

1. joven	A. *brain*
2. el/la bebé	B. *polite*
3. la anciana	C. *to breathe*
4. el hombro	D. *young*
5. la piel	E. *baby*
6. gordo	F. *shoulder*
7. el dedo	G. *skin*
8. cortés	H. *fat*
9. el cerebro	I. *finger*
10. respirar	J. *old woman*

II. Fill in the blanks with the appropriate Spanish word.

1. *The opposite of* pesimista *is* _____.
2. *The opposite of* humilde *is* _____.
3. *The Spanish word for knee is* _____.
4. Hay cinco _____ (*fingers*) en una _____ (*hand*).
5. La muchacha es _____ (*tall*), _____ (*young*) y _____ (*pretty*).

ANSWERS: I. 1. D, 2. E, 3. J, 4. F, 5. G, 6. H, 7. I, 8. B, 9. A, 10. C
II. 1. *THE OPPOSITE OF* PESIMISTA *IS* **OPTIMISTA**. 2. *THE OPPOSITE OF* HUMILDE *IS* **ARROGANTE**. 3. *THE SPANISH WORD FOR KNEE IS* **RODILLA**. 4. HAY CINCO **DEDOS** EN UNA **MANO**. 5. LA MUCHACHA ES **ALTA, JOVEN** Y **BONITA**.

Feelings & Thoughts

Opiniones e ideas

EXPRESSING LIKES AND DISLIKES

Cómo expresar gustos

POSITIVE ADJECTIVES

bueno	*good*
estupendo	*great*
excelente	*excellent*
maravilloso	*wonderful*
favorito	*favorite*

POSITIVE VERBS

gustar	*to like*
encantar	*to love*
preferir	*to prefer*
interesarse por	*to be interested in*
disfrutar	*to enjoy*
agradecer	*to appreciate*
pasarlo bien	*to have a good time*
divertirse	*to have fun*
entretener	*to amuse*
entusiasmarse por	*to be excited by*
apasionar	*to excite*

NEGATIVE ADJECTIVES

malo	*bad*
atroz	*awful*
aburrido	*boring*
terrible	*terrible*

NEGATIVE VERBS

no gustar	*to dislike*
tenerle antipatía a algo	*to dislike*
disgustar	*to displease, to annoy*
odiar	*to hate*

no soportar	*to be unable to stand (something)*
pasarlo mal	*to have a bad time*
aburrirse de algo	*to be bored by*
aburrir	*to bore*

NOTE: More words for expressing likes and dislikes can be found in other categories in this book, such as General Descriptive Words & Phrases.

Words In Use

Me **encanta** mirar la televisión los jueves. *I love watching TV on Thursdays.*

En el campamento ella lo **pasó mal**. *She had a bad time during camp.*

Fue una película **aburrida**. *It was a boring film.*

"Los Vikingos" es mi restaurante **favorito**. *"Los Vikingos" is my favorite restaurant.*

Yo **disfruto** del buen vino. *I enjoy good wine.*

A él le **gusta** el pollo frito. *He likes fried chicken.*

EMOTIONS, MOODS, AND FEELINGS

Emociones, genio y sensaciones

POSITIVE NOUNS

el sentimiento	*feeling*
el pensamiento	*thought*
la felicidad	*happiness*
la dicha	*bliss*
la satisfacción	*contentment*
la emoción	*emotion, excitement*
el entusiasmo	*enthusiasm*
la euforia	*elation*
el júbilo	*joy*
el humor	*mood*
el genio	*mood*

POSITIVE ADJECTIVES

feliz	*happy*
contento	*content*
maravilloso	*blissful*
emocionado	*excited*
entusiástico	*enthusiastic*
eufórico	*elated*
ilusionado	*harboring hopes for something*
intrigado	*intrigued*

POSITIVE VERBS

estar de buen humor	*to be in a good mood*
estar de buen genio	*to be in a good mood*
tener una buena actitud	*to have a good outlook/attitude*

NEGATIVE NOUNS

la tristeza	*sadness*
la ira	*anger*
la furia	*rage*
los celos	*jealousy*
el aburrimiento	*boredom*
el miedo	*fear*
la ansiedad	*anxiety*
la inquietud	*worry, concern, anxiety*

NEGATIVE ADJECTIVES

triste	*sad*
enojado	*angry*
celoso	*jealous*
aburrido	*bored*
asustado	*frightened*
nervioso	*nervous*
inquieto	*worried, anxious*

NEGATIVE VERBS

tener miedo de	*to be afraid of*
estar de mal humor	*to be in a bad mood*
estar enojado con	*to be upset by*
tener una mala actitud	*to have a bad outlook/attitude*
preocuparse	*to worry*
tener morriña	*to be blue*

OTHER ADJECTIVES

estresado	*stressed*
tenso	*tense*
ansioso	*anxious*
deprimido	*depressed*
impresionado	*impressed*
con vértigo	*light-headed*
mareado	*dizzy*
enfermo	*sick*

3

Expressing Likes
and Dislikes

**Emotions, Moods
and Feelings**

Expressions of
Emotions

General Mental
Activities and
States

horrorizado	*horrified*
escandalizado	*shocked*
sorprendido	*surprised*
indignado	*indignant*

OTHER VERBS

estresar	*to stress*
deprimir	*to depress*
horrorizar	*to horrify*
impresionar	*to impress, to shock*
escandalizar	*to shock*
sorprender	*to surprise*
añorar	*to be homesick*
echar de menos	*to be homesick*
sentir náuseas	*to feel nauseated*

Words In Use

Me impresionó la **horrible** noticia. *The horrible news shocked me.*

El accidente nos **sorprendió** a todos. *The accident surprised all of us.*

La señora García estuvo una semana **enferma**. *Mrs. Garcia spent a week sick.*

Siempre me siento **ansioso** antes de un viaje. *I always feel anxious before a trip.*

Después del concierto el público quedó **eufórico**. *After the concert the audience felt elated.*

La conversación me dejó **intrigado**. *The conversation left me intrigued.*

EXPRESSIONS OF EMOTIONS

Términos para expresar emociones

NOUNS OF EXPRESSION

el beso	*kiss*
el abrazo	*hug*
la sonrisa	*smile*
la risa	*laughter*
las lágrimas	*tears*
la piel de gallina	*goosebumps*

VERBS OF EXPRESSION

besar	*to kiss*
abrazar	*to hug*
estar abrazados	*to cuddle, to hug*

Feelings & Thoughts Opiniones e ideas

arrimarse	*to cuddle, to snuggle up*
reír	*to laugh*
llorar	*to cry*
sonreír	*to smile*
fruncir el ceño	*to frown*
gritar	*to shout, to yell*
suspirar	*to sigh*
gruñir	*to groan*
gemir	*to moan*
quejarse	*to complain, to whine*
gimotear	*to whine*
atacar	*to attack*
pelear	*to fight*
golpear	*to hit, to slap*
abofetear	*to slap in the face*
dar un puño	*to punch*
asentir con la cabeza	*to nod one's head*
negar con la cabeza	*to shake one's head*
tiritar	*to shiver*

3

Expressing Likes
and Dislikes

Emotions, Moods
and Feelings

**Expressions of
Emotions/
General Mental
Activities and
States**

Words In Use

Él permaneció en silencio, pero **asintió con la cabeza**. *He remained silent but he nodded in approval.*

Ella tiene una **sonrisa** muy bonita. *She has a beautiful smile.*

No me gusta cuando **frunces el ceño**. *I don't like it when you frown.*

El discurso me dejó la **piel de gallina**. *The speech gave me goosebumps.*

El niño le dio un **abrazo** a su madre. *The child gave his mother a hug*

Hacía tanto frío que comencé a **tiritar**. *It was so cold that I started to shiver.*

GENERAL MENTAL ACTIVITIES AND STATES
Estados mentales
MENTAL ADJECTIVES

pensativo	*pensive*
atento	*thoughtful*
desatento	*inattentive*
olvidadizo	*forgetful*
casquivano	*scatterbrained*
confundido	*confused*
listo	*clever, smart*

ingenioso	*ingenious, witty*
estúpido	*dumb, stupid*

MENTAL VERBS

pensar	*to think*
volver a pensar	*to rethink*
entender	*to understand*
darse cuenta de	*to realize*
inspirar	*to inspire*
influir	*to influence*
provocar	*to provoke*
persuadir	*to persuade*
convencer	*to convince*
disuadir	*to dissuade*
memorizar	*to memorize*
calcular	*to calculate*
decidir	*to decide*
estimar	*to estimate*
imaginar	*to imagine*
concentrarse en	*to concentrate (on)*
enfocarse	*to focus (on)*
considerar	*to consider*
contemplar	*to contemplate*
suponer	*to assume*
percibir	*to perceive*
evaluar	*to evaluate*
juzgar	*to judge*
recordar	*to remember*
olvidar	*to forget*
confundir	*to confuse*
quedarse en blanco	*to blank out*
entender mal	*to mistake*

Words In Use

Tengo que **enfocarme** en mis estudios. *I have to focus on my studies.*

A ella siempre se le **olvida** mi nombre. *She always forgets my name.*

No es bueno **juzgar** a los demás. *It's not good to judge others.*

No vas a poder **convencerme**. *You won't be able to convince me.*

Nunca **asumas** que sabes toda la verdad. *Never assume that you know the whole truth.*

EXERCISES

I. Match the Spanish word on the left with the English word on the right.

1. entretener
2. la furia
3. gritar
4. disfrutar
5. la risa
6. la emoción
7. ansioso
8. el beso
9. encantar
10. preocuparse

A. *to love*
B. *excitement*
C. *rage*
D. *anxious*
E. *to amuse*
F. *to worry*
G. *kiss*
H. *to enjoy*
I. *laughter*
J. *to shout*

3

Expressing Likes
and Dislikes

Emotions, Moods
and Feelings

Expressions of
Emotions

**General Mental
Activities and
States**

II. Fill in the blanks with the appropriate Spanish word.

1. No sé _____ (*to calculate*) el total.
2. Tienes que _____ (*to memorize*) muchas palabras.
3. No me gusta verte _____ (*to cry*).
4. No me vas a _____ (*to convince*).
5. Fue una película _____ (*boring*).

ANSWERS: I. 1. E, 2. C, 3. J, 4. H, 5. I, 6. B, 7. D, 8. G, 9. A, 10. F
II. 1. NO SÉ **CALCULAR** EL TOTAL. 2. TIENES QUE **MEMORIZAR** MUCHAS
PALABRAS. 3. NO ME GUSTA VERTE **LLORAR**. 4. NO ME VAS A **CONVENCER**.
5. FUE UNA PELÍCULA **ABURRIDA**.

4

Actions
Acciones

GENERAL PHYSICAL ACTIVITIES
Actividades físicas

abrir	*to open*
agarrar	*to catch*
bailar	*to dance*
beber	*to drink*
caminar	*to walk*
cerrar	*to close*
coger	*to catch**
comer	*to eat*
correr	*to run*
dar	*to give*
despertarse	*to wake up*
dormir	*to sleep*
entrar	*to enter, to go in*
enviar	*to send*
lanzar	*to throw*
levantar	*to lift*
llamar	*to call*
llevar	*to carry*
mover	*to move*
pararse	*to stop*
poner	*to put*
ponerse de pie	*to stand*
recibir	*to receive*
salir	*to leave*
saltar	*to jump*
sentarse	*to sit*
tomar	*to take*

NOTE: More Action words can be found in other categories of this books, such as the Sports and Leisure category.

* Coger *has a vulgar meaning in some Latin American countries.*

Me **despierto** a las seis de la mañana. *I wake up at 6 a.m.*

Debes **poner** el sello en la carta. *You should put a stamp on the letter.*

¿No vas a **abrir** tu regalo? *Aren't you going to open your present?*

No me gusta mucho **bailar**. *I don't like to dance much.*

El muchacho **corre** muy rápido. *That guy runs very fast.*

PHYSICAL STATES
Estados físicos

atento	*attentive, focused*
despierto	*awake*
energético	*energetic*
alerta	*alert*
dinámico	*dynamic*
vigilante	*vigilant*
activo	*active*
cansado	*tired*
agotado	*exhausted*
en forma	*in good shape*
fuera de forma	*out of shape*
acostado	*lying down*
sentado	*sitting*
de pie	*standing*

Words In Use

Después del café me siento muy **alerta**. *After drinking coffee I feel very alert.*

Debo ir al gimnasio; estoy **fuera de forma**. *I should join a gym, I'm feeling out of shape.*

¿Estaba **de pie** o estaba **sentado**? *Was he standing or sitting?*

SPEECH AND COMMUNICATION
Lenguaje y comunicación

NOUNS OF COMMUNICATION

la comunicación	*communication*
el idioma	*language*
la lengua	*language*
el discurso	*speech*
el acento	*accent*
el diálogo	*dialogue*

el entendimiento	understanding
el malentendido	misunderstanding
la palabra	word
el vocabulario	vocabulary
la oración	sentence
el tartamudeo	stutter

ADJECTIVES OF COMMUNICATION

fuerte	loud
tranquilo	quiet
silencioso	silent
hablador	talkative
inteligible	articulate
vocal	vocal

VERBS OF COMMUNICATION

hablar	to talk, to speak
decir	to say, to tell
platicar	to chat
repetir	to repeat
discutir	to argue
debatir	to debate
deliberar	to deliberate
oír	to hear
escuchar	to listen
callarse	to keep quiet
entenderse	to be understood
entender	to mean, to intend
comprender	to understand
suspirar	to whisper
musitar	to mumble
gritar	to shout, to yell
dar alaridos	to yell
tartamudear	to stutter
bromear	to joke
hacer gestos	to gesture
declarar	to assert, to claim, to declare
pronunciar	to pronounce
anunciar	to announce

explicar	*to explain*
comentar	*to comment*

Words In Use

El niño les **gritó** a sus amigos. *The boy shouted at his friends.*

No me gusta **discutir**; prefiero el **diálogo**. *I don't like to argue, I prefer to have a dialogue.*

Como la radio estaba alta, no pude **escuchar**. *Because the radio was so loud, I was not able to listen.*

Él tiene un **vocabulario** muy extenso; conoce el significado de muchas **palabras**. *He has an extensive vocabulario; he knows the meaning of many words.*

EXERCISES

I. Match the Spanish word on the left with the English word on the right.

1. platicar		A.	*to run*
2. alerta		B.	*to joke*
3. en forma		C.	*word*
4. correr		D.	*to close*
5. levantar		E.	*awake*
6. cerrar		F.	*to chat*
7. la oración		G.	*alert*
8. despierto		H.	*in shape*
9. bromear		I.	*to lift*
10. la palabra		J.	*sentence*

II. Fill in the blanks with the appropriate Spanish word.

1. *The opposite of* en forma *is* _____.

2. *The opposite of* cerrar *is* _____ .

3. *The opposite of* de pie *is* _____.

4. Es una persona que sabe _____ (*to listen*).

5. Me gusta _____ (*to hear*) música clásica cuando como.

ANSWERS: I. 1. F, 2. G, 3. H, 4. A, 5. I, 6. D, 7. J, 8. E, 9. B, 10. C
II. 1. *THE OPPOSITE OF* EN FORMA *IS* **FUERA DE FORMA**. 2. *THE OPPOSITE OF* CERRAR *IS* **ABRIR**. 3. *THE OPPOSITE OF* DE PIE *IS* **SENTADO**. 4. ES UNA PERSONA QUE SABE **ESCUCHAR**. 5. ME GUSTA **ESCUCHAR** MÚSICA CLÁSICA CUANDO COMO.

The Five Senses

Los cinco sentidos

5

SIGHT

La vista

SIGHT NOUNS

la forma	*shape*
el círculo	*circle*
el rectángulo	*rectangle*
el cuadrado	*square*
el triángulo	*triangle*
el losange	*diamond*
el trapecio	*trapezoid*
el óvalo	*oval*

SIGHT ADJECTIVES

circular	*round*
oblongo	*oblong*
cuadrado	*square*
rectangular	*rectangular*
brillante	*bright*
oscuro	*dark*
cerca	*near*
lejos	*far*
borroso	*blurry*
con niebla	*foggy*
claro	*clear*
enfocado	*focused*
visible	*visible*
invisible	*invisible*

SIGHT VERBS

ver	*to see*
mirar	*to look at, to watch*
observar	*to watch, to observe*
reparar	*to notice, to observe*

| enfocar | *to focus* |
| mirar fijamente | *to stare* |

NOTE: More words related to Sight can be found in other categories of this book, such as People or Entertainment and Media.

Words In Use

¿Qué **forma** tiene la casa? *What shape is the house?*

Es de **forma rectangular**. *It has a rectangular shape.*

No me gustó como ella me **miró fijamente**. *I didn't like how she stared at me.*

Él revela sus fotos en su propio cuarto **oscuro**. *He develops his pictures in his own dark room.*

HEARING
El oído

HEARING NOUNS

el sonido	*noise, sound*
el ruido	*noise*
la alarma	*alarm*
el estallido	*bang*
el estrépito	*crash*
el zumbido	*hum*
el golpe	*knock*
el ruido sordo	*thud*
el batacazo	*thud*
el tañido	*ring*
la llamada a la puerta	*knock*
la llamada por teléfono	*ring*
el gruñido	*growl*
el bocinazo	*hoot*
el chirrido	*screech*
el chillido	*screech*
la sirena	*siren*
el silbato	*whistle*

HEARING ADJECTIVES

audible	*audible*
inaudible	*inaudible*
ruidoso	*noisy*
alto	*loud*

estridente	*piercing*
silencioso	*quiet, silent*
bajo	*quiet*
tenue	*faint*
débil	*faint*

HEARING VERBS

oír	*to hear*
escuchar a	*to listen to*
hacer ruido	*to make noise*
escuchar furtivamente	*to eavesdrop*
gruñir	*to growl*
gemir	*to moan*
sonar	*to ring*
tañer	*to ring*
silbar	*to whistle*
castañetear	*to rattle*
traquetear	*to rattle*
llamar a la puerta	*to knock (on the door)*
llamar por teléfono	*to ring (on the phone)*

NOTE: More words related to Hearing can be found in other categories of this book, such as Entertainment and Media.

Words In Use

Me despertó un **sonido estridente**. *A piercing noise woke me up.*

El detective estaba **escuchándolo furtivamente**. *The detective was eavesdropping on the man.*

Siempre he querido aprender a **silbar**. *I've always wanted to learn how to whistle.*

El **estallido** se pudo **oír** en varios pueblos. *The bang was heard in several towns.*

Baja el volumen, ¡está muy **alto**! *Lower the volume, it's too loud!*

SMELL
El olfato

SMELL NOUNS

el olor	*odor, smell*
el aroma	*aroma*
el perfume	*perfume*
el hedor	*stench*
la peste	*stench*

SMELL ADJECTIVES

con olor	*scented*
perfumado	*scented*
aromático	*aromatic*
a flor	*floral, flowery*
floral	*floral*
fresco	*fresh*
a fruta	*fruity*
afrutado	*fruity*
dulce	*sweet*
almizcleño	*musky*
pútrido	*putrid*

SMELL VERBS

oler	*to smell (something)*
oler a	*to smell (to give off an odor)*
olfatear	*to scent, to sniff*
perfumar	*to perfume, to scent*
apestar	*to stink*

Words In Use

El **olor a fruta** llenaba el salón. *The fruity smell filled the room.*

El perro comenzó a **olfatear** todos los árboles. *The dog began to sniff every tree.*

A María le gustan los **perfumes florales**. *Mary likes floral perfumes.*

Prefiero darme un baño **aromático**. *I prefer to take an aromatic bath.*

Es un **olor** bastante **fresco**. *It's a rather fresh smell.*

TOUCH
El tacto

TOUCH NOUNS

el tacto	*touch*
la textura	*texture*

TOUCH ADJECTIVES

duro	*hard*
suave	*soft*
áspero	*rough*
liso	*smooth*
afilado	*sharp*

| espinoso | *prickly* |
| accidentado | *bumpy* |

TOUCH VERBS

tocar	*to touch*
sentir	*to feel*
frotar	*to rub*
acariciar	*to caress*
acariciar a un animal	*to pet (an animal)*

Words In Use

No vayas por esa ruta; el camino es **accidentado**. *Don't take that route, it's a bumpy road.*

Necesito que me **frotes** la espalda. *I need you to rub my back.*

¡Qué **suave** tienes la piel! *How soft is your skin!*

Es importante que las madres **acaricien** a sus bebés. *It's important that mothers caress their babies.*

Los cocodrilos tienen la piel **áspera**. *Crocodiles have rough skin.*

TASTE
El gusto

TASTE NOUNS

el sabor	*taste*
la amargura	*bitterness*
la dulzura	*sweetness*

TASTE ADJECTIVES

salado	*salty*
dulce	*sweet*
ácido	*sour*
amargo	*bitter*
acre	*pungent*
picante	*spicy*
delicioso	*delicious*
repugnante	*disgusting*
asqueroso	*revolting, loathsome, filthy*

TASTE VERBS

degustar	*to taste*
probar	*to try, to taste*
saborear	*to savor*

NOTE: More words related to Taste can be found in the Food category of this book.

Words In Use

A José le gustan los caramelos **ácidos**. *Jose likes sour candy.*

Deberías **probar** muchos tipos de comida. *You should try different types of food.*

¡Qué cena tan **deliciosa**! *What a delicious dinner!*

Al señor le gusta **degustar** vinos. *The man loves wine tasting.*

EXERCISES

I. Match the Spanish word on the left with the English word on the right.

1. saborear	A. *odor*
2. tocar	B. *to rub*
3. afilado	C. *round*
4. olor	D. *to savor*
5. el gruñido	E. *sweet*
6. llamar a la puerta	F. *to make noise*
7. hacer ruido	G. *to touch*
8. circular	H. *sharp*
9. frotar	I. *to knock*
10. dulce	J. *growl*

II. Fill in the blanks with the appropriate Spanish word.

1. *The opposite of* liso *is* _____ .

2. *The opposite of* oscuro *is* _____.

3. No pongas mucha sal; ya está _____ (*salty*).

4. Me gusta la comida _____ (*spicy*).

5. Tienes que _____ (*listen*) lo que dicen los mayores.

ANSWERS: I. 1. D, 2. G, 3. H, 4. A, 5. J, 6. I, 7. F, 8. C, 9. B, 10. E
II. 1. *THE OPPOSITE OF* LISO *IS* **ÁSPERO**. 2. *THE OPPOSITE OF* OSCURO *IS* **CLARO**. 3. NO PONGAS MUCHA SAL; YA ESTÁ **SALADO**. 4. ME GUSTA LA COMIDA **PICANTE**. 5. TIENES QUE **ESCUCHAR** LO QUE DICEN LOS MAYORES.

6 Family & Relationships

Familia y relaciones

FAMILY

La familia

FAMILY NOUNS—PEOPLE

los padres	*parents*
la madre	*mother, parent (female)*
la mamá	*mother*
el padre	*father, parent (male)*
el papá	*father*
el niño	*child (male)*
la niña	*child (female)*
el hijo	*son*
la hija	*daughter*
la hermana	*sister, sibling (female)*
el hermano	*brother, sibling (male)*
la tía	*aunt*
el tío	*uncle*
el primo	*cousin (male)*
la prima	*cousin (female)*
la sobrina	*niece*
el sobrino	*nephew*
la abuela	*grandmother*
el abuelo	*grandfather*
la nieta	*granddaughter, grandchild (female)*
el nieto	*grandson, grandchild (male)*
la bisabuela	*great-grandmother*
el bisabuelo	*great-grandfather*
el bisnieto	*great-grandson, great-grandchild (male)*
la bisnieta	*great-granddaughter, great-grandchild (female)*
el marido	*husband*
el esposo	*husband, spouse (male)*

la esposa	*wife, spouse (female)*
la mujer	*wife*
el compañero	*male partner*
la compañera	*female partner*
la suegra	*mother-in-law*
el suegro	*father-in-law*
el cuñado	*brother-in-law*
la cuñada	*sister-in-law*
el padrastro	*stepfather*
la madrastra	*stepmother*
el hijastro	*stepson*
la hijastra	*stepdaughter*
el medio hermano	*half-brother*
la media hermana	*half-sister*
la viuda	*widow*
el viudo	*widower*
los antepasados	*ancestors*
los descendientes	*descendants*
los familiares	*relatives*

FAMILY NOUNS—SITUATIONS

el matrimonio	*marriage*
la unión civil	*civil union*
el compromiso	*commitment*
la separación	*separation*
el divorcio	*divorce*

FAMILY ADJECTIVES

soltero	*single*
casado	*married*
separado	*separated*
divorciado	*divorced*
adoptivo	*adopted*
emparentado	*related*

FAMILY VERBS

casarse	*to marry*
comprometerse	*to get engaged*
divorciarse	*to divorce*
adoptar	*to adopt*

6

Words In Use

Mis mejores amigos **adoptaron** a un niño. *My best friends adopted a child.*

Yo me reúno con mis **familiares** en Navidad. *I get together with my relatives for Christmas.*

Ella **se divorció** hace dos años. *She got divorced a couple of years ago.*

No podría encontrar un mejor **esposo**. *I could not find a better husband.*

Es un **padre** estupendo. *He is a great father.*

Mi **abuela** es mayor que mi **abuelo**. *My grandmother is older than my grandfather.*

DATING AND FRIENDSHIP
Amor y amistad

FRIENSHIP NOUNS—POSITIVE

el amigo	*friend*
el mejor amigo	*best friend*
el compinche	*"pal"/"buddy"*
el pana	*"pal"/"buddy"*
el colega	*"pal"/"buddy", colleague*
el compañero de escuela	*schoolmate*
el compañero de clase	*classmate*
la novia	*girlfriend*
el novio	*boyfriend*
la novia seria	*serious girlfriend*
el novio serio	*serious boyfriend*
el prometido	*fiancé*
la prometida	*fiancée*
el esposo	*husband*
el marido	*husband*
el esposa	*wife*
la mujer	*wife*
el compañero	*partner (male)*
la compañera	*partner (female)*
el conocido	*acquaintance*
el compañero	*peer (male)*
la compañera	*peer (female)*

FRIENDSHIP NOUNS—NEGATIVE

el ex novio	*ex-boyfriend*
la ex novia	*ex-girlfriend*
el ex marido	*ex-husband*

la ex mujer	*ex-wife*
el enemigo	*enemy (male)*
la enemiga	*enemy (female)*
el rival	*rival (male)*
la rival	*rival (female)*
el desconocido	*stranger (male)*
la desconocida	*stranger (female)*

Family

Dating and Friendship/ Positive Relationship Verbs

Negative Relationship Verbs

Other Relationships Verbs

Childbirth, Children, and Care for Children

Words In Use

Su **ex mujer** se casó muy rápido. *His ex-wife got married quickly.*

Mi **mejor amigo** se fue de viaje ayer. *My best friend went on a trip yesterday.*

Mi **compañero** es muy responsable. *My partner is very responsible.*

Te presento a mi **prometida**. *Let me introduce you to my fiancée.*

Somos **novios** desde que éramos **compañeros de escuela**. *We've been boyfriend and girlfriend since we were schoolmates.*

POSITIVE RELATIONSHIP VERBS

Relaciones, verbos positivos

adorar	*to adore*
apreciar	*to appreciate, to cherish*
volverse loco por	*to be crazy about*
gustar	*to like*
amar	*to love*
proponerle a	*to propose to*
comprometerse	*to get engaged*
casarse	*to marry*
ir tomados de las manos	*to hold hands*
abrazar	*to hug*
besar	*to kiss*
valorar	*to treasure*
tenerle mucho cariño	*to cherish*
disfrutar	*to enjoy*

Words In Use

Juana y Pedro **iban tomados de las manos** por el parque. *Juana and Pedro were holding hands in the park.*

¡Me estoy **volviendo loco** por ella! *I'm crazy about her!*

Carlos acaba de **comprometerse**. *Carlos has just gotten engaged.*

Yo **aprecio** mucho mi relación con él. *I cherish my relationship with him.*

NEGATIVE RELATIONSHIP VERBS

Relaciones, verbos negativos

no gustar	*to dislike*
tenerle antipatía a alguien	*to dislike*
molestar	*to annoy*
detestar	*to detest*
odiar	*to hate*
no soportar	*to be unable to stand*
discutir	*to argue*
pelear	*to fight*
gritar	*to yell*
pegar	*to hit*
dar un puñetazo	*to punch*
dar una bofetada	*to slap*
burlarse de	*to make fun of*
poner en ridículo	*to mock*
provocar	*to tease*
romper con	*to break up*
separarse	*to separate*
divorciarse	*to divorce*

Words In Use

El **se divorció** hace un mes. *He got divorced a month ago.*

No te **burles** de ella. *Don't make fun of her!*

Después de la pelea **se separaron**. *They separated after the fight.*

Es difícil **romper** con tu pareja. *Breaking up is a hard thing.*

Odio tener peleas. *I hate having fights.*

OTHER RELATIONSHIPS VERBS

Relaciones, verbos generales

saludar	*to greet*
dar la bienvenida	*to welcome*
conocer	*to meet*
llegar a conocer	*to get to know*
pasar tiempo con	*to spend time with*
hacerse amigos	*to befriend, to become friends*
ponerse en contacto	*to contact*
distanciarse	*to grow apart*
echar de menos	*to miss*

Words In Use

No te olvides de **ponerte en contacto** conmigo. *Don't forget to contact me.*

Echo de menos los viejos tiempos. *I miss the old times.*

El anfitrión les **dio la bienvenida** a sus huéspedes. *The host welcomed all his guests.*

¿**Conoces** al padre de Roberto? *Do you know Robert's father?*

CHILDBIRTH, CHILDREN, AND CARE FOR CHILDREN

Parto, niños y cuidado de los niños

CHILDREN NOUNS—STAGES

el bebé	baby
el embrión	embryo
el feto	fetus
el infante	infant
el niño que empieza a andar	toddler

CHILDREN NOUNS—PREGNANCY

la inseminación	insemination
el embarazo	pregnancy
el cuidado prenatal	pre-natal care
la ecografia	ultrasound
el cordón umbilical	umbilical cord
el vientre	womb
la cesárea	Caesarean section
el parto natural	natural birth
la depresión postnatal	post-natal depression

CHILDREN NOUNS—ITEMS

la cuna	cradle, crib
la canción de cuna	lullaby
el corralito para niños	play-pen
el cajón de arena	sandbox
la mesa para cambiar	changing table
los pañales	diapers
los paños	wipes
el biberón	bottle
el tetero	bottle
la comida de bebé	baby formula
la fórmula de bebé	baby formula

los juguetes	*toys*
el animalito de peluche	*stuffed animal*
el osito de peluche	*teddy bear*
el sonajero	*rattle*
los bloques	*blocks*
la muñeca	*doll*

CHILDREN NOUNS—CHILDCARE

el cuidado diurno	*daycare*
la niñera	*baby-sitter*
el desarrollo	*development*
el entrenamiento para controlar las esfínteres	*toilet training*

CHILDREN ADJECTIVES

embarazada	*pregnant*
saludable	*healthy*
prematuro	*premature*
parto de nalgas	*breech*

CHILDREN VERBS

tener un hijo	*to have a baby/give birth*
dar de pecho	*to breast-feed/nurse a baby*
amamantar	*to breast-feed/nurse a baby*
sacar gases	*to burp*
ayudar a un bebé a eructar	*to burp (a baby)*
cambiar pañales	*to change a baby's diaper*
mecer al niño	*to rock to sleep*
criar	*to raise*
atender al niño	*to take care of*
cuidar niños	*to baby sit*
estar pendiente del niño	*to watch (after) a child*

NOTE: More words related to Children can be found in the School category of this book.

Words In Use

El bebé **nació por cesárea**. *The baby was born through a Caesarean section.*

¿Necesitas que te **cuide a los niños**? *Do you need me to baby sit?*

Hay que darle el **biberón** a las seis. *I have to give him the bottle at 6 p.m.*

Le compré un **juguete** a Alex. *I bought a toy for Alex.*

Ya es hora de **cambiarle los pañales** al niño. *It's time to change the baby's diapers.*

EXERCISES

I. Match the Spanish word on the left with the English word on the right.

1. la hija	A. *niece*
2. criar	B. *single*
3. besar	C. *stepfather*
4. soltero	D. *marriage*
5. saludar	E. *daughter*
6. la sobrina	F. *to raise*
7. el padrastro	G. *to enjoy*
8. el tío	H. *to kiss*
9. el matrimonio	I. *uncle*
10. disfrutar	J. *to greet*

II. Fill in the blanks with the appropriate Spanish word.

1. *Your mother's mother is your _____.*

2. *Your cousin's mother is your _____.*

3. *Your mother's brother is your _____.*

4. *Your aunt's daughter is your_____.*

5. *Your spouse's father is your _____.*

Family

Dating and Friendship

Positive Relationship Verbs

Negative Relationship Verbs

Other Relationships Verbs

Childbirth, Children, and Care for Children

ANSWERS: I. 1. E, 2. F, 3. H, 4. B, 5. J, 6. A, 7. C, 8. I, 9. D, 10. G
II. 1. *YOUR MOTHER'S MOTHER IS YOUR* **ABUELA**. 2. *YOUR COUSIN'S MOTHER IS YOUR* **TÍA**. 3. *YOUR MOTHER'S BROTHER IS YOUR* **TÍO**. 4. *YOUR AUNT'S DAUGHTER IS YOUR* **PRIMA**. 5. *YOUR SPOUSE'S FATHER IS YOUR* **SUEGRO**.

Clothing

Ropa

CLOTHING

Ropa

CLOTHING NOUNS—TOPS

la camisa	*shirt*
la playera	*t-shirt*
la camiseta	*t-shirt*
la camiseta de manga sisa	*tank top*
la camiseta interior	*undershirt*
la camiseta sin mangas	*tank top*
la blusa	*blouse*
el chaleco	*vest*
el jersey	*sweater*
el suéter	*sweater*

CLOTHING NOUNS—BOTTOMS

los pantalones	*pants, trousers*
los vaqueros	*jeans*
los jeans	*jeans*
los pantalones cortos	*shorts*
la falda	*skirt*
la minifalda	*miniskirt*
los pantalones de bota campana	*bell-bottoms*

CLOTHING NOUNS—SUITS

el traje	*suit*
el traje de tres piezas	*three-piece suit*
el traje cruzado	*double-breasted suit*
el traje de etiqueta	*tuxedo*
el esmoquin	*tuxedo*
el saco	*suit jacket*

CLOTHING NOUNS—JACKETS

el abrigo	*coat, overcoat*
el impermeable	*raincoat*
la chaqueta	*jacket*
la chaqueta formal	*dinner jacket*
la chaqueta de sport	*blazer*
la americana de sport	*blazer*

CLOTHING NOUNS—DRESSES

el vestido	*dress*
el vestido largo	*gown*

CLOTHING NOUNS—NIGHTWEAR AND UNDERWEAR

el albornoz	*robe*
la bata	*robe*
el pijamas	*pajamas*
el traje de noche	*nightgown*
la ropa interior	*underwear*
el sostén	*bra*
las bombachas	*panties*
las bragas	*panties (Spain)*
el calzón	*panties*
los calzoncillos	*underpants*
los calcetines	*socks*
las medias	*stockings*

CLOTHING ADJECTIVES

casual	*casual*
informal	*informal, casual*
formal	*formal*
de última moda	*fashionable*
chic	*chic*
elegante	*stylish*
a la moda	*in style*
fuera de moda	*out of style*
pasado de moda	*old fashioned*
profesional	*professional*
bien arreglado	*neat*
desarreglado	*disheveled*
arrugado	*wrinkled*

CLOTHING VERBS

usar	*to wear*
llevar puesto	*to wear*
ponerse	*to put on*
quitarse	*to take off*
estirar	*to stretch*
rasgar	*to tear*
limpiar	*to clean*
lavar	*to wash*
lavar en seco	*to dry clean*
planchar	*to iron*
combinar	*to accessorize*

NOTE: More words related to Clothing can be found in other sections of this book, such as Shopping or Running Errands.

Words In Use

No se usan mucho los **trajes cruzados**. *Double-breasted suits are not very popular.*

Hace mucho sol. **Ponte** un sombrero. *It's too sunny, put on a hat.*

En el verano siempre me pongo **pantalones cortos**. *In the summer I always wear shorts.*

No te pongas esa **camisa**; está **arrugada.** *Don't put on that shirt; it's wrinkled.*

Los **pantalones de bota campana** eran populares en los sesenta. *Bell-bottoms were popular in the sixties.*

Ricardo siempre se ve muy **bien arreglado**. *Richard always looks so neat.*

SHOES
Zapatos

los zapatos	*shoes*
las botas	*boots*
los mocasines	*loafers*
los zapatos deportivos	*sneakers, tennis shoes, sports shoes*
los zapatos tenis	*tennis shoes*
los zapatos de tacón	*high heel shoes*
los zapatos de tacón de aguja/puntiagudos	*stiletto heel*
los zapatos de plataforma	*platform shoes*
el calce	*wedge (heel)*

las zapatillas	*slippers*
las pantuflas	*slippers*
las babuchas	*slippers*

Clothing

Shoes/Jewelry

Accessories/
Miscellaneous

Patterns

Fabrics

Sewing and
Repairs

Words In Use

Hay mucha nieve. Deberías ponerte tus **botas.** *It's very snowy, you should wear your boots.*

Para el trabajo me gusta llevar **mocasines.** *I like to wear loafers for work.*

Se me olvidó traer mis **zapatos deportivos**. *I forgot to bring my sneakers.*

Estos **zapatos de tacón** son muy incómodos. *These high heel shoes are very uncomfortable.*

JEWELRY
Joyería

la joya	*jewel*
el anillo	*ring*
el brazalete	*bracelet*
la pulsera	*bracelet*
el arete	*earring*
el pendiente	*pendant, earring*
la gargantilla	*necklace*
el collar	*necklace*
la cadena	*chain*
el dije	*locket*
el colgante	*pendant*
el broche	*brooch*
el prendedor	*brooch*
el alfiler	*pin*
el alfiler de corbata	*tie pin*
los gemelos	*cufflink*
el reloj	*watch*

Words In Use

No te metas en la piscina con el **reloj.** *Don't get in the pool with your watch on.*

Me encanta tu **brazalete.** *I love your bracelet.*

¿Son de oro tus **pendientes**? *Are your earrings made of gold?*

Es un **collar** de perlas. *It's a pearl necklace.*

ACCESSORIES/MISCELLANEOUS

Accesorios y misceláneos

GENERAL

el estilo	style
las prendas sueltas	separates
la imagen	image

HEAD

el sombrero	hat
la gorra	cap
las orejeras	ear muffs
el velo	veil

EYES

las gafas	glasses
los anteojos	glasses
los espejuelos	spectacles
los lentes de contacto	contact lenses
los anteojos de sol	sunglasses

NECK

la corbata	tie, necktie
el corbatín	bow tie
el pañuelo	scarf (silk/foulard)
la bufanda	scarf (winter)
la banda	sash
el ceñidor	sash
el pañuelo de hombre para el cuello	cravat
el chal	shawl

HANDS

los guantes	gloves
los mitones	mittens
el manguito	muff

WAIST

el cinturón	belt
la trabilla	belt loop

RAINWEAR

el impermeable	*raincoat*
la capa	*raincoat*
el paraguas	*umbrella*
la sombrilla	*umbrella*

UNDERWEAR

el albornoz	*bathrobe*
la bata	*bathrobe*
los calzones	*boxers*
la lencería	*lingerie*
el corsé	*corset*
la faja	*girdle, sash*
el vestido entubado	*sheath*

PARTS OF CLOTHING

la hebilla	*buckle*
el botón	*button*
el velcro	*Velcro*
la cremallera	*zipper*
el cierre	*clasp*
el broche	*clasp, brooch*
el lazo	*bow*
la capucha	*hood*
el cuello	*collar*
la manga	*sleeve*
el puño	*cuff*
la solapa	*lapel*
el dobladillo	*hem*
el ruedo	*hem*
el bajo	*hemline*
la costura	*seam*
el pliegue	*pleat*
el bolsillo	*pocket*
el tirante	*strap*
las hombreras	*shoulder pads*
el tacón	*heel*
el talón	*heel*
el largo	*length*
la cintura	*waist*

7

Clothing

Shoes

Jewelry

**Accessories/
Miscellaneous**

Patterns

Fabrics

Sewing and
Repairs

MISCELLANEOUS ADJECTIVES

hecho a la medida	*tailored*
pierna recta	*straight-legged*

Words In Use

¿Cuánto mides de **cintura**? *What's your waist size?*

El **largo** de los pantalones es 32 pulgadas. *The length of the pants is 32 inches.*

Está lloviendo; busca un **paraguas.** *It's raining, get your umbrella.*

Hacía tanto frío que necesitábamos **guantes**. *It was so cold that we needed gloves.*

Me molestan mis **lentes de contacto**. *My contact lenses are bothering me.*

Dejé mi **bufanda** en el autobús. *I left my scarf on the bus.*

PATTERNS

Patrones

PATTERN NOUNS

el estampado	*print*
la raya diplomática	*pinstripe*
los lunares	*polka-dot*
los puntos	*polka-dot*
el diseño de cachemira	*paisley*
el punto de espiga	*herringbone*
el punto de espinapez	*herringbone*
el estampado con tinte	*tie-dye*
el prelavado	*stone wash*
el lavado con ácido	*acid wash*

PATTERN ADJECTIVES

de un solo color	*solid color*
a rayas	*striped*
de rayas finas	*pinstriped*
de cuadros a la esocesa	*plaid*
de guinga	*gingham*
floral	*floral*
geométrico	*geometric*

PATTERN VERBS

combinar	*to match*
complementar	*to complement*
desentonar	*to clash*

Words In Use

Esa falda no **combina** con esos zapatos. *That skirt doesn't match those shoes.*

Ella llevaba una bufanda de **cuadros a la escocesa**. *She was wearing a plaid scarf.*

No me gustan las camisas con diseños **florales**. *I don't like shirts that have floral patterns.*

Prefiero el vestido de **lunares** negros. *I prefer the black polka dot dress.*

Siempre que la veo lleva ropa **de un solo color**. *I always see her wearing solid colors.*

7

Clothing

Shoes

Jewelry

Accessories/
Miscellaneous

Patterns/Fabrics

Sewing and
Repairs

FABRICS

Telas

FABRIC NOUNS

la tela	*fabric*
la fibra artificial	*man-made fiber*
la fibra natural	*natural fiber*
el algodón	*cotton*
el lino	*linen, flax*
el lienzo	*linen*
el hilo	*yarn*
la lana	*wool*
la seda	*silk*
el terciopelo	*velvet*
el fieltro	*felt*
el yute	*jute*
el brocado	*brocade*
el damasco	*damask*
el encaje	*lace*
el tapiz	*tapestry*
el cuero	*leather*
la gamuza	*suede*
el ante	*suede*
la piel	*fur, leather*
el acrílico	*acrylic*
el poliéster	*polyester*
el nailon	*nylon*
el nilón	*nylon*
el rayón	*rayon*

el spándex elástico	spandex
la mezcla	blend

FABRIC ADJECTIVES

artificial	fake
sintético	synthetic
tejido	knitted, woven
impermeable	water-repellent
estampado	printed

Words In Use

¿Cuál es tu tipo de **tela** favorito? *What's your favorite type of fabric?*

El material del sofá es **impermeable**. *The fabric of the sofa is water-repellent.*

Ella tenía un vestido de **terciopelo** elegantísimo. *She had a very elegant velvet dress.*

El **algodón** y el **hilo** son los mejores materiales para el verano. *Cotton and linen are the best fabrics for the summer.*

¿Es perjudicial el **acrílico** para la piel? *Is acrylic bad for your skin?*

En Bélgica se consigue muy buen **encaje**. *You can get beautiful lace in Belgium.*

Sus pantalones eran una **mezcla** de **nailon** y **poliéster**. *His pants were a blend of nylon with polyester.*

SEWING AND REPAIRS

Costura y arreglos

SEWING AND REPAIRS NOUNS

la mancha	stain
la lejía	bleach
el cloro	bleach
el lavado en seco	dry-cleaning
el rasgón	tear
la rasgadura	tear
la aguja	needle
el hilo	thread

SEWING AND REPAIRS VERBS

emborronar	to smudge
manchar	to stain
lavar	to wash
blanquear	to bleach

descolorar	*to discolor*
rasgar	*to rip, to tear*
cortar	*to cut*
remendar	*to mend*
reparar	*to repair*
coser	*to sew*

7

Clothing

Shoes

Jewelry

Accessories/
Miscellaneous

Patterns

Fabrics

**Sewing and
Repairs**

Words In Use

Tengo que **lavar** estas sábanas por separado. *I have to wash these sheets separately.*

Se me **rasgaron** los pantalones cuando me caí. *My pants tore when I fell down.*

Estaba tan sucio que tuvimos que **lavarlo** con **lejía**. *It was so dirty that we had to wash it with bleach.*

¿Me puedes prestar **hilo** y **aguja**? *May I borrow a needle and thread?*

El **rasgón** es tan grande que me temo que no pueda **remendarlo**. *The tear is so big that I'm afraid I can't mend it.*

EXERCISES

I. Match the Spanish word on the left with the English word on the right.

1. la mancha
2. artificial
3. el zapato
4. combinar
5. lavar
6. la tela
7. el lavado en seco
8. planchar
9. la camisa
10. desentonar

A. *shirt*
B. *to iron*
C. *dry-cleaning*
D. *to clash*
E. *fabric*
F. *shoe*
G. *stain*
H. *to wash*
I. *to match*
J. *fake*

II. Fill in the blanks with the appropriate Spanish word.

1. Me gusta mucho tu _____ (*chain*) de oro.
2. Tengo problemas con esta _____ (*zipper*).
3. Yo llevo mi dinero en el _____ (*pocket*) de enfrente.
4. Se me perdió uno de mis _____ (*gloves*).
5. No me gusta el _____ (*dress*) que llevaba puesto.

ANSWERS: I. 1. G, 2. J, 3. F, 4. I, 5. H, 6. E, 7. C, 8. B, 9. A, 10. D
II. 1. ME GUSTA MUCHO TU **CADENA** DE ORO. 2. TENGO PROBLEMAS CON ESTA **CREMALLERA**. 3. YO LLEVO MI DINERO EN EL **BOLSILLO** DE ENFRENTE. 4. SE ME PERDIÓ UNO DE MIS **GUANTES**. 5. NO ME GUSTA EL **VESTIDO** QUE LLEVABA PUESTO.

Health, Hygiene & Safety

Salud, higiene y seguridad

PERSONAL HYGIENE

Higiene personal

HYGIENE NOUNS

el jabón	soap
la toalla	towel
el paño para lavarse	washcloth
la toallita para lavarse	washcloth
la esponja	sponge
la toalla para la cara	face cloth
el astringente	astringent
el cepillo de dientes	toothbrush
la pasta de dientes	toothpaste
el dentífrico	toothpaste
el enjuague bucal	mouthwash
el hilo dental	dental floss
el champú	shampoo
el cepillo	brush
el peine	comb
el secador de pelo	hair dryer
el rulo	curler
las tenacillas para rizar el pelo	curling iron
el rizador	curling iron
la navaja de afeitar	razor
la hoja de afeitar	razor blade
la cuchilla de afeitar	razor blade
la máquina de afeitar eléctrica	electric shaver
la crema de afeitar	shaving cream
las pinzas	tweezers
la lima para las uñas	nail file

HYGIENE VERBS

bañarse	*to take a bath*
ducharse	*to take a shower*
lavarse	*to wash*
fregar	*to scrub*
restregar	*to scrub*
enjuagar	*to rinse*
aclarar	*to rinse*
secar	*to dry*
cepillarse el pelo	*to brush one's hair*
cepillarse los dientes	*to brush one's teeth*
peinarse	*to comb one's hair*
cortarse el pelo	*to get a haircut*
afeitarse	*to shave*

NOTE: More words related to Personal Hygiene can be found in the Bathroom section of this book.

Words In Use

La **higiene personal** debe enseñarse desde pequeño. *Personal hygiene should be taught since childhood.*

El dentista me sugirió usar **hilo dental**. *The dentist suggested that I use dental floss.*

Debes usar **astringente** después de lavarte la cara. *You should use astringent after washing your face.*

No me gusta el olor de ese **champú**. *I don't like the smell of that shampoo.*

Esta **toalla** está muy mojada. *This towel is too wet.*

Le voy a regalar una **máquina de afeitar eléctrica**. *I'm going to get him an electric shaver.*

Mañana voy a ir a **cortarme el pelo**. *Tomorrow I'm getting a haircut.*

COSMETICS

Cosméticos

COSMETIC NOUNS—MAKEUP

el maquillaje	*make-up*
la base	*foundation*
el delineador de ojos	*eye liner*
la sombra para los ojos	*eye shadow*
el rímel	*mascara*
el colorete	*blush*
el lápiz labial	*lipstick*

el brillo labial	*lip gloss*
el delineador de labios	*lip liner*
el polvo	*powder*
el esmalte de uñas	*nail polish*

COSMETICS NOUNS—FACE CARE

la crema humectante	*moisturizer*
la crema	*cream*
el espejo	*mirror*

COSMETICS NOUNS—HAIR CARE

el gel para el pelo	*hair gel*
la laca para el pelo	*hairspray*
el mousse	*mousse*

COSMETICS NOUNS—SCENTS

el perfume	*perfume*
la colonia	*cologne*
la loción para después de afeitarse	*aftershave*

NOTE: More words related to Cosmetics can be found in the Bathroom section of this book.

Words In Use

A ella no le gusta usar mucho **maquillaje**. *She doesn't like to wear too much make-up.*

El color de ese **lápiz labial** es demasiado rojo. *The color of that lipstick is too red.*

Yo nunca uso **laca para el pelo** después de ducharme. *I never use hairspray after taking a shower.*

Es importante usar **crema humectante** desde que se es joven. *It's important to use moisturizer from the time you're young.*

El **espejo** nunca miente. *The mirror never tells lies.*

Julia debe usar una **base** más tenue. *Julia should use a lighter foundation.*

HEALTH AND SICKNESS

Salud y enfermedad

HEALTH NOUNS—DISEASE AND SICKNESS

la enfermedad	*disease*
la bacteria	*bacteria*
el virus	*virus*
la infección	*infection*

el catarro	*cold*
el resfriado	*cold*
la influenza	*flu, influenza*
la gripe	*flu*
la alergia	*allergy*
la acidez estomacal	*heartburn*
la pulmonía	*pneumonia*
la neumonía	*pneumonia*
la diabetes	*diabetes*
el ataque al corazón	*heart attack*
la enfermedad del corazón	*heart disease*
el cáncer	*cancer*
el derrame	*stroke*
la enfermedad de Alzheimer	*Alzheimer's disease*
la enfermedad de Parkinson	*Parkinson's disease*
la enfermedad de transmisión sexual	*sexually transmitted disease*
el sida	*AIDS*
la hepatitis	*hepatitis*
el cólera	*cholera*
la desnutrición	*malnutrition*

8

Personal Hygiene

Cosmetics

Health and Sickness

Physical Ability

Accidents and Emergencies

Safety and Security

HEALTH NOUNS—SYMPTOMS

la presión arterial	*blood pressure*
el pulso	*pulse*
el latido	*heartbeat*
la erupción en la piel	*rash (skin)*
la congestión	*congestion*
la fiebre	*fever*

HEALTH NOUNS—CARE

el tratamiento	*treatment*
la vacuna	*vaccine*
la medicina	*drug, medicine*
el medicamento	*drug, medicine*
el medicamento genérico	*generic drugs*
el medicamento sin receta	*over-the-counter*
la medicina con receta	*prescription drug*
el medicamento veterinario	*veterinary drug*
la píldora	*pill*

la pastilla	*pill, tablet*
la tableta	*tablet*
la cápsula	*capsule*
los antibióticos	*antibiotics*
la vacuna	*vaccine*
el antídoto	*antidote*
el placebo	*placebo*
el veneno	*poison*
la cirugía de conductos	*root canal*
el empaste	*filling*
la anestesia	*anesthesic*
las vitaminas	*vitamins*

HEALTH NOUNS—CHECK-UP AND EXAM

la visita de rutina	*check-up*
el examen	*exam, test*
el pronóstico	*prognosis*
la toxicología	*toxicology*
los rayos x	*x-ray*

HEALTH NOUNS—PLACES

el hospital	*hospital*
la farmacia	*pharmacy*
la compañía farmacéutica	*pharmaceutical company*
el laboratorio	*laboratory*

HEALTH NOUNS—PEOPLE

el/la paciente	*patient*
el/la médico/a	*doctor*
el/la doctor/a	*doctor*
el/la enfermero/a	*nurse*
el/la médico/a general	*general practitioner*
el/la pediatra	*pediatrician*
el/la dentista	*dentist*
el/la ginecólogo/a	*gynecologist*
el/la neurólogo/a	*neurologist*
el/la oncólogo/a	*oncologist*
el/la optómetra	*optometrist*
el/la oculista	*eye doctor*
el/la oftalmólogo/a	*ophthalmologist*

| el/la farmacéutico/a | *pharmacist* |
| el/la farmacólogo/a | *pharmacologist* |

HEALTH ADJECTIVES

saludable	*healthy*
no saludable	*unhealthy*
enfermo	*sick, ill*
en forma	*fit*
desnutrido	*malnourished*
senil	*senile*
neurológico	*neurological*
físico	*physical*

HEALTH VERBS

dar un catarro	*to catch a cold*
toser	*to cough*
tener fiebre	*to have a fever*
temblar	*to shiver*
vomitar	*to vomit*
estornudar	*to sneeze*
tener la nariz tupida	*to have a stuffy nose*
estar constipado	*to have a stuffy nose*
tener alergia	*to have allergies*
ser alérgico a algo	*to be allergic to something*
examinar	*to examine*
tomarse la temperatura	*to take one's temperature*
examinarse	*to test*
recetar	*to prescribe*
recuperar	*to recover*
romperse (algo)	*to break (something)*
torcerse el tobillo	*to twist one's ankle*

Words In Use

El **sida** está arrasando el continente africano. *AIDS is sweeping through the African continent.*

Tenía una **fiebre** tan alta que estaba **temblando**. *I had such a high fever that I was shivering.*

Mi padre siempre ha sido una persona muy **saludable.** *My father has always been a very healthy person.*

La **desnutrición** es un problema que todavía afecta a la humanidad. *Malnutrition is still a problem that affects mankind.*

El **catarro** se convirtió en una peligrosa **pulmonía**. *The cold turned into a dangerous pneumonia.*

¿Qué te **recetó** el médico? *What did the doctor prescribe?*

El padre de Roberto es **médico general**. *Roberto's father is a general practitioner.*

¿Tomas **vitaminas** todos los días? *Do you take vitamins every day?*

No me gusta ir a los **hospitales**. *I don't like to visit hospitals.*

Tuve que tomar **antibióticos** durante ocho días. *I had to be on antibiotics for 8 days.*

PHYSICAL ABILITY

Aptitud física

PHYSICAL ABILITY NOUNS

el bastón	*cane*
las muletas	*crutches*
la abrazadera	*brace*
el aparato	*brace*
la silla de ruedas	*wheelchair*
la silla de ruedas eléctrica	*electric wheelchair*
las gafas	*eyeglasses*
los anteojos	*eyeglasses*
los lentes de contacto	*contact lenses*
el audífono	*hearing aid*
la prótesis auditiva	*hearing aid*
el perro guía	*guide dog*
el lazarillo	*seeing-eye dog*
el Braille	*Braille*
el lenguaje por señas	*sign language*

PHYSICAL ABILITY ADJECTIVES

minusválido	*disabled*
discapacitado	*handicapped*
impedido físicamente	*handicapped*
ciego	*blind*
que tiene mala visión	*vision impaired*
sordo	*deaf*
duro de oído	*hearing impaired*
mudo	*mute*
paralizado	*paralyzed*

Words In Use

Después del accidente tuve que usar **muletas**. *After the accident I had to use crutches.*

Y yo tuve que usar un **bastón**. *And I had to use a cane.*

El señor perdió la vista hasta quedar **ciego**. *The man lost his vision to the extent that he went blind.*

A veces pienso que te haces el **sordo**. *Sometimes I think you play deaf with me.*

¿Qué tipo de **lentes de contacto** usas? *What type of contact lenses do you wear?*

Yo prefiero usar **gafas**. *I prefer to wear eyeglasses.*

El edificio no está equipado para los **minusválidos**. *The building is not equipped for the disabled.*

ACCIDENTS AND EMERGENCIES

Accidentes y emergencias

EMERGENCY NOUNS

la emergencia	*emergency*
la urgencia	*emergency, urgency*
la sala de emergencias	*emergency room*
la sangre	*blood*
la transfusión de sangre	*blood transfusion*
el brazo roto	*broken arm*
la herida	*cut, wound*
la cortadura	*cut*
la quemadura	*burn*
la herida profunda	*gash*
el rasguño	*scrape*
los accidentes	*accidents*
el choque	*crash*
la colisión	*crash*
el fuego	*fire*
la explosión	*explosion*
el veneno	*poison*
el seguro	*insurance*

EMERGENCY ADJECTIVES

roto	*broken*
dislocado	*sprained*
torcido	*twisted*

lacerado	*lacerated*
peligroso	*dangerous*
fatal	*fatal*
tóxico	*toxic*
resbaladizo	*slippery*
cubierto de hielo	*icy*

EMERGENCY VERBS

caerse	*to fall*
resbalarse	*to slip*
chocar	*to crash*
cortarse	*to cut*
romperse un hueso	*to break a bone*

Words In Use

Él se **rompió un hueso** con la caída. *He broke a bone after the fall.*

Sí, el piso estaba **resbaladizo**. *Yes, the floor was slippery.*

Y la carretera estaba **cubierta de hielo**. *And the road was icy.*

Fue un día muy **peligroso** para estar fuera. *It was a dangerous day to be outdoors.*

Hubo muchos **accidentes** ese día. *There were many accidents that day.*

Gracias a Dios el **accidente** no fue **fatal**. *Thank goodness the accident was not fatal.*

Sólo tuve un pequeño **rasguño**. *I only had a minor scrape.*

SAFETY AND SECURITY

Seguridad

SAFETY NOUNS

la seguridad física	*safety*
la seguridad	*security*
la defensa personal	*self-defense*
el aerosol irritante	*mace*
el aerosol lacrimógeno	*pepper spray*
el/la guardia/guardiana	*guard*
el guardaespaldas	*bodyguard*
el perro de presa	*attack dog*
la alarma	*alarm*
la alarma contra incendios	*smoke alarm*
la pared	*wall*

la valla	*fence*
la cerca	*fence*
el alambre de púas	*barbed wire*
la puerta	*gate, door*
la salida	*gate, exit*
la cerradura	*lock*
el cerrojo	*bolt (door lock)*
el pestillo	*bolt (door lock)*
la falleba	*bolt (door lock)*
el código personal	*personal code*
la salida de emergencia	*fire escape*
el extintor/extinguidor de incendios	*fire extinguisher*
la manta protectora	*fire blanket*
el repelente de fuego	*fire retardant*
el simulacro contra incendios	*fire drill*
el plan de evacuación	*escape plan*
el botiquín	*first aid kit*

8

Personal Hygiene

Cosmetics

Health and
Sickness

Physical Ability

Accidents and
Emergencies

**Safety and
Security**

SAFETY ADJECTIVES

seguro	*safe*
protegido con alarma	*alarmed*
cercado	*fenced-in*
protegido por verja	*gated*

SAFETY VERBS

estar seguro	*to be safe*
asegurar	*to secure*
proteger	*to protect*
detectar fuego	*to detect smoke*
proteger con alarma	*to rig with an alarm*

Words In Use

Mi casa está **protegida con alarma**. *My house is protected with an alarm.*

Mi barrio está **protegido por verja**. *My neighborhood is a gated community.*

Tengo que instalar una nueva **alarma contra incendios**. *I have to install a new smoke alarm.*

¿No tienes que cambiar la **cerradura**? *Don't you have to change your lock?*

No, la **seguridad** aquí es buena. *No, security here is good.*

¿Hay suficientes **guardias**? *Are there enough guards?*

No, pero yo sé **defensa personal**. *No, but I know self-defense.*

Necesito comprar un nuevo **botiquín**. *I have to get a new first aid kit.*

EXERCISES

I. Match the Spanish word on the left with the English word on the right.

1. el esmalte de uñas	A. *sponge*
2. la cápsula	B. *brush*
3. el cepillo	C. *filling*
4. la esponja	D. *poison*
5. ciego	E. *nail polish*
6. el veneno	F. *mute*
7. mudo	G. *blind*
8. secar	H. *capsule*
9. el tratamiento	I. *to dry*
10. el empaste	J. *treatment*

II. Fill in the blanks with the appropriate Spanish word.

1. ¿Ya estuvo aquí la _____ (*nurse*)?
2. Él estuvo una semana usando una _____ (*wheelchair*).
3. ¿Cuál es tu tipo de _____ (*blood*)?
4. Necesito comprarme un nuevo _____ (*hair dryer*).
5. Mi tía sufrió un _____ (*stroke*).

ANSWERS: I. 1. E, 2. H, 3. B, 4. A, 5. G, 6. D, 7. F, 8. I, 9. J, 10. C
II. 1. ¿YA ESTUVO AQUÍ LA **ENFERMERA**? 2. ÉL ESTUVO UNA SEMANA
USANDO UNA **SILLA DE RUEDAS**. 3. ¿CUÁL ES TU TIPO DE **SANGRE**?
4. NECESITO COMPRARME UN NUEVO **SECADOR DE PELO**. 5. MI TÍA SUFRIÓ
UN **DERRAME**.

Human Society

La sociedad humana

CONTINENTS AND COUNTRIES OF THE WORLD

Continentes y países del mundo

GENERAL NOUNS

los continentes	*continents*
los países	*countries*

NORTH AMERICA

América del Norte	*North America*
Norteamérica	*North America*
Bahamas	*Bahamas*
Belice	*Belize*
Canadá	*Canada*
el Caribe	*Caribbean*
Costa Rica	*Costa Rica*
Cuba	*Cuba*
El Salvador	*El Salvador*
los Estados Unidos	*United States*
Guatemala	*Guatemala*
Haití	*Haiti*
Honduras	*Honduras*
Jamaica	*Jamaica*
México	*Mexico*
Nicaragua	*Nicaragua*
Panamá	*Panama*
Puerto Rico	*Puerto Rico*
República Dominicana	*Dominican Republic*
Trinidad y Tobago	*Trinidad & Tobago*

SOUTH AMERICA

América del Sur	*South America*
Argentina	*Argentina*
Bolivia	*Bolivia*

Brasil	*Brazil*
Colombia	*Colombia*
Chile	*Chile*
Ecuador	*Ecuador*
Guayana	*Guyana*
Paraguay	*Paraguay*
Perú	*Peru*
Sudamérica	*South America*
Surinam	*Surinam*
Uruguay	*Uruguay*
Venezuela	*Venezuela*

AFRICA

África	*Africa*
Angola	*Angola*
Argelia	*Algeria*
Burundi	*Burundi*
Camerún	*Cameroon*
Congo (República Democrática)	*Congo (Dem. Rep.)*
Congo	*Congo*
Costa de Marfil	*Ivory Coast*
Chad	*Chad*
Egipto	*Egypt*
Eritrea	*Eritrea*
Etiopía	*Ethiopia*
Ghana	*Ghana*
Kenia	*Kenya*
Lesotho	*Lesotho*
Liberia	*Liberia*
Libia	*Libya*
Madagascar	*Madagascar*
Marruecos	*Morocco*
Nigeria	*Nigeria*
República Central Africana	*Central African Republic*
Ruanda	*Rwanda*
Senegal	*Senegal*
Somalia	*Somalia*
Sudáfrica	*South Africa*
Sudán	*Sudan*
Tanzania	*Tanzania*

Túnez	*Tunisia*
Uganda	*Uganda*
Zambia	*Zambia*
Zimbabwe	*Zimbabwe*

ASIA

Asia	*Asia*
Afganistán	*Afghanistan*
Arabia Saudita	*Saudi Arabia*
Bangladesh	*Bangladesh*
Birmania	*Burma (Myanmar)*
Camboya	*Cambodia*
China	*China*
Corea del Norte	*North Korea*
Corea del Sur	*South Korea*
Filipinas	*Philippines*
India	*India*
Indonesia	*Indonesia*
Irak	*Iraq*
Irán	*Iran*
Israel	*Israel*
Japón	*Japan*
Jordania	*Jordan*
Kuwait	*Kuwait*
Líbano	*Lebanon*
Malasia	*Malaysia*
Mongolia	*Mongolia*
Nepal	*Nepal*
Pakistán	*Pakistan*
Qatar	*Qatar*
Rusia (Federación Rusa)	*Russia (Russian Federation)*
Singapur	*Singapore*
Siria	*Syria*
Tailandia	*Thailand*
Taiwán	*Taiwan*
Turquía	*Turkey*
Uzbekistán	*Uzbekistan*
Vietnam	*Vietnam*

Continents
and Countries
of the World

Races,
Nationalities,
and Languages

Beliefs and
Religions

Supernatural

Human, Social,
and Political
Identities

EUROPE

Europa	*Europe*
Alemania	*Germany*
Austria	*Austria*
Bélgica	*Belgium*
Bulgaria	*Bulgaria*
Croacia	*Croatia*
Dinamarca	*Denmark*
España	*Spain*
Estonia	*Estonia*
Finlandia	*Finland*
Francia	*France*
Grecia	*Greece*
Hungría	*Hungary*
Inglaterra	*England*
Irlanda	*Ireland*
Islandia	*Iceland*
Italia	*Italy*
Latvia	*Latvia*
Lituania	*Lithuania*
Luxemburgo	*Luxembourg*
Noruega	*Norway*
Países Bajos	*Netherlands*
Polonia	*Poland*
Portugal	*Portugal*
Reino Unido	*United Kingdom*
República Checa	*Czech Republic*
Rumanía	*Romania*
Suecia	*Sweden*
Suiza	*Switzerland*
Ucrania	*Ukraine*
Yugoslavia	*Yugoslavia*

OCEANIA

Oceanía	*Oceania*
Australia	*Australia*
Fiji	*Fiji*
Nueva Zelanda	*New Zealand*
Papua Nueva Guinea	*Papua New Guinea*
Antártica	*Antarctica*

Words In Use

Muchas personas de **México** viven en los **Estados Unidos**. *Many people from Mexico live in the United States.*

Cuba, Puerto Rico y la **República Dominicana** están en el Caribe. *Cuba, Puerto Rico, and the Dominican Republic are in the Caribbean.*

En el **Brasil** se habla el portugués. *They speak Portuguese in Brazil.*

Quisiera visitar las pirámides de **Egipto**. *I would love to visit the pyramids in Egypt.*

Yo estuve en el canal de **Panamá**. *I went to the Panama Canal.*

El estrecho de Gibraltar separa **España** de **Marruecos**. *The Strait of Gibraltar divides Spain from Morocco.*

Italia y **Grecia** son países mediterráneos. *Italy and Greece are Mediterranean countries.*

Noruega, **Suecia** y **Finlandia** son países escandinavos. *Norway, Sweden, and Finland are Scandinavian countries.*

Continents
and Countries
of the World

**Races,
Nationalities,
and Languages**

Beliefs and
Religions

Supernatural

Human, Social,
and Political
Identities

RACES, NATIONALITIES, AND LANGUAGES
Razas, nacionalidades e idiomas

GENERAL NOUNS

la raza	*race*
la nacionalidad	*nationality*
los idiomas	*languages*
el ser humano	*human being*

GENERAL ADJECTIVES

blanco	*white, Caucasian*
negro	*black*
africano	*African*
hispano	*Hispanic*
asiático	*Asian*
europeo	*European*
americano	*American*
norteamericano	*North American*
sudamericano	*South American*
centroamericano	*Central American*
caribeño	*Caribbean Islander*
indígena americano	*Native American*
indígena australiano	*Native Australian*
indígena	*indigenous, native*

RACES, NATIONALITIES, AND LANGUAGES— NORTH AMERICA

americano	*American*
costarricense	*Costa Rican*
cubano	*Cuban*
dominicano	*Dominican*
estadounidense	*American, citizen of the United States*
canadiense	*Canadian*
haitiano	*Haitian*
hondureño	*Honduran*
jamaicano	*Jamaican*
mexicano	*Mexican*
nicaragüense	*Nicaraguan*
panameño	*Panamanian*
puertorriqueño	*Puerto Rican*
salvadoreño	*Salvadorian*

RACES, NATIONALITIES, AND LANGUAGES— SOUTH AMERICA

argentino	*Argentinian*
boliviano	*Bolivian*
brasileño	*Brazilian*
brasilero	*Brazilian*
colombiano	*Colombian*
chileno	*Chilean*
ecuatoriano	*Ecuadorian*
paraguayo	*Paraguayan*
peruano	*Peruvian*
uruguayo	*Uruguayan*
venezolano	*Venezuelan*

RACES, NATIONALITIES, AND LANGUAGES—AFRICA

argelino	*Algerian*
egipcio	*Egyptian*
eritreo	*Eritrean*
etíope	*Ethiopian*
keniano	*Kenyan*
libio	*Libyan*
marroquí	*Moroccan*
nigeriano	*Nigerian*
senegalés	*Senegalese*

somalí	*Somali*
sudafricano	*South African*
tanzano	*Tanzanian*
tunecino	*Tunisian*
ugandés	*Ugandan*
zambiano	*Zambian*
zimbabuo	*Zimbabwean*

RACES, NATIONALITIES, AND LANGUAGES—ASIA

afgano	*Afghan*
árabe	*Arab*
bangladesí	*Bangladeshi*
burmés	*Burmese*
camboyano	*Cambodian*
coreano	*Korean*
chino	*Chinese*
hindú	*Indian*
indonés	*Indonesian*
iraní	*Iranian*
iraquí	*Iraqi*
israelí	*Israeli*
japonés	*Japanese*
jordano	*Jordanian*
kuwaití	*Kuwaiti*
libanés	*Lebanese*
malasio	*Malaysian*
mongol	*Mongolian*
palestino	*Palestinian*
paquistaní	*Pakistani*
ruso	*Russian*
saudí	*Saudi*
sirio	*Syrian*
tailandés	*Thai*
turco	*Turkish*
vietnamita	*Vietnamese*

RACES, NATIONALITIES, AND LANGUAGES—EUROPE

| alemán | *German* |
| austríaco | *Austrian* |

belga	*Belgian*
británico	*British*
búlgaro	*Bulgarian*
croata	*Croatian*
checo	*Czech*
danés	*Danish*
escocés	*Scottish*
español	*Spanish*
estonio	*Estonian*
finlandés	*Finnish*
francés	*French*
griego	*Greek*
holandés	*Dutch*
húngaro	*Hungarian*
inglés	*English*
irlandés	*Irish*
islandés	*Icelandic*
italiano	*Italian*
latvio	*Latvian*
lituano	*Lithuanian*
noruego	*Norwegian*
polaco	*Polish*
portugués	*Portuguese*
rumano	*Romanian*
sueco	*Swedish*
suizo	*Swiss*

RACES, NATIONALITIES, AND LANGUAGES—OCEANIA

australiano	*Australian*
filipino	*Philippine*
neozelandés	*New Zealander*

Words In Use

En la excursión había **canadienses** y **australianos**. *There were Canadians and Australians on the excursion.*

Fue una excursión por las islas **griegas**. *It was an excursion through the Greek Isles.*

¡Me encanta la comida **turca**! *I love Turkish food!*

A mí la paella **española.** *I like Spanish paella.*

¿Te gustan las crepes **franceses**? *Do you like French crepes?*

Sí, y también los vinos **chilenos**. *Yes, and Chilean wines too.*

¿Quieres ir al restaurante **tailandés** o al **vietnamita**? *Do you want to go to the Thai or to the Vietnamese restaurant?*

Prefiero ir al restaurante **chino**. *I prefer to go to the Chinese restaurant.*

Está cerrado; vamos al **japonés**. *It's closed, let's go to the Japanese restaurant.*

BELIEFS AND RELIGIONS
Creencias y religiones

RELIGIOUS NOUNS—GENERAL

la religión	*religion*
la teología	*theology*
la ética	*ethics*
la moralidad	*morality*
la creencia	*belief*
la fe	*faith*
el principio	*tenet*
el dogma	*dogma, tenet*
la doctrina	*doctrine, tenet*
la vida eterna	*eternal life*
la reencarnación	*reincarnation*
el pecado	*sin*
el alma	*soul*
la oración	*prayer*
el ídolo	*idol*
la idolatría	*idolatry*
el dios	*god*
el ángel	*angel*
el diablo	*devil*
la secta	*sect*
el culto	*cult*
la Biblia	*Bible*
la parábola	*parable*

RELIGIOUS NOUNS—RELIGIONS

el cristianismo	*Christianity*
el judaísmo	*Judaism*
el islam	*Islam*
el hinduismo	*Hinduism*
el budismo	*Buddhism*

9

Continents
and Countries
of the World

Races,
Nationalities,
and Languages

**Beliefs and
Religions**

Supernatural

Human, Social,
and Political
Identities

el confucianismo	Confucianism
el taoísmo	Taoism
el ateísmo	atheism
el agnosticismo	agnosticism
el humanismo	humanism

RELIGIOUS NOUNS—EVENTS

la ceremonia	ceremony
el servicio	service
el bautismo	baptism
la comunión	communion

RELIGIOUS NOUNS—PLACES

la iglesia	church
el templo	church, temple
la sinagoga	synagogue
la mezquita	mosque

RELIGIOUS NOUNS—PEOPLE

el/la predicador/a	preacher
el pastor	preacher, pastor
el sacerdote	priest
el cura	priest
el monje	monk
la monja	nun
el rabino	rabbi
el chamán	shaman
el curandero	medicine man
el/la santo/a	saint
el/la pecador/a	sinner

RELIGIOUS ADJECTIVES

protestante	Protestant
católico	Roman-Catholic
cristiano	Christian
judío	Jewish
musulmán	Muslim
hindú	Hindu
budista	Buddhist
confuciano	Confucian
taoísta	Taoist

ateo	*atheist*
agnóstico	*agnostic*
humanista	*humanist*
religioso	*religious*
ético	*ethical*
moral	*moral*
virtuoso	*moral, virtuous*
sagrado	*holy*
piadoso	*pious*
pío	*pious*
fundamentalista	*fundamentalist*
ortodoxo	*orthodox*
humanista	*humanist*
reformado	*reformed*
vuelto a nacer	*born-again*
estricto	*strict*
pagano	*pagan*
ateo	*atheist*
laico	*secular*
secular	*secular*

Continents
and Countries
of the World

Races,
Nationalities,
and Languages

**Beliefs and
Religions**

Supernatural

Human, Social,
and Political
Identities

RELIGIOUS VERBS

creer	*to believe*
creer en	*to believe in*
tener fe	*to have faith*
seguir	*to follow*
aceptar	*to accept*
atenerse a	*to adhere to*
cuestionar	*to question*
rechazar	*to reject*

Words In Use

Fue una **ceremonia** muy bonita. *It was a beautiful ceremony.*

Yo no **creo** en la **reencarnación**. *I don't believe in reincarnation.*

Pero sí **creo** en la **vida eterna**. *But I do believe in eternal life.*

Hay que respetar todas las **creencias religiosas**. *One must respect all religious beliefs.*

Yo prefiero **seguir** varios **dogmas**. *I prefer to follow several dogmas.*

Mi primo estudió **teología** en la universidad. *My cousin studied theology at the University.*

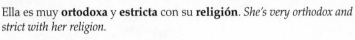
Ella es muy **ortodoxa** y **estricta** con su **religión**. *She's very orthodox and strict with her religion.*

Tengo fe en que todo saldrá bien. *I have faith that everything will go well.*

Él no es **religioso**, pero tiene un gran sentido de **ética** y justicia. *He's not religious but he has a high sense of ethics and justice.*

SUPERNATURAL
Sobrenatural

el espíritu	*spirit*
el fantasma	*ghost*
el vampiro	*vampire*
la bruja	*witch*
la casa embrujada	*haunted house*
el/la clarividente	*clairvoyant*
el/la médium	*medium*
el/la psíquico/a	*psychic*
las cartas del tarot	*tarot cards*
la sesión espiritista	*séance*

Words In Use

¿Crees en lo **sobrenatural**? *Do you believe in supernatural powers?*

Nunca he visto un **fantasma.** *I've never seen a ghost.*

Dicen que ella vive en una **casa embrujada**. *They say she lives in a haunted house.*

¿Alguna vez has visitado a un **psíquico**? *Have you ever visited a psychic?*

No, pero me han leído las **cartas** del **tarot**. *No, but I've had my tarot cards read.*

Tengo un buen disfraz de **bruja**. *I have a good witch costume.*

HUMAN, SOCIAL, AND POLITICAL IDENTITIES
Identidad humana, social y política

IDENTITY NOUNS

la identidad humana	*human identity*
la identidad social	*social identity*
la identidad política	*political identity*

IDENTITY ADJECTIVES—ECONOMIC

millonario	*millionaire*
rico	*rich*

acaudalado	*wealthy*
adinerado	*wealthy*
pobre	*poor*
indigente	*destitute*
clase media	*middle class*
clase alta	*upper class*
clase baja	*low class*
clase trabajadora	*working class*
obrero	*blue-collar*
clase profesional	*white-collar*

IDENTITY ADJECTIVES — SOCIAL

promiscuo	*promiscuous*
abstinente	*abstinent*
virgen	*virgin*
célibe	*celibate*
fiel	*faithful*
heterosexual	*straight*
bisexual	*bisexual*
gay	*gay*
heterosexual	*heterosexual*
homosexual	*homosexual*
lesbiana	*lesbian*
transexual	*transsexual*
travesti	*transvestite*
travestido	*transvestite*

IDENTITY ADJECTIVES — POLITICAL

liberal	*liberal*
moderado	*moderate*
conservador	*conservative*
pacifista	*pacifist*
vegetariano	*vegetarian*
ambientalista	*environmentalist*
ecologista	*conservationist*
socialista	*socialist*
comunista	*communist*
anarquista	*anarchist*
militante	*militant*
extremista	*extremist*

Words In Use

Siempre he apoyado las causas **ambientalistas**. *I've always supported environmentalist causes.*

El país tiene una **clase media** muy fuerte. *The country has a strong middle class.*

Sí, pero la **clase baja** está olvidada. *Yes, but the lower class has been forgotten.*

Es un artista muy **rico**. *He's a very rich artist.*

Mi mejor amiga es **lesbiana**. *My best friend is a lesbian.*

Es una muchacha muy **fiel** a sus amigos. *She's very loyal to her friends.*

También es muy **pacifista**. *She's also a pacifist.*

EXERCISES

I. Match the Spanish word on the left with the English word on the right.

1. sueco	A. *holy*
2. suizo	B. *preacher*
3. el/la predicador/a	C. *Danish*
4. la monja	D. *Dutch*
5. sagrado	E. *faithful*
6. sudamericano	F. *German*
7. danés	G. *Swedish*
8. alemán	H. *nun*
9. fiel	I. *Swiss*
10. holandés	J. *South American*

II. Fill in the blanks with the appropriate Spanish word.

1. Dicen que en la casa hay muchos _____ (*spirits*).

2. Nunca he estado en el continente _____ (*Asian*).

3. La comunidad _____ (*homosexual*) de la ciudad participa activamente en la política.

4. Me gusta mucho la comida _____ (*Italian*).

5. Mi primo es _____ (*priest*).

ANSWERS: I. 1. G, 2. I, 3. B, 4. H, 5. A, 6. J, 7. C, 8. F, 9. E, 10. D
II. 1. DICEN QUE EN LA CASA HAY MUCHOS **ESPÍRITUS**. 2. NUNCA HE ESTADO EN EL CONTINENTE **ASIÁTICO**. 3. LA COMUNIDAD **HOMOSEXUAL** DE LA CIUDAD PARTICIPA ACTIVAMENTE EN LA POLÍTICA. 4. ME GUSTA MUCHO LA COMIDA **ITALIANA**. 5. MI PRIMO ES **SACERDOTE**.

Money & the Economy

Dinero y economía

ECONOMIC WORDS

Términos económicos

ECONOMIC NOUNS

el mercado	*market*
la inflación	*inflation*
el déficit	*deficit*
la recesión	*recession*
la depresión	*depression*
la riqueza	*wealth*
la pobreza	*poverty*
el pago	*payment*
el millonario	*millionaire*
el multi-millonario	*multi-millionaire*
el billonario	*billionaire*
la clase alta	*upper class*
la clase media	*middle class*
la clase baja	*lower class*

ECONOMIC ADJECTIVES

económico	*economic*
pobre	*poor*
rico	*rich*
acaudalado	*wealthy*
adinerado	*wealthy*
en bancarrota	*broke*
del tercer mundo	*third-world*
sin ánimo de lucro	*non-profit*
sin fines de lucro	*non-profit*
fiscal	*fiscal*

ECONOMIC VERBS

comprar	*to buy, to purchase*
adquirir	*to purchase*
poseer	*to own*
ser dueño	*to own*
vender	*to sell*
gastar	*to spend*
disminuir el tamaño	*to downsize*
estar sin dinero	*to be broke*

ECNOMIC EXPRESSIONS

"Cárguelo a mi tarjeta".	*"Charge it to my credit card."*

NOTE: More Economic words can be found in other sections of this book, such as Accounting and Shopping.

Words In Use

La **inflación** parece estar bajo control. *Inflation seems to be under control.*

Necesito **comprar** un carro nuevo. *I need to buy a new car.*

Pero no quiero **gastar** mucho dinero. *But I don't want to spend too much money.*

¿No vas a **vender** el otro carro? *Aren't you going to sell the other car?*

¡Sí, pero no soy tan **adinerado**! *Yes, but I'm not that wealthy!*

Mejor que yo. . . ¡estoy en **bancarrota**! *Better than me . . . I'm broke!*

MONEY, INVESTMENTS, AND BANKING

Dinero, inversiones y banca

MONEY, INVESTMENTS, AND BANKING NOUNS—GENERAL

la deuda	*debt*
la deuda a corto plazo	*short-term debt*
la deuda a largo plazo	*long-term debt*
el débito	*charge*
el déficit	*deficit*
la inflación	*inflation*
la deflación	*deflation*
los beneficios netos	*net*
los bienes	*assets*
el billete	*bill*
el capital	*capital*
el estancamiento económico	*economic stagnation*
el excedente	*surplus*
la factura	*invoice*

la fecha de vencimiento	*due date*
la ganancia	*profit*
las ganancias	*earnings*
el cargo	*charge*
la cuota	*fee*
los honorarios	*fee*
el impuesto	*tax*
los ingresos brutos	*gross income*
los ingresos	*earnings, income*
el interés	*interest*
el límite de crédito	*credit limit*
el límite de deuda	*debt limit*
la línea de crédito	*credit line*
la pérdida o ganancia	*bottom line*
la pérdida	*loss*
el porcentaje	*percent*
el precio	*price*
el precio de mercado	*market price*
la reactivación económica	*economic recovery*
la recesión	*recession*
la política económica	*economic policy*
la política fiscal	*fiscal policy*
la política monetaria	*monetary policy*
el pago subsecuente	*repayment*
el pago	*payment*
los indicadores económicos	*economic indicators*
la industria	*industry*
el inventario	*inventory*
la marca registrada	*trade mark*
el margen de ganancia	*profit margin*
el margen de interés neto	*net interest margin*

MONEY, INVESTMENTS, AND BANKING NOUNS—MONEY

la tarjeta de crédito	*credit card*
el dinero	*money*
la divisa	*currency*
la economía	*economy*
el efectivo	*cash*
la moneda	*coin, currency*
el cheque	*check*

| los cheques de viajero | *traveler's checks* |
| el crédito | *credit* |

MONEY, INVESTMENTS, AND BANKING NOUNS—BANKING

la banca	*banking*
la banca privada	*private banking*
el banco comercial	*commercial bank*
la banca al detalle	*retail banking*
la banca al por menor	*retail banking*
la banca al por mayor	*wholesale banking*
la banca comercial	*commercial banking*
la banca corresponsal	*correspondent banking*
la banca de comerciantes	*merchant banking*
el banco de inversiones	*investment bank*
la banca de inversiones	*investment banking*
el banco de comerciantes	*merchant bank*
el depósito	*deposit, safe-deposit box*
la caja fuerte	*safe-deposit box*
el cajero automático	*automatic teller machine (ATM)*
el cambio	*change, exchange*
la divisa	*foreign exchange*
el certificado de depósito	*certificate of deposit (CD)*
la cuenta	*account, bill, check*
la cuenta corriente	*checking account*
la cuenta de ahorros	*savings account*
el costo de la transacción	*transaction costs*
la sucursal	*branch*
la tasa	*rate*
la tasa de cambio de divisas	*foreign exchange*
la tasa de cambio	*exchange rate*
la tasa de incumplimiento de pago	*delinquency rate*
la tasa de interés (fijo, flexible)	*interest rate (fixed, floating)*
la transacción	*transaction*
el sobregiro	*overdraft*
el retiro	*withdrawal*
el préstamo	*loan*
el préstamo a corto plazo	*short-term loan*
el préstamo a largo plazo	*long-term loan*
el préstamo asegurado	*secured loan*

Money & the Economy Dinero y economía

el préstamo sindicado	*syndicated loan*
el préstamo vencido	*overdue loan*
la hipoteca	*mortgage*
el préstamo	*borrowing*
la cuota inicial	*down payment*
el envío de dinero por cable	*wire*

MONEY, INVESTMENTS, AND BANKING NOUNS—INVESTMENT

la inversión	*investment*
el mercado bursátil	*stock market*
el mercado de bonos	*bond market*
el mercado de valores	*stock market*
la acción preferencial	*preferred stock*
la acción	*stock*
la comisión	*commission, fee*
la cotización	*share price*
el bono comercial	*corporate bond*
el bono	*bond*
los bonos del tesoro	*treasury bonds*
la carta de crédito	*letter of credit (L/C)*
la cartera	*portfolio*
la depreciación	*depreciation*
la devaluación	*devaluation*
el fideicomiso	*trust*
el fondo de inversión	*trust*
el fondo de inversiones	*mutual fund*
el fondo mutualista	*mutual fund*
el fondo	*fund*
la obligación	*bond, obligation*
el producto	*commodity*
el pronóstico	*forecast*
los recursos propios	*equity*
el patrimonio	*equity*
el riesgo	*risk*
los servicios para inversionistas	*investment services*
el sindicato	*syndicate*
los títulos	*security/securities*
los valores	*security/securities*

MONEY, INVESTMENTS, AND BANKING NOUNS—OTHER

el dividendo	*dividend*
las obligaciones	*liability, obligations*
el pasivo	*liability, debit side*
la deuda	*debt, liability*
la proporción de rendimiento	*efficiency ratio*
el proveedor	*supplier*
la relación precio/beneficio	*price/earnings (p/e) ratio*
el subsidio	*subsidy*
la subvención	*subsidy*
la prima	*subsidy, bonus, premium*
el superávit	*surplus*
la adquisición	*acquisition, takeover*
el alquiler	*lease*
la competencia	*competition*
la concesión	*grant*
el costo de los fondos	*cost of funds*
el costo fijo	*fixed cost*
la utilidad bruta	*gross income*
el valor de mercado	*market value*
las ventas brutas	*gross sales*
la franquicia	*franchise*
la fusión	*merger*
la gama	*spread*

MONEY, INVESTMENTS, AND BANKING NOUNS—PEOPLE

el/la directora/a de sucursal	*branch manager*
el/la gerente	*branch manager*
el/la cajero/a	*cashier, teller*
el/la prestamista	*loan officer*
el/la acreedor/a	*creditor*
el/la accionista	*stockholder*
el/la gerente de cartera	*portfolio manager*
el/la comerciante	*trader*
el/la inversionista activo/a	*day trader*
el/la operador/a	*dealer*
el administrador del fondo	*trust officer*
el/la agente del fideicomiso	*trust officer*
el/la asegurador/a	*underwriter*

10

Money & the Economy Dinero y economía

el/la asesor/a financiero/a	*financial adviser*
el/la inversionista institucional	*institutional investor*
el/la abastecedor/a	*supplier*
el/la licenciatario/a	*franchisee*

MONEY, INVESTMENTS, AND BANKING ADJECTIVES

bruto	*gross*
cobrado	*withdrawn*
retirado	*withdrawn*
en bancarrota	*bankrupt*
insolvente	*bankrupt*
neto	*net*
líquido	*liquid*

MONEY, INVESTMENTS, AND BANKING VERBS

comprar	*to buy*
vender	*to sell*
comerciar	*to trade*
tomar prestado	*to borrow*
pedir prestado	*to borrow*
dar un préstamo	*to loan*
prestar	*to lend*
hipotecar	*to mortgage*
pagar	*to pay*
abrir una cuenta	*to open an account*
cerrar una cuenta	*to close an account*
depositar	*to deposit*
ingresar	*to deposit*
retirar	*to withdraw*
acumular	*to accrue*
adquirir	*to acquire*
ahorrar	*to save*
invertir	*to invest*
sacar beneficios	*to profit*
tener ganancias	*to profit*
valorar	*to price*
tasar	*to price*
cobrar	*to cash*
hacer efectivo	*to cash*
transferir dinero	*to transfer money*

enviar dinero por cable	*to wire money*
cambiar dinero	*to exchange/to change money*
abrir una carta de crédito	*to open a letter of credit*
hacer una transacción	*to transact*
negociar	*to transact, to negotiate*
imponer contribuciones	*to tax*
fusionarse	*to merge*
asegurar	*to underwrite*
guardar	*to hedge*
proteger	*to hedge*
liquidar	*to liquidate*
poner en un fideicomiso	*to trust*
sacar de un apuro financiero	*to bail out*

Words In Use

Mi banco ha cerrado mi **sucursal** local. *My bank closed my local branch.*

Ya es tarde; pide la **cuenta**. *It's getting late, get the check.*

No puedo pagar en **efectivo** hoy. *I can't pay cash today.*

Debes usar tu **tarjeta de crédito**. *You should use your credit card.*

La **economía** se ha recuperado. *The economy has improved.*

La **tasa de interés** se ha estabilizado. *Interest rates have stabilized.*

¿Es alta la **comisión** en ese banco? *Is the commission high in that bank?*

La **política económica** ha cambiado. *The economic policy has changed.*

La **tasa de cambio** está alta. *The exchange rate is high.*

La **devaluación** del dólar afecta a los turistas. *The dollar's devaluation affects toursits.*

¿Cuál es la **moneda** de Argentina? *What's the national currency of Argentina?*

No encontré un **cajero automático**. *I couldn't find an ATM.*

No tengo suficiente **dinero**. *I don't have enough money.*

No creo que fue una buena **inversión**. *I don't think it was a good investment.*

La **fusión** de las compañías ha creado consolidación en esa **industria**. *The merger of the companies has created consolidation in that industry.*

Mucha gente **invierte** en **fondos comunes de inversión**. *Many people invest in mutual funds.*

El **pronóstico** financiero es bueno. *The financial forecast is bright.*

Te recomiendo **comprar acciones** en esa compañía. *I suggest you buy stock in that company.*

La **adquisición** de la compañía ha reducido la competencia. *The company's takeover has curtailed competition.*

Fue una **transacción** secreta. *It was a secret transaction.*

Tuve que **tomar prestados** veinte dólares. *I had to borrow twenty dollars.*

Tengo dos mil dólares para **invertir**. *I have two thousand dollars to invest.*

Ella **pagó** un **precio** muy alto por ese apartamento. *She paid too high a price for that apartment.*

Money,
Investments,
and Banking

EXERCISES

I. Match the Spanish word on the left with the English word on the right.

1. la pobreza
2. el/la cajero/a
3. el subsidio
4. la factura
5. el impuesto
6. el bono
7. el mercado
8. adquirir
9. la pérdida
10. la moneda

A. *market*
B. *coin*
C. *loss*
D. *invoice*
E. *to purchase*
F. *cashier*
G. *subsidy*
H. *poverty*
I. *tax*
J. *bond*

II. Fill in the blanks with the appropriate Spanish word.

1. Mi hijo universitario tiene que abrir una _____ (*checking account*).
2. Tengo que ir al banco para hacer un _____ (*deposit*).
3. Mi fondo común de inversión paga buenos _____ (*dividends*).
4. Cuando vendí mis acciones obtuve una buena _____ (*profit*).
5. Mucha gente le tiene miedo al _____ (*stock market*).

ANSWERS: I. 1. H, 2. F, 3. G, 4. D, 5. I, 6. J, 7. A, 8. E, 9. C, 10. B
II. 1. MI HIJO UNIVERSITARIO TIENE QUE ABRIR UNA **CUENTA CORRIENTE**.
2. TENGO QUE IR AL BANCO PARA HACER UN **DEPÓSITO**. 3. MI FONDO COMÚN
DE INVERSIÓN PAGA BUENOS **DIVIDENDOS**. 4. CUANDO VENDÍ MIS
ACCIONES OBTUVE UNA BUENA **GANANCIA**. 5. MUCHA GENTE LE TIENE
MIEDO AL **MERCADO DE VALORES**.

Politics & Government

Política y gobierno

POLITICAL WORDS

Términos políticos

POLITICAL NOUNS—GENERAL

el gobierno	*government*
la rama ejecutiva	*executive branch*
la rama judicial	*judicial branch*
la rama legislativa	*legislative branch*
el derecho	*law*
la ley	*law*
la legislación	*legislation*
el cuerpo legislativo	*legislature*
el senado	*senate*
el parlamento	*parliament*
la política	*politics*
las elecciones	*election*
la junta de los dirigentes de un partido político	*caucus*
el partido	*party*
la ciudadanía	*citizenship*
la población	*population*
la sociedad	*society*
la negociación	*negotiation*
el pacto	*pact*
el tratado	*treaty*
la paz	*peace*
la propuesta	*proposal*
la recomendación	*recommendation*
el plan	*plan*
la política de	*policy*
el procedimiento	*procedure*
la regulación	*regulation*

la regla	regulation
el formulario	form
la subvención	grant
la concesión	grant
la información	information
el informe	report
la investigación	research
los recursos	resources
el servicio	service

POLITICAL NOUNS—ORGANIZATIONS

las organizaciones gubernamentales	government organizations
el ministerio	department
la administración	administration
el gobierno	administration
el instituto	institute
la comisión	commission
el comité	committee
la asociación	association
la delegación	delegation
la comunidad	community
la región	region
la oficina regional	regional office
la oficina	office
la agencia	agency
la agencia regulatoria	regulatory agency
la agencia no gubernamental	non-government agency
la embajada	embassy
el consulado	consulate
el Departamento de Estado	State Department
el Ministerio de Hacienda	Department of Treasury
el Ministerio del Interior	Department of Interior
el Ministerio de Agricultura	Department of Agriculture
el Ministerio de Defensa	Department of Defense

POLITICAL NOUNS—ISSUES

el desarrollo	development
las artes	arts
la educación	education

el medio ambiente	*environment*
la vivienda	*housing*
la vivienda pública	*public housing*
el servicio público	*public service*
las relaciones internacionales	*international relations*

POLITICAL NOUNS—PEOPLE

el/la ciudadano/a	*citizen*
el rey	*king*
la reina	*queen*
el príncipe	*prince*
la princesa	*princess*
el emperador	*emperor*
la emperatriz	*empress*
el dictador	*dictator*
el/la presidente/a	*president*
el/la vicepresidente/a	*vice president*
el/la líder	*leader*
el/la dirigente/a	*leader*
el/la primer/a ministro/a	*prime minister, premier*
el/la canciller	*chancellor*
el embajador	*ambassador*
la embajadora	*ambassadress*
el zar	*tsar*
el/la dirigente/a	*ruler*
el/la representante	*representative*
el/la cabildero/a	*lobbyist*
el/la consejero principal	*chief counsel*
el/la consejero/a	*advisor*
el/la planificador/a	*planner*

POLITICAL NOUNS—SYSTEMS

la monarquía	*monarchy*
la democracia	*democracy*
la teocracia	*theocracy*
la dictadura	*dictatorship*
la meritocracia	*meritocracy*
la autocracia	*autocracy*
la anarquía	*anarchy*
el capitalismo	*capitalism*

el conservadurismo	*conservatism*
el conservatismo	*conservatism*
el fascismo	*fascism*
el feudalismo	*feudalism*
el globalismo	*globalism*
el liberalismo	*liberalism*
el marxismo	*marxism*
el socialismo	*socialism*
el comunismo	*communism*

POLITICAL ADJECTIVES

político	*political*
público	*public*
internacional	*international*
regional	*regional*
sin fines de lucro	*non-profit*
sin ánimo de lucro	*non-profit*
gubernamental	*governmental*
económico	*economic*
social	*social*
cultural	*cultural*
liberal	*liberal*
conservador	*conservative*
democrático	*democratic*
republicano	*republican*
verde	*green*
socialista	*socialist*
comunista	*communist*
fascista	*fascist*
largo alcance	*long range*
militar	*military*

POLITICAL VERBS

votar	*to vote*
elegir	*to elect*
acusar	*to impeach*
denunciar	*to impeach*
gobernar	*to rule*
derrocar	*to overthrow*
vetar	*to veto*

debatir	*to debate*
negociar	*to negotiate*
planificar	*to plan*
gravar	*to tax*
poner impuesto	*to tax*

NOTE: More words related to Politics can be found in the Social Problems and Controversial Issues category.

Words In Use

¿Cuál fue la **recomendación** del juez? *What was the judge's recommendation?*

El sindicato está en medio de **negociaciones**. *The union is in the middle of negotiations.*

El **pacto** entre los dos países traerá la **paz**. *The pact between the two countries will bring peace.*

Este **gobierno** no promueve las **artes**. *This administration does not promote the arts.*

¿Por qué el **partido verde** no tiene popularidad? *Why isn't the green party more popular?*

El **líder** africano fue **derrocado**. *The African leader was overthrown.*

¿Qué tipo de **monarquía** hay en España? *What type of monarchy do they have in Spain?*

No he leído aún el **informe**. *I haven't read the report yet.*

Tienes que llenar este **formulario**. *You have to fill out this form.*

¿Cuándo se celebran **elecciones** en Puerto Rico? *When are elections held in Puerto Rico?*

El problema de la **vivienda pública** ha mejorado. *The problem with public housing has improved.*

La **rama legislativa** se ocupa de crear las **leyes**. *The legislative branch is in charge of making laws.*

La isla tiene un gran número de **autovías**. *The island has a large number of highways.*

LIST OF MAJOR WORLD ORGANIZATIONS
Listado de las principales organizaciones mundiales

las Naciones Unidas	*United Nations*
el Banco Mundial	*World Bank*
la Organización Mundial del Comercio	*World Trade Organization*
la OTAN	*NATO*
la Unión Europea (UE)	*EU*
la Mancomunidad de Estados Independientes	*CIS*

el NASDAQ	*NASDAQ*
la Bolsa de Londres (FTSE)	*FTSE*
la Unión Económica Europea (UEE)	*EEC*
la Organización Mundial de la Salud	*World Health Organization*
el NAFTA	*NAFTA*
Amnistía Internacional	*Amnesty International*
la UNICEF	*UNICEF*

Words In Use

El **Banco Mundial** le ofreció un préstamo a Argentina. *The World Bank offered a loan to Argentina.*

Italia, Noruega y Turquía son miembros de la **OTAN**. *Italy, Norway and Turkey are NATO member countries.*

La **Bolsa de Londres** terminó el día en alza. *The FTSE ended the day higher.*

La **Organización Mundial de la Salud** declaró emergencia en la ciudad. *The World Health Organization declared an emergency in the city.*

El **NASDAQ** ha fluctuado mucho este año. *The NASDAQ has fluctuated a lot this year.*

¿Eres miembro de **Amnistía Internacional**? *Are you a member of Amnesty International?*

CIVIL LIBERTIES

Libertades civiles

CIVIL LIBERTIES NOUNS—RIGHTS

los derechos civiles	*civil rights*
la igualdad de derechos	*equal rights*
los derechos de los homosexuales	*gay rights*
los derechos de los gays	*gay rights*
los derechos de las lesbianas	*lesbian rights*
los derechos en el lugar de trabajo	*workplace rights*
los derechos por incapacidad	*disability rights*
el derecho a la reproducción	*reproductive rights*
los derechos humanos	*human rights*
el derecho de igualdad de los sexos	*gender rights*
el derecho al sufragio universal	*voting rights*

CIVIL LIBERTIES NOUNS—GENERAL

la libertad	*freedom, liberty*
la libre expresión	*free expression, free speech*
la libertad de expresión	*freedom of expression, freedom of speech*
la igualdad	*equality*
la raza	*race*
las minorías	*minorities*
la acción afirmativa	*affirmative action*
el prejuicio	*bias, prejudice*
el sexo	*gender*
el feminismo	*feminism*
la justicia	*justice*
la justicia criminal	*criminal justice*
la pena de muerte	*death penalty*
los crímenes por prejuicio	*hate crime*
el individuo	*individual*
la privacidad	*privacy*

CIVIL LIBERTIES ADJECTIVES

heterosexual	*straight*
bisexual	*bisexual*
homosexual	*gay, homosexual*
gay	*gay*
lesbiana	*lesbian*
transexual	*transsexual*
transgénero	*transgendered*
feminista	*feminist*
racista	*racist*
nacionalista	*nationalist*
sexista	*sexist*
parcial	*biased, partial*
prejuiciado	*biased, prejudiced*

CIVIL LIBERTIES VERBS

tratar a alguien justamente	*to treat someone equally*
tratar a alguien injustamente	*to treat someone unfairly*
discriminar	*to discriminate*
prohibir	*to ban*
censurar	*to censor*
luchar por una causa	*to fight for a cause*

Words In Use

A ella le pareció el comentario demasiado **sexista**. *She found the comment to be too sexist.*

El gobierno autoritario **censuró** la película. *The authoritarian government censored the film.*

Political Words

List of
Major World
Organizations

Es bueno **luchar por una causa** importante. *It's good to fight for an important cause.*

La **libertad** es una de nuestras mayores virtudes. *Freedom is one of our greatest virtues.*

Es importante tener **igualdad de derechos**. *It's important to have equal rights.*

Todas las **minorías** merecen tener **derechos civiles**. *All minorities deserve to have civil rights.*

Así habra **justicia** para todos. *That way there will be justice for all.*

Civil Liberties

EXERCISES

I. Match the Spanish word on the left with the English word on the right.

1. feminista
2. igualdad
3. el príncipe
4. la reina
5. sin fines de lucro
6. el ciudadano
7. prohibir
8. la privacidad
9. el embajador
10. la propuesta

A. *to ban*
B. *proposal*
C. *equality*
D. *feminist*
E. *queen*
F. *ambassador*
G. *prince*
H. *privacy*
I. *citizen*
J. *non-profit*

II. Fill in the blanks with the appropriate Spanish word.

1. Nuestro sistema económico es el _____ (*capitalism*).
2. La conferencia de prensa fue desde el _____ (*Department of State*).
3. La _____ (*death penalty*) es legal en varios estados.
4. El país lleva veinte años de _____ (*dictatorship*).
5. Las _____ (*United Nations*) tienen sede en la ciudad de Nueva York.

ANSWERS: I. 1. D, 2. C, 3. G, 4. E, 5. J, 6. I, 7. A, 8. H, 9. F, 10. B
II. 1. NUESTRO SISTEMA ECONÓMICO ES EL **CAPITALISMO**. 2. LA CONFERENCIA DE PRENSA FUE DESDE EL **DEPARTAMENTO DE ESTADO**. 3. LA **PENA DE MUERTE** ES LEGAL EN VARIOS ESTADOS. 4. EL PAÍS LLEVA VEINTE AÑOS DE **DICTADURA**. 5. LAS **NACIONES UNIDAS** TIENEN SEDE EN LA CIUDAD DE NUEVA YORK.

Social Problems & Controversial Issues

Problemas sociales y temas polémicos

SOCIAL PROBLEMS

Problemas sociales

SOCIAL PROBLEM NOUNS—GENERAL

el delito	crime
el delito grave	serious crime
el crimen	crime
el genocidio	genocide
el asesinato en masa	mass murder
la prostitución	prostitution
los disturbios civiles	civil unrest
el disturbio	riot
el motín	riot
el toque de queda	curfew
el maltrato	abuse
el nacionalismo	nationalism
el racismo	racism
el hostigamiento	harassment
la desigualdad	inequality
la sobrepoblación	overpopulation
la pobreza	poverty
la enfermedad	disease
la plaga	plague
la enfermedad sexualmente transmitida	sexually transmitted disease
el hambre	hunger, starvation
la inanición	starvation
el desamparo	homelessness

SOCIAL PROBLEM NOUNS—PEOPLE

el/la refugiado/a	*refugee*
el/la refugiado/a político/a	*political refugee*

SOCIAL PROBLEM ADJECTIVES

maltratado	*abused*
injurioso	*abusive*
sin hogar	*homeless*

SOCIAL PROBLEM VERBS

tener hambre	*to be hungry*
matar	*to kill*

NOTE: More words related to Social Problems can be found in the Politics and Government category.

Words In Use

Hubo un **disturbio** peligroso en el parque. *There was a dangerous riot in the park.*

El **nacionalismo** en exceso no es bueno. *Extreme nationalism is not good.*

El gobierno de la ciudad ha podido controlar la **prostitución** en el área. *The city government has been able to control prostitution in the area.*

El **hostigamiento** sexual es un **delito** en este país. *Sexual harassment is a crime in this country.*

A pesar de décadas de progreso, el **racismo** sigue siendo un problema. *In spite of decades of progress, racism is still a problem.*

CONTROVERSIAL ISSUES

Temas polémicos

CONTROVERSIAL NOUNS—ISSUES

el aborto	*abortion*
la protesta	*protest*
el control de armas de fuego	*gun control*
la controversia	*controversy*
la contracultura	*counterculture*
el movimiento	*movement*
el escándalo	*scandal*

CONTROVERSIAL NOUNS—PEOPLE

el/la activista	*activist*
el/la manifestante	*protester*

CONTROVERSIAL ADJECTIVES

liberal	*liberal*
conservador	*conservative*

CONTROVERSIAL VERBS

estar de acuerdo	*to agree*
estar en desacuerdo	*to disagree*
protestar	*to protest*
provocar disturbios	*to riot*
amotinarse	*to riot*

NOTE: More words related to Controversial Issues can be found in the Politics and Government category

Words In Use

Los dos actores han sido **activistas** desde hace años. *Both actors have been activists for years.*

El **escándalo** afectó mucho su carrera. *The scandal affected his career.*

El actor Charlton Heston está en contra del **control de armas de fuego**. *Actor Charlton Heston is against gun control.*

Es un **tema polémico** para muchos. *It's a controversial issue.*

La **controversia** continúa. *The controversy continues.*

DRUGS

Drogas

DRUG NOUNS—DRUGS

la marihuana	*marijuana*
la cocaína	*cocaine*
el crack	*crack, crack cocaine*
la cocaína en piedra	*crack cocaine*
el éxtasis	*ecstasy*
la dietilamida del ácido lisérgico	*LSD*
el LSD	*LSD*
la anfetamina	*amphetamine*
las anfetas	*speed, amphetamines*
el speed	*speed*
la heroína	*heroin*
el opio	*opium*
la metadona	*methadone*
la morfina	*morphine*

el Valium	*Valium*
el estimulante	*upper*
el sedante	*downer*

DRUG NOUNS—PEOPLE

el/la consumidor/a	*user*
el/la adicto/a	*addict*
el/la traficante de drogas	*drug dealer*
el/la repartidor/a	*drug runner*
el/la distribuidor/a de drogas	*drug runner*
el/la contrabandista de drogas	*drug smuggler*

DRUG NOUNS—OTHER NOUNS

la redada de drogas	*drug bust*
el contrabando de drogas	*drug trade*
la guerra contra las drogas	*drug war*
el cartel	*cartel*
la legalización	*legalization*
la pastilla	*pill*
la jeringuilla	*syringe*
la aguja	*needle*
la inyección	*injection*
las medidas enérgicas	*crackdown*

DRUG ADJECTIVES

adicto	*addicted*
que crea hábito	*addictive*
emporrado	*high*

DRUG VERBS

abusar	*to abuse*
estar adicto	*to be addicted (to)*
inyectar	*to inject*
tener una sobredosis	*to overdose*
recuperar	*to recover*
pasar de contrabando	*to smuggle*
despenalizar	*to decriminalize*
legalizar	*to legalize*

Words In Use

Las **medidas enérgicas** contra las drogas han dado buenos resultados. *The drug crackdown has given good results.*

Hay quienes piensan que es bueno **legalizar** la **marihuana**. *Some people believe that it would be good to legalize marijuana.*

La **guerra contra las drogas** ha sido un tema político importante. *The war on drugs has been an important political topic.*

La **heroína** es una droga muy peligrosa. *Heroin is a very dangerous drug.*

En la **redada de drogas** capturaron miles de **pastillas** de **éxtasis**. *They recovered thousands of ecstasy pills in the drug bust.*

CRIME AND JUSTICE

Crimen y justicia

CRIME AND JUSTICE NOUNS—LAW

la ley	*law*
la ley civil	*civil law*
la ley internacional	*international law*
la ley municipal	*bylaw*
el afidávit	*affidavit*
la bancarrota	*bankruptcy*
la cláusula de un documento legal	*boilerplate*
el contrato	*contract*
el copyright	*copyright*
los derechos de autor	*copyright*
la patente	*patent*
la marca registrada	*trademark*
el corpus	*corpus*
el cuerpo del delito	*corpus*
el agravio	*tort*
el convenio	*covenant*
el bufete de abogados	*law firm*
el barrote	*bar*
la validación	*probate*
la legalización	*probate*

CRIME AND JUSTICE NOUNS—COURT AND PUNISHMENT

la justicia	*justice*
la corte	*court*
el juzgado	*courthouse*

la audiencia	*hearing*
el juicio	*judgement, suit, trial*
la coartada	*alibi*
la defensa	*defense*
la demanda	*lawsuit*
la demencia temporal	*temporary insanity*
el descubrimiento	*discovery*
la precedencia	*precedence*
la moción	*motion*
el interrogatorio	*cross-examination*
la evidencia	*evidence*
el expediente	*brief*
el litigio	*litigation*
el pleito	*lawsuit, suit*
el tribunal	*bench*
el veredicto	*finding, verdict*
la decisión	*decision, judgement*
el dictamen	*judgement*
el fallo	*finding, judgement, sentence*
la sentencia	*judgement, sentence*
la absolución	*acquittal*
la acusación	*indictment*
la convicción	*conviction*
la apelación	*appeal*
la consideración	*consideration*
la libertad condicional	*parole*
los daños	*damages*
la prisión preventiva	*remand*
el mandamiento judicial	*cease and desist order*
el mandato de restricción	*restraining order*
la cadena perpetua	*life sentence*
la pena de muerte	*death penalty*
la policía	*police*
la prisión	*prison*
la cárcel	*jail*
la buena conducta	*good behavior*
la obediencia	*obedience*
la fianza	*bail, bond*

12

Social Problems

Controversial
Issues

Drugs

**Crime and
Justice**

War

Historical
Experience

CRIME AND JUSTICE NOUNS—CRIMES

el delito mayor	*felony*
el delito menor	*misdemeanor*
el asesinato	*murder*
el homicidio	*murder, homicide*
el ataque	*assault*
la agresión	*assault*
la violación	*rape*
el robo	*burglary, robbery*
la traición	*treason*
el perjurio	*perjury*
el libelo	*libel*
la difamación	*slander, defamation*
la calumnia	*slander*
la desobediencia pública	*public disobedience*
el fraude	*fraud*
la estafa	*defraud*
la negligencia	*negligence, malpractice*
el procedimiento incompetente	*malpractice*
el delito corporativo	*corporate crime*

CRIME AND JUSTICE NOUNS—PEOPLE

el/la juez/a	*judge*
el/la acusado/a	*defendant*
el/la demandado/a	*defendant*
el/la demandante	*plaintiff*
el querellante	*plaintiff*
el jurado	*jury*
el/la abogado/a	*attorney, lawyer, barrister, solicitor*
el/la acusador/a	*prosecutor*
el/la fiscal	*prosecutor*
el/la alcaide	*warden*
el/la carcelero/a	*warden*
la guardia	*guard*
el/la guardián/guardiana	*guard*
el/la delincuente	*criminal*
el/la atracador/a	*thief*
el/la ladrón/ladrona	*burglar, thief*
el estafador	*con man*
el homicida	*murderer*

el/la asesino/a	murderer
el/la asesino/a múltiple	serial killer
el/la contrabandista	smuggler
el cártel	cartel
el/la falsificador/a	forger
la prostituta	prostitute
el macarra	pimp
el proxeneta	pimp
el alcahuete	pimp
el chulo	pimp
el violador	rapist

CRIME AND JUSTICE ADJECTIVES

legal	legal
ilegal	illegal
presunto	alleged
culpable	guilty
no culpable	not guilty
inocente	innocent
honesto	honest
deshonesto	dishonest
inmoral	immoral
corrupto	corrupt
de seguridad máxima	maximum security
de seguridad mínima	minimum security

CRIME AND JUSTICE VERBS

violar la ley	to break the law
cometer un delito grave	to commit a crime
matar	to kill
asesinar	to murder
violar	to rape
robar	to rob, to steal
hurtar	to steal
cometer fraude	to fraud
defraudar	to defraud
ir a juicio	to go to trial
demandar	to sue
alegar culpabilidad	to plead guilty
alegar inocencia	to plead innocent

enjuiciar	*to prosecute*
entablar un juicio contra	*to prosecute*
interrogar	*to cross-examine*
acusar	*to indict*
juzgar	*to judge*
ordenar	*to order*
impedir	*to restrain*
ser absuelto	*to be acquitted of a crime*
ser declarado culpable	*to be convicted of a crime*
apelar	*to appeal*
pagar fianza	*to pay bail*
poner una multa	*to fine*
registrar los derechos de autor	*to copyright*
patentar	*to patent*

Words In Use

Si **violas la ley** tienes que esperar consecuencias. *If you break the law you have to expect consequences.*

El famoso actor **fue absuelto** del delito. *The famous actor was acquitted of his crime.*

El **abogado** piensa **entablar un juicio contra** el famoso **criminal** pronto. *The lawyer expects to prosecute soon the famous criminal.*

Fue una transacción **ilegal**. *It was an illegal transaction.*

Pero él dice que es **inocente**. *But he says he's innocent.*

La **violación** ocurrió en pleno día. *The rape took place in broad daylight.*

Tuvo que pagar mucho por la **fianza**. *He had to pay a very high bail.*

El **jurado** era muy heterogéneo. *The jury was very heterogeneous.*

Salió de la cárcel bajo **libertad condicional**. *He left jail on parole.*

El **demandante** reclama **justicia**. *The plaintiff demands justice.*

WAR

Guerra

WAR NOUNS—GENERAL

la invasión	*invasion*
la batalla	*battle*
la frontera	*border*
la defensa	*defense*
el ataque aéreo	*air strike*
la tierra de nadie	*no-man's land*

la sanción	sanction
el tratado	treaty
la tregua	truce
la baja	casualty
las pérdidas	casualties, losses
la ayuda	aid
el peligro	danger

WAR NOUNS—FORCES

los militares	military
las fuerzas	forces
las fuerzas terrestres	ground forces
las fuerzas armadas	army, military
la fuerza aérea	air force
la marina de guerra	navy
la armada	navy, armada

WAR NOUNS—WEAPONRY

el arma	weapon
el arma de fuego	gun
la metralleta	machine gun
el cañón	cannon
la bomba	bomb
la mina	mine
la mina terrestre	land mine
el arma nuclear	nuclear weapon
el tanque	tank

WAR NOUNS—PEOPLE

las tropas	troops
el/la capitán	captain
el/la teniente/a	lieutenant
el/la cabo	corporal
el/la sargento	sergeant
el/la general	general
el/la soldado raso	private
el héroe	hero
la heroína	heroine
el/la rehén	hostage
el/la villano/a	villain

el enemigo	*enemy*
el aliado	*ally*
el/la pacifista	*pacifist*
el objetor de consciencia	*conscientious objector*

WAR ADJECTIVES

sangriento	*bloody*
peligroso	*dangerous*
traicionero	*treacherous*
alargado	*drawn out*
más largo	*drawn out*
neutral	*neutral*
pacífico	*peaceful*
seguro	*safe*
desaparecido en acción	*missing in action*
ausente	*AWOL*

WAR VERBS

pelear	*to fight*
luchar	*to battle*
hacer la guerra a	*to wage war*
conquistar	*to conquer*
invadir	*to invade*
ponerse del lado de	*to side with*
apoyar	*to support*
rendirse	*to surrender*

NOTE: More words related to War can be found in the Politics & Government category.

Words In Use

Hubo muchas **guerras** en el siglo XX. *There were many wars in the twentieth century.*

La **invasión** duró varios meses. *The invasion lasted several months.*

El **tratado** puso fin al **conflicto**. *The treaty put an end to the conflict.*

El país no tuvo ningún **aliado** en esta **guerra**. *The country didn't have any allies in this war.*

Solamente tuvieron que usar la **fuerza aérea**. *They only had to use air forces.*

El **enemigo** usó **fuerzas terrestres**. *The enemy used ground forces.*

La **ayuda** humanitaria vino tarde. *Humanitarian aid arrived late.*

Gandhi fue uno de los más importantes **pacifistas**. *Gandhi was one of the most important pacifists.*

HISTORICAL EXPERIENCE
El paso de la historia

HISTORICAL NOUNS—PEOPLE

el/la pionero/a	*pioneer*
el/la explorador/a	*explorer*
el/la peregrino/a	*pilgrim*
la tribu	*tribe*
el clan	*clan*
el neandertal	*neanderthal*
el homo sapiens	*homo sapien*
el homo erectus	*homo erectus*
el/la cavernícola	*caveman*
el/la antepasado	*ancestor*
el conquistador	*conqueror, conquistador*
el/la nazi	*Nazi*
el bárbaro	*barbarian*
el vikingo	*Viking*

HISTORICAL NOUNS—ACTIONS AND EVENTS

la civilización	*civilization*
la evolución	*evolution*
el viaje	*voyage, trip, journey*
la travesía	*voyage, crossing*
la migración	*migration*
la inmigración	*immigration*
la emigración	*emigration*
la exploración	*exploration*
el descubrimiento	*discovery*
el hito	*landmark, milestone*
el punto de referencia	*landmark, point of reference*
la peste	*The Black Plague*
el imperio	*empire*
el holocausto	*Holocaust*
la esclavitud	*slavery*
la cruzada	*crusade*

HISTORICAL ADJECTIVES

antiguo	*ancient*
histórico	*historical*

12

Social Problems

Controversial
Issues

Drugs

Crime and
Justice

War

**Historical
Experience**

tribal	*tribal*
medieval	*medieval*
barroco	*baroque*
renacentista	*renaissance*
arcaico	*archaic*

HISTORICAL VERBS

inmigrar	*to immigrate*
emigrar	*to emigrate*
explorar	*to explore*

NOTE: More Historical words can be found in the Politics and Government category.

Words In Use

España logró crear un **imperio** en las Américas. *Spain managed to create an empire in the Americas.*

Mi familia tuvo que **inmigrar** desde Irlanda. *My family had to immigrate from Ireland.*

La **esclavitud** fue una de las causas de la guerra. *Slavery was one of the causes of the war.*

El **explorador** nunca llegó a su tierra deseada. *The explorer never got to his desired land.*

Los **peregrinos** le dieron gracias a Dios al final de su travesía. *The pilgrims thanked God when they ended their voyage.*

Todos esperamos el **descubrimiento** de una vacuna contra el sida. *We all hope for the discovery of an AIDS vaccine.*

EXERCISES

I. Match the Spanish word on the left with the English word on the right.

1. peligroso	A. *protester*
2. antiguo	B. *curfew*
3. el/la contrabandista	C. *bond*
4. la fianza	D. *alibi*
5. el toque de queda	E. *ancient*
6. la pobreza	F. *dangerous*
7. el/la manifestante	G. *border*
8. la coartada	H. *poverty*
9. el descubrimiento	I. *smuggler*
10. la frontera	J. *discovery*

II. Fill in the blanks with the appropriate Spanish word.

1. Supermán es un _____ (*hero*) de las tiras cómicas.

2. La _____ (*war*) duró tres meses.

3. El actor parece ser _____ (*guilty*) de varios cargos.

4. El muchacho es _____ (*addict*) a las anfetaminas.

5. El _____ (*lawyer*) tiene que leer muchos casos.

ANSWERS: I. 1. F, 2. E, 3. I, 4. C, 5. B, 6. H, 7. A, 8. D, 9. J, 10. G
II. 1. SUPERMÁN ES UN **HÉROE** DE LAS TIRAS CÓMICAS. 2. LA **GUERRA** DURÓ
TRES MESES. 3. EL ACTOR PARECE SER **CULPABLE** DE VARIOS CARGOS.
4. EL MUCHACHO ES **ADICTO** A LAS ANFETAMINAS. 5. EL **ABOGADO** TIENE
QUE LEER MUCHOS CASOS.

Social Problems

Controversial
Issues

Drugs

Crime and
Justice

War

**Historical
Experience**

Food & Cooking

Comida y cocina

13

MEALS

Comidas

la comida	*meal, lunch, dinner*
el desayuno	*breakfast*
el almuerzo	*lunch*
la cena	*dinner*
el brunch	*brunch*
el bocado	*snack*
la merienda	*snack*

Words In Use

¿Cuál es tu **comida** principal del día? *What's your main meal of the day?*

Mi **almuerzo** suele ser ligero. *My lunch is usually light.*

Los fines de semana como **brunch**. *On weekends I have brunch.*

A media tarde tomo una **merienda**. *I have a snack in the middle of the afternoon.*

APPETIZERS AND SIDE DISHES

Aperitivos y acompañantes

el aperitivo	*appetizer*
el acompañante	*side dish*
la ensalada	*salad*
la sopa	*soup*
el panecillo	*roll*

Words In Use

¿Desea algún **aperitivo**? *Would you like an appetizer?*

Sí, una **sopa** de tomate, por favor. *Yes, a tomato soup, please.*

¿Desea comer la **ensalada** griega? *Would you like to have the Greek salad?*

No, pero quiero más **panecillos**. *No, but I'd like more bread rolls.*

MEAT

Carne

MEAT NOUNS—BEEF

la carne de res	*beef*
la carne de vaca	*beef*
el bistec	*steak*
el filete	*steak fillet*
la carne curada con sal	*corned beef*
la cecina	*corned beef*
el salami	*salami*
la salchicha	*sausage*
la ternera	*veal*
la hamburguesa	*hamburger*

MEAT NOUNS—PORK

el cerdo	*pork*
el jamón	*ham*

MEAT NOUNS—LAMB

el cordero	*lamb*
la oveja	*mutton*

MEAT NOUNS—POULTRY

el pollo	*chicken*
la pechuga de pollo	*chicken breast*
el muslo de pollo	*chicken leg*
el hígado de pollo	*chicken liver*
el ala de pollo	*chicken wing*
las vísceras	*giblets*
la molleja	*gizzards*
el pollito	*young chicken*
el pollo joven	*young chicken*
el pavo	*turkey*
el pato	*duck*
la codorniz	*quail*

MEAT NOUNS—OTHER

el venado	*venison*
la rana	*frog*
el caracol	*snail*

MEAT ADJECTIVES

poco cocida	*rare*
a medio	*medium*
bien cocida	*well done*

Words In Use

¿Has pedido la carne de **venado**? *Did you order venison?*

No, pedí el **cordero**. *No, I ordered lamb.*

¿Te gusta el **pavo**? *Do you like turkey?*

Sí, pero me gusta más el **pollo**. *Yes, but I prefer chicken.*

La ensalada viene con **pechuga de pollo**. *The salad comes with chicken breast.*

Hace tiempo que no como **hamburguesas**. *I haven't had a hamburger in a long time.*

SEAFOOD AND FISH

Pescados y mariscos

SEAFOOD NOUNS

el abulón	*abalone*
la almeja	*clam*
el berberecho	*cockle*
el cangrejo	*crab*
la langosta	*lobster*
el pulpo	*octopus*
la ostra	*oyster*
el langostino	*prawn*
el escalope	*scallops*
el marisco	*shellfish*
el camarón	*shrimp*
el calamar	*squid*
el chipirón	*squid*

FISH NOUNS

el bacalao	*cod*
el filete	*fillet*
la platija	*flounder*
el lenguado	*flounder*
el arenque	*herring*
la caballa	*mackerel*
la macarela	*mackerel*

el lucio	pike
el salmón	salmon
el róbalo	sea bass
la lubina	sea bass
el tiburón	shark
la trucha	trout
el atún	tuna

Words In Use

¿Prefieres **langostinos** o **camarones** en la paella? *Do you prefer prawn or shrimp in your paella?*

El **salmón** es muy bueno para la salud. *Salmon is very good for your health.*

¿Con qué frecuencia comes **pescado**? *How frequently do you eat fish?*

Como algún tipo de **marisco** una vez a la semana. *I eat some kind of seafood once a week.*

Nunca he probado el **tiburón**. *I've never tried shark.*

Dicen que sabe mejor que la **platija**. *They say it tastes better than flounder.*

VEGETABLES
Verduras

el ajo	garlic
el apio	celery
la arveja china	snow pea
las arvejas	peas
la batata	sweet potato
el boniato	sweet potato
la berenjena	eggplant
el brécol	broccoli
los brotes de soja	bean sprouts
el calabacín	squash
la calabaza	pumpkin
la cebolla	onion
la cebolleta	chives
el cebollino	chives
el champiñón	mushroom
la col	cabbage
las coles de Bruselas	Brussels sprouts
la coliflor	cauliflower
el espárrago	asparagus
la espinaca	spinach
el frijol de soja	soybean

13

Meals

Appetizers and
Side dishes

Meat

**Seafood and
Fish/Vegetables**

Fruits

Nuts and Grains

Condiments
and Sauces

Spices

Sweets

Dairy

Beverages

Preparation

Cooking Methods

Cooking Utensils

Cooking
Measurements

Describing Food

el frijol	*bean*
el guisante chino	*snow peas*
los guisantes	*peas*
la habichuela	*bean*
la habichuela de caritas	*black-eyed pea*
la habichuela pinta	*black-eyed pea*
las habichuelas de soja	*soybeans*
el jenjibre	*ginger*
la judía	*bean*
la judía verde	*green bean*
la lechuga	*lettuce*
el maíz	*corn*
la papa	*potato*
la patata	*potato*
el pepino	*cucumber*
el perejil	*parsley*
el pimiento rojo	*red pepper*
el pimiento verde	*green pepper*
el puerro	*leek*
el quimbombó	*okra*
la seta	*mushroom*
el tofu	*tofu*
el tofú	*tofu*
el tomate	*tomato*
el vegetal	*vegetable*
la verdura	*vegetable, green*
la zanahoria	*carrot*

Words In Use

Voy a pedir la ensalada de **espinaca**. *I'm going to order the spinach salad.*

No le pongas **cebolla** a la hamburguesa. *Don't put onion on the hamburger.*

Tengo **perejil** en mi jardín. *I grow parsley in my garden.*

Mi madre prepara una excelente sopa de **puerros**. *My mother makes an excellent leek soup.*

Pon más **pimientos rojos** en la ensalada. *Put more red peppers in the salad.*

No me gustan las **papas** al horno; las prefiero fritas. *I don't like baked potatoes, I prefer them fried.*

FRUITS

Frutas

el albaricoque	*apricot*
el arándano amargo	*cranberry*
los arándanos	*blueberries*
la banana	*banana*
la cereza	*cherry*
la ciruela	*plum*
la ciruela pasa	*prune*
el coco	*coconut*
la frambuesa	*raspberry*
la fresa	*strawberry*
la granada	*pomegranate*
el higo	*fig*
la lima	*lime*
el limón	*lemon, lime*
el mango	*mango*
la manzana	*apple*
el melocotón	*peach*
el melón	*melon, cantaloupe*
la naranja	*orange*
la papaya	*papaya*
la pera	*pear*
la piña	*pineapple*
el plátano	*banana*
el pomelo	*grapefruit*
la sandía	*watermelon*
la toronja	*grapefruit*
las uvas	*grapes*
las uvas pasas	*raisins*

Words In Use

¿Quieres jugo de **naranja**? *Would you like an orange juice?*

Prefiero el jugo de **pomelo**. *I prefer grapefruit juice.*

Tengo néctar de **melocotón**. *I have peach nectar.*

¿Cuántos **limones** usaste para preparar esa limonada? *How many lemons did you use for that lemonade?*

¿Llevamos una **sandía** a la playa? *Should we bring a watermelon to the beach?*

Me gustan las **fresas**, pero no las cerezas. *I like strawberries but not cherries.*

NUTS AND GRAINS
Frutos secos y cereales

NUTS AND GRAINS NOUNS—NUTS

las nueces	*nuts*
los frutos secos	*nuts*
la castaña	*chestnut*
la castaña tostada	*roasted chestnut*
la nuez	*walnut*
la almendra	*almond*
el cacahuete	*peanut*
el anacardo	*cashew*

NUTS AND GRAINS NOUNS—BREAD

el pan	*bread*
la barra de pan	*loaf*
la hogaza de pan	*loaf*
la barra de pan francés	*baguette*
el panecillo	*bun, roll*

NUTS AND GRAINS NOUNS—RICE

el arroz	*rice*
el arroz blanco	*white rice*
el arroz integral	*brown rice*

NUTS AND GRAINS NOUNS—SEEDS

las semillas de sésamo	*sesame seeds*
las semillas de amapola	*poppy seeds*
las semillas de girasol	*sunflower seeds*

NUTS AND GRAINS NOUNS—GRAINS

el cereal	*grain, cereal*
el grano	*grain*
la harina	*flour*
la harina de trigo	*wheat flour*
el trigo	*wheat*
el centeno	*rye*

NUTS AND GRAINS NOUNS—PASTA

la pasta	*pasta*
los fideos	*noodles*

Words In Use

¿Ya compraste el **pan**? *Did you buy bread?*

Sí, compré una **barra de pan francés**. *Yes, I bought a baguette.*

El **arroz integral** es bueno para la salud. *Brown rice is good for your health.*

Sí, pero yo prefiero el **arroz blanco**. *Yes, but I prefer white rice.*

Debes poner **semillas de sésamo** en la ensalada china. *You should put sesame seeds in the Chinese salad.*

CONDIMENTS AND SAUCES
Condimentos y salsas

CONDIMENTS AND SAUCES NOUNS—SAVORY

el ketchup	*ketchup*
el catsup	*ketchup*
la salsa de tomate	*tomato sauce, ketchup*
el condimento	*relish*
la mayonesa	*mayonnaise*
la mostaza	*mustard*
el rábano picante	*horseradish*
la salsa Worcestershire	*Worchestershire sauce*
la salsa inglesa	*Worchestershire sauce*
la salsa para bistec	*steak sauce*
la salsa picante	*hot sauce*

CONDIMENTS AND SAUCES NOUNS—JAMS AND BUTTERS

la mermelada	*jam, marmalade*
la jalea de menta	*jelly (mint)*
la mantequilla	*butter*
la mantequilla de maní	*peanut butter*

CONDIMENTS AND SAUCES NOUNS—OILS

el aceite de girasol	*sunflower oil*
el aceite de oliva	*olive oil*
el aceite de sésamo	*sesame oil*
el aceite vegetal	*vegetable oil*

CONDIMENTS AND SAUCES NOUNS—VINEGARS

el vinagre	*vinegar*
el vinagre balsámico	*balsamic vinegar*
el vinagre de Módena	*balsamic vinegar*

Words In Use

Me gusta el pan con mucha **mantequilla**. *I like bread with a lot of butter.*

Pon más **aceite de oliva** en la **salsa**. *Put more olive oil in the sauce.*

¿Quieres **mayonesa** en tu emparedado? *Do you want mayonnaise on your sandwich?*

No, con **mostaza** por favor. *No, with mustard please.*

SPICES
Especias

la albahaca	basil
el azafrán	saffron
la canela	cinnamon
el cilantro	coriander
el comino	cumin
el culantro	coriander
la cúrcuma	turmeric
el curry	curry powder
el eneldo	dill
el estragón	tarragon
la hoja de laurel	bay leaf
la menta	mint
el orégano	oregano
el pimentón	paprika
la pimienta	pepper
la pimienta de cayena	cayenne pepper
la sal	salt
la vainilla	vanilla

Words In Use

Me gustan las margaritas con **sal** y limón. *I like margaritas with lemon and salt.*

La salsa de espaguetis necesita más **orégano**. *The spaghetti sauce needs more oregano.*

Camarero, quisiera un té de **menta**, por favor. *Waiter, I'd like a mint tea, please.*

Le pusiste mucha **pimienta** a la sopa. *You put too much pepper in the soup.*

SWEETS

Dulces

el azúcar	*sugar*
la miel	*honey*
el chocolate	*chocolate*
la menta	*mint*
el pastel	*cake*
el bizcocho	*cake*
la torta	*cake*
el caramelo	*candy*
las galletas	*cookies*
el chicle	*gum*
la goma de mascar	*gum*
el helado	*ice cream*

Words In Use

No le pongas **azúcar** al café. *Don't put sugar in my coffee.*

¡Me encantan los **dulces**! *I love sweets!*

Prefiero **miel** en mi té. *I prefer honey in my tea.*

¿Me das un **chicle**, por favor? *Would you give me a piece of gum, please?*

DAIRY

Productos lácteos

la leche	*milk*
la mantequilla	*butter*
el suero de leche	*buttermilk*
la leche cortada	*buttermilk*
el queso	*cheese*
el requesón	*cottage cheese*
la cuajada	*curds*
la crema de leche	*curds*
el yogur	*yogurt*
la creme de leche	*cream*
la crema agria	*sour cream*
el helado	*ice cream*

Words In Use

Ella no puede comer **productos lácteos**. *She can't eat dairy products.*

Me encanta el **queso** suizo. *I love Swiss cheese.*

Los niños deben tomar mucha **leche**. *Children should drink a lot of milk.*

Hace calor. Vamos a tomarnos un **helado**. *It's hot. Let's go get ice cream.*

BEVERAGES

Bebidas

BEVERAGES NOUNS—NON-ALCOHOLIC

el agua	*water*
el jugo	*juice*
el zumo	*juice*
el jugo/zumo de naranja	*orange juice*
el jugo/zumo de manzana	*apple juice*
el jugo/zumo de arándano amargo	*cranberry juice*
el jugo/zumo de uva	*grape juice*
el jugo/zumo de toronja	*grapefruit juice*
el café	*coffee*
el té	*tea*
el té negro	*black tea*
el té verde	*green tea*
la infusión	*herbal tea*
el té de hierbas	*herbal tea*
el chocolate caliente	*hot cocoa/hot chocolate*
la leche	*milk*
la leche de soja	*soy milk*

BEVERAGES NOUNS—ALCOHOLIC

la cerveza	*beer*
el vino	*wine*
el vino blanco	*white wine*
el vino tinto	*red wine*
el cóctel	*cocktail*
la ginebra	*gin*
el ron	*rum*
el vodka	*vodka*
el whisky	*whiskey*
el whisky escocés	*scotch*

BEVERAGES ADJECTIVES

sin alcohol	*non-alcoholic*
alcohólico	*alcoholic*
en las rocas	*on the rocks*
con hielo	*on the rocks, with ice*
puro	*neat*
solo	*neat*

Words In Use

Quiero un **vodka en las rocas**. *I'll have a vodka on the rocks.*

¿De dónde es el **vino**? *Where's the wine from?*

El **vino blanco** es de Chile. *The white wine is from Chile.*

El **vino tinto** es de la Rioja. *The red wine is from Rioja.*

Me gusta la **cerveza** alemana. *I like German beer.*

Debes tomar ocho vasos de **agua** al día. *You should drink eight glasses of water per day.*

PREPARATION

Preparación

batir	*to beat, to whip*
cernir	*to sift*
colar	*to sift*
cortar a rebanadas	*to slice*
cortar en dados	*to dice*
cortar en trozos gruesos	*to cube*
cortar en trozos	*to chop*
deshuesar	*to pit*
despepitar	*to seed*
espolvorear	*to sprinkle*
mezclar	*to blend, to mix*
pelar	*to peel*
picar	*to chop*
prensar	*to press*
rallar	*to grate*
revolver	*to stir*
tajar	*to slice*
tamizar	*to sift*
triturar	*to crush*
vertir	*to pour*

La carne tiene que ser **cortada en dados** primero. *The beef has to be diced first.*

Mezcla la leche en polvo con un litro de agua. *Mix the powdered milk with a liter of water.*

Se te olvidó **triturar** el ajo. *You forgot to crush the garlic.*

Hay que **vertir** el jugo sobre el pescado. *You have to pour the lime juice over the fish.*

COOKING METHODS

Métodos para cocinar

COOKING METHODS ADJECTIVES

asado a la parrilla	*broiled*
cocido al horno	*baked*
cocido al vapor	*steamed*
escalfado	*poached*
estofado	*stewed*
frito	*fried*
hervido	*boiled, poached*
muy cocido	*hard-boiled*
quemado	*burnt*
salteado	*sautéed*
soasado	*seared*

COOKING METHODS VERBS

asar	*to bake*
asar a la parrilla	*to broil*
cocer	*to bake*
cocer al vapor	*to steam*
escalfar	*to poach*
estofar	*to stew*
freír	*to fry*
guisar	*to stew*
hervir	*to boil, to poach*
hornear	*to bake*
saltear	*to sauté*
soasar	*to sear*
tostar	*to sear*

Words In Use

Es muy sano comer las verduras **cocidas al vapor**. *It's very healthy to eat steamed vegetables.*

En este restaurante el pollo **asado a la parrilla** es muy bueno. *The broiled chicken is very good in this restaurant.*

Él pidió el pollo **frito**. *He ordered fried fish.*

COOKING UTENSILS

Utensilios de cocina

COOKING UTENSILS NOUNS — POTS AND PANS

la olla	*pot*
el cazo	*saucepan*
el perol	*saucepan*
la cacerola	*pot, saucepan, casserole dish*
la cazuela	*casserole dish*
la sartén para freír	*frying pan*
la parrilla	*grill*

COOKING UTENSILS NOUNS — KNIVES AND TOOLS

el cuchillo	*knife*
el cuchillo para carne	*butcher's knife*
el cuchillo para la mantequilla	*butter knife*
la cuchilla de carnicero	*cleaver*
el cuchillo para pescado	*fish knife*
el rallador de queso	*cheese grater*

COOKING UTENSILS NOUNS — MEASURING

la taza para medir	*measuring cup*
la cuchara para medir	*measuring spoon*

COOKING UTENSILS NOUNS — OTHER UTENSILS

el colador	*sieve*
la espátula	*spatula*
el batidor	*whisk*
la cuchara	*spoon*
el cuenco grande	*mixing bowl*
el tazón	*mixing bowl*
la fuente	*mixing bowl*
la bandeja para hornear	*baking sheet*

la batidora	*mixer*
los palitos chinos	*chopsticks*
el papel de aluminio	*aluminum foil*
el papel encerado	*wax paper*

NOTE: More words related to Cooking Utensils can be found in the Kitchen section of this book.

Words In Use

No me dieron **palitos chinos**. *They didn't give me chopsticks.*

Esa **olla** me costó mucho dinero. *That pot cost me a lot of money.*

Quiero comprar una **parrilla** para mi patio. *I'd like to buy a grill for my backyard.*

La **cacerola** es de acero inoxidable. *The saucepan is made of stainless steel.*

COOKING MEASUREMENTS
Medidas de cocina

la taza	*cup*
la pizca	*dash, pinch*
la pinta	*pint*
el cuarto de galón	*quart*
la cucharada	*tablespoon*
la cucharadita	*teaspoon*

Words In Use

La receta dice que es una **cucharada** de vinagre. *The recipe calls for a tablespoon of vinegar.*

Y dos **cucharaditas** de jugo de naranja. *And two teaspoons of orange juice.*

Hace falta un **pizca** de sal. *We still need a pinch of salt.*

DESCRIBING FOOD
Describiendo la comida

DESCRIBING FOOD NOUNS

la cocina	*cuisine*
el arte culinario	*culinary arts, cuisine*

DESCRIBING FOOD ADJECTIVES

dulce	*sweet*
salado	*salty*
amargo	*bitter*
ácido	*tart*

agrio	*tart*
picante	*spicy*
no muy picante	*mild*
suave	*mild*
fuerte y picante	*tangy*
insípido	*tasteless*
soso	*tasteless, bland*
deleitable	*delectable*
delicioso	*delicious*
de gastronomía	*gourmet*
fuerte	*hearty*
copioso	*hearty*
frío	*cold*
tibio	*lukewarm*
sabroso	*palatable*
refrescante	*refreshing*
maduro	*ripe*
crujiente	*crispy, crunchy*
rancio	*stale*
mojado	*soggy*
pastoso	*soggy*
mohoso	*moldy*
enmohecido	*moldy*
vegetariano	*vegetarian*

DESCRIBING FOOD VERBS

estar pasado	*to be off*
estar cortado	*to be off*

NOTE: More words related to Describing Food can be found in the General Descriptive Words and Five Senses categories.

Words In Use

No le sirvas carne; ella es **vegetariana**. *Don't serve any meat; she's a vegetarian.*

La cena fue un desastre. . . el pan estaba **rancio**. *The dinner was a disaster . . . the bread was stale.*

El consomé quedó **insípido**. *The consommé was tasteless.*

La sopa estaba **tibia**. *The soup was lukewarm.*

¡Y la ensalada de pollo demasiado **fría**! *And the chicken salad was too cold!*

EXERCISES

I. Match the Spanish word on the left with the English word on the right.

1. sabroso		A.	*corn*
2. el cuchillo		B.	*butter*
3. la bebida		C.	*candy*
4. el caramelo		D.	*cup*
5. el melocotón		E.	*knife*
6. el maíz		F.	*peach*
7. la lechuga		G.	*refreshing*
8. refrescante		H.	*palatable*
9. la taza		I.	*beverage*
10. la mantequilla		J.	*lettuce*

II. Fill in the blanks with the appropriate Spanish word.

1. Mi abuela preparó una _____ (*delicious*) cena.

2. En el Caribe se produce muy buen _____ (*rum*).

3. En el verano me gusta tomar _____(*beer*).

4. La _____ (*sauce*) de espaguetis está muy espesa.

5. El _____ (*garlic*) es muy bueno para el corazón.

ANSWERS: I. 1. H, 2. E, 3. I, 4. C, 5. F, 6. A, 7. J, 8. G, 9. D, 10. B
II. 1. MI ABUELA PREPARÓ UNA **DELICIOSA** CENA. 2. EN EL CARIBE SE
PRODUCE MUY BUEN **RON**. 3. EN EL VERANO ME GUSTA TOMAR **CERVEZA**.
4. LA **SALSA** DE ESPAGUETI ESTÁ MUY ESPESA. 5. EL **AJO** ES MUY BUENO
PARA EL CORAZÓN.

Around the House— The Home and Home Activities

En la casa: El hogar y las actividades domésticas

HOUSE AND REAL ESTATE TERMS

Términos para el hogar y las bienes raíces

HOUSE AND REAL ESTATE NOUNS—TYPES OF HOMES

la casa	*house*
la casa de ladrillo	*brick house*
la casa de playa	*beach house*
el rancho	*ranch house*
la casa de granja	*farmhouse*
la mansión	*mansion*
el piso	*apartment*
el apartamento	*apartment*
el condominio	*condominium (condo)*
la cooperativa	*cooperative (co-op)*
el dúplex	*duplex*
el bungalow	*bungalow*
la cabaña	*cabin, hut*
la casucha	*shack*
la choza	*shack*
el iglú	*igloo*
el tipi	*teepee*
la tienda de campaña	*tent*
el edificio	*building*
el hotel	*hotel*
la oficina	*office*

HOUSE AND REAL ESTATE NOUNS—PARTS OF THE HOUSE

el techo	*ceiling, roof*
los pisos	*floors*
la puerta	*door*
las paredes	*walls*
la pared de soporte	*bearing wall*
la división	*partition*
el tabique	*partition*
las escaleras	*stairs*
la baranda	*banister*
el pasamanos	*banister*
la ventana	*window*
el apoyo de la ventana	*windowsill*
la claraboya	*skylight*
la chimenea	*chimney*
el porche	*porch, stoop*
el pórtico	*stoop*
el terreno	*land*
la tierra	*land*
el adjunto	*attachment*
el almacenamiento	*self-storage*
los servicios públicos	*utilities*
el agua y la luz	*water and light, utilities*

HOUSE AND REAL ESTATE NOUNS— RENTING AND BUYING A HOUSE

los bienes raíces	*real estate*
la inmobiliaria	*real estate, realtor (company)*
el alquiler	*rent*
el arrendamiento	*lease*
la escritura	*deed*
la escritura de garantía	*warranty deed*
el título	*title*
el compromiso	*commitment*
el acuerdo	*agreement*
el contrato	*contract*
la búsqueda de título	*title search*
el cierre	*closing*
los costos de cierre	*closing costs*
la compra por debajo	*buy-down*

la opción	*option*
la hipoteca	*mortgage*
la primera hipoteca	*first mortgage*
la segunda hipoteca	*second mortgage*
el seguro de hipoteca privada	*private mortgage insurance*
la tasa de porcentaje anual	*annual percentage rate*
el préstamo puente	*bridge loan*
el pago inicial	*down-payment*
la cuota inicial	*down-payment*
el capital	*capital, principal*
la garantía	*collateral*
el interés	*interest*
la valoración	*appraisal, assessment*
la tasación	*assessment*
la depreciación	*depreciation*
el embargo preventivo	*lien*
la equidad	*equity*
el fideicomiso	*trust*
el incumplimiento de contrato	*breach of contract*
la indemnización	*indemnity*
el juicio hipotecario	*foreclosure*
la subasta	*auction*
la venta pública	*public sale*
la propiedad	*property*
la construcción	*construction, building*
el código de construcción	*building codes*
la licencia de construcción	*building permit*
la zonificación	*zoning*
la construcción prefabricada	*prefabricated construction*
la vivienda fabricada	*manufactured housing*
la ocupación	*occupancy*
el inquilinato	*occupancy*
el diseño de jardines	*landscaping*
los barrios residenciales	*suburbs*
los barrios suburbanos	*suburbs*
la censura	*condemnation*
el seguro	*insurance*
el seguro contra inundación	*flood insurance*

| el seguro contra riesgos | *hazard insurance* |
| el seguro de título | *title insurance* |

HOUSE AND REAL ESTATE NOUNS—PEOPLE

el/la propietario/a	*owner*
el/la dueño/a	*owner*
el/la inquilino/a	*tenant*
el/la que alquila	*renter*
el/la casero/a	*renter*
el/la arrendador/a	*lessor*
el/la arrendatario/a	*lessee*
el/la agente	*agent, broker*
el/la agente de bienes raíces	*realtor*
el contratista general	*general contractor*

HOUSE AND REAL ESTATE ADJECTIVES

arriba	*upstairs*
abajo	*downstairs*
adjunto	*attached*
de alquiler	*rental*
de arriendo	*rental*
de un nivel	*one-storey*
de dos pisos	*two-storey*
de tres pisos	*three-storey*
de nivel dividido	*split-level*
rural	*rural*
urbano	*urban*
residencial	*residential*
vacante	*vacant*
vacío	*vacant*

HOUSE AND REAL ESTATE VERBS

ser dueño/a	*to own*
alquilar	*to lease, to rent*
arrendar	*to rent, to let, to lease*
realquilar	*to sublet*
subarrendar	*to sublet*
acordar	*to settle*
comprar	*to buy*
vender	*to sell*

apostar	*to bid*
hacer una oferta	*to bid*
rescindir	*to rescind*
evaluar	*to appraise*
refinanciar	*to refinance*
asignar	*to assign*
incumplir un acuerdo	*to default*
transmitir	*to convey*

House and Real
Estate Terms

Living Room

Bedroom

Bathroom

Attic

Basement

Kitchen

Dining Room

Storage and
Containers

Outside

Cleaning

Tools

Home Decoration

Plumbing and
Electricity

Words In Use

Ella es **dueña** de dos **apartamentos** en Manhattan. *She owns two apartments in Manhattan.*

Tuvo que **refinanciar** uno de ellos. *She had to refinance one of them.*

¿Piensas que va a **vender** el otro? *Do you think she'll sell the other one?*

Es una **mansión** con **pisos** de mármol. *It's a mansion with marble floors.*

¿Qué tipo de **edificio** es? *What type of building is it?*

Creo que es un **condominio**. *I think it's a condominium.*

Estoy en el proceso de buscar una **hipoteca**. *I'm in the process of getting a mortgage.*

¿Encontraste una buena **tasa de porcentaje anual**? *Did you find a good annual percentage rate?*

¿Cuál es la **valoración** de la **casa**? *What's the appraisal of the house?*

LIVING ROOM

La sala

LIVING ROOM NOUNS

el sofá	*sofa*
la silla	*chair*
el sillón	*armchair*
el descanso para los pies	*footrest*
el taburete	*stool*
la mesa	*table*
la mesita para el café	*coffee table*
la mesita lateral	*side table*
el piso	*floor*
el suelo	*floor*
los pisos de madera	*hardwood floors*
la alfombra	*carpet, rug*
la alfombra de felpa	*shag carpet*

el techo	ceiling
el ventilador de techo	ceiling fan
las paredes	walls
la ventana	window
la cortinas	curtains
el reloj	clock
el reloj de péndulo	grandfather clock
la lámpara	lamp
la iluminación superior	overhead lighting
la pintura	picture
el cuadro	picture
el marco	picture frame
el estante	shelf
el estante para libros	bookshelf
el televisor	television
la chimenea	fireplace

LIVING ROOM ADJECTIVES

acogedor	cozy
relajante	relaxing
cálido	warm
bien iluminado	well-lit
lleno de color	colorful
vistoso	flashy, colorful

LIVING ROOM VERBS

sentarse	to sit
ponerse de pie	to stand
visitar	to visit
reunirse	to gather
relajarse	to relax
leer	to read
mirar la televisión	to watch television

Words In Use

Le voy a regalar a Pedro un **televisor** nuevo. *I'm getting Pedro a new television.*

A él le gusta mucho **mirar la televisión**. *He loves to watch television.*

Me gusta **leer** en la **sala**. *I like to read in the living room.*

La **alfombra** tiene un color muy bonito. *The carpet has a beautiful color.*

Combina muy bien con el **sofá**. *It matches with the sofa.*

Tengo que mandar a pintar las **paredes**. *I have to have the walls painted.*

Casi nunca uso la **chimenea**. *I rarely ever use the fireplace.*

BEDROOM
El dormitorio

BEDROOM NOUNS

la cama	*bed*
la cama con dosel	*canopy bed*
la cabecera	*headboard*
la almohada	*pillow*
la sábana	*sheet*
la manta	*blanket*
el edredón	*duvet, comforter*
la mesita de noche	*bedside table*
la lámpara	*lamp*
el armario	*closet*
la percha	*hanger*
el gancho	*hanger, hook*
el tocador	*dresser*
el espejo	*mirror*
el sueño	*dream*
la pesadilla	*nightmare*
el insomnio	*insomnia*

BEDROOM ADJECTIVES

oscuro	*dark*
claro	*bright*
cómodo	*comfortable*
acogedor	*cozy*
cansado	*tired*
despierto	*awake*
inquieto	*restless*

BEDROOM VERBS

dormir	*to sleep*
despertarse	*to wake up*
vestirse	*to get dressed*
bostezar	*to yawn*
soñar	*to dream*

Words In Use

¿Cuántos **dormitorios** tiene la casa? *How many bedrooms does the house have?*

Este **dormitorio** es el más **oscuro** de la casa. *This bedroom is the darkest one in the house.*

Éste es más **claro**, pero no es tan **cómodo**. *This one is brighter but it's not as comfortable.*

No puedo **dormir** bien. *I can't sleep well.*

¿Por qué? ¿Padeces de **insomnio**? *Why, do you suffer from insomnia?*

BATHROOM

El baño

BATHROOM NOUNS

el agua	*water*
el inodoro	*toilet*
el váter	*toilet*
el papel higiénico	*toilet paper*
el lavabo	*sink*
el lavamanos	*sink*
el grifo	*faucet*
la ducha	*shower*
la cortina de baño	*shower curtain*
la bañera	*bathtub*
el desagüe	*drain*
la lechada	*grout*
el tapete de baño	*bath mat*
la alfombrita de baño	*bath mat*
el piso de baldosas	*tile floor*
el espejo	*mirror*
la toalla	*towel*
la toalla de manos	*hand towel*
la toallita para lavarse	*washcloth*
el paño para lavarse	*washcloth*
el toallero	*towel rack*
el jabón	*soap*
el champú	*shampoo*
el acondicionador	*conditioner*
el cepillo para el cabello	*hair brush*
el peine	*comb*

la navaja de afeitar	*razor*
la espuma para afeitar	*shaving foam*
el cepillo de dientes	*toothbrush*
el dentrífico	*toothpaste*
la pasta de dientes	*toothpaste*

BATHROOM ADJECTIVES

caliente	*hot*
frío	*cold*
limpio	*clean*
sucio	*dirty*
lleno de vapor	*steamy*
empañado	*steamy*
húmedo	*moist*
sanitario	*sanitary*
antihigiénico	*unsanitary, unhygienic*
insalubre	*unhealthy, unsanitary*

BATHROOM VERBS

lavarse	*to wash oneself*
enjabonarse	*to lather*
enjuagar	*to rinse*
aclarar	*to rinse*
peinarse	*to comb*
afeitarse	*to shave*
cepillarse los dientes	*to brush your teeth*
orinar	*to urinate*
defecar	*to defecate*
tirar de la cadena	*to flush*

NOTE: More words related to the Bathroom can be found in the Personal Hygiene and Cosmetics sections of this book.

Words In Use

Esta **bañera** es importada de Italia. *This bathtub is imported from Italy.*

No vayas al **baño** del restaurante. ¡Está **sucio**! *Don't use the bathroom in the restaurant; it's dirty!*

El **baño** de los hombres está **limpio**. *The men's bathroom is clean.*

Es importante **cepillarse los dientes** después de cada comida. *It's important to brush one's teeth after each meal.*

No te olvides de comprar **pasta de dientes** y **jabón**. *Don't forget to buy toothpaste and soap.*

ATTIC
El ático

ATTIC NOUNS

la escalera	*ladder*
las vigas	*rafters*
el aislamiento	*insulation*
el almacenamiento	*storage*
las cajas	*boxes*
la telaraña	*cobwebs*

ATTIC ADJECTIVES

oscuro	*dark*
polvoriento	*dusty*
rancio	*musty, rancid*
que huele a moho	*musty, smelling of mold*
rechinador	*creaky*
poco sólido	*creaky*
viejo	*old*

ATTIC VERBS

trepar	*to climb*
almacenar	*to store*
buscar	*to search*
encontrar	*to find*

Words In Use

Yo **almaceno** mis discos viejos en el **ático**. *I store my old records in the attic.*

Busqué por todas partes y no los pude **encontrar**. *I searched everywhere but could not find them.*

¿Los buscaste en esta **caja**? *Did you look for them in this box?*

Ten cuidado con esa **escalera**. *Be careful with that ladder.*

BASEMENT
El sótano

BASEMENT NOUNS

la caldera	*boiler*
la lavandería	*laundry*
la lavadora	*washer*
la secadora	*dryer*

BASEMENT ADJECTIVES

húmedo	*damp*
mohoso	*moldy*

BASEMENT VERBS

lavar la ropa	*to do the laundry*

Words In Use

Yo **lavo la ropa** los sábados. *I do the laundry on Saturdays.*

¿Tienes **secadora** en tu casa? *Do you have a dryer in your house?*

No, pero tengo **lavadora**. *No, but I have a washer.*

Nunca he estado en el **sótano** del edificio. *I've never been to the basement in this building.*

KITCHEN
La cocina

KITCHEN NOUNS—GENERAL

el mostrador	*counter*
el armario	*cupboard*
la despensa	*pantry*
el fregadero	*sink*
el cubo de basura	*trash can*
la caneca	*trash can*

KITCHEN NOUNS—APPLIANCES

la nevera	*refrigerator*
el horno	*oven*
la parrilla	*grill*
el horno de microondas	*microwave*
la tostadora	*toaster*
la batidora	*blender*
el robot de cocina	*food processor*
la procesadora de alimentos	*food processor*
el triturador de basura	*garbage disposal*
el molinillo de café	*coffee grinder*
la cafetera	*coffee maker*

KITCHEN ADJECTIVES

sanitario	*sanitary*
antihigiénico	*unsanitary, unhygienic*
insalubre	*unhealthy, unsanitary*

KITCHEN VERBS

comer	*to eat*
beber	*to drink*
cocinar	*to cook*
cocinar en microondas	*to microwave*
preparar	*to prepare*
mezclar	*to blend*
moler	*to grind*
tostar	*to toast*
servir la comida	*to serve a meal*
lavar los platos	*to wash the dishes*
secar los platos	*to dry the dishes*

NOTE: More words related to the Kitchen can be found in the Food category of this book.

Words In Use

Me gusta **moler** mi propio café. *I like to grind my own coffee.*

¿A qué hora vas a **servir la comida**? *At what time are you serving the meal?*

Ayúdame a **lavar los platos**. *Help me wash the dishes.*

¿Dónde está el **cubo de basura**? *Where's the garbage can?*

No lo sé preparar en el **horno de microondas**. *I don't know how to prepare it in the microwave oven.*

DINING ROOM

El comedor

DINING ROOM NOUNS

la mesa de comedor	*dining table*
el aparador	*sideboard*
la vajilla fina	*china*
el plato	*plate*
el platillo para ensalada	*salad plate*
el platillo	*saucer*
la fuente	*bowl*
el cuenco	*bowl*
el tazón	*bowl*
la vajilla de plata	*silverware*
los cubiertos	*cutlery*
el tenedor	*fork*
la cuchara	*spoon*
la cucharita	*teaspoon*

el cuchillo	*knife*
el cuchillo para la mantequilla	*butter knife*
el cuchillo para el pescado	*fish knife*
el centro de mesa	*centerpiece*

DINING ROOM VERBS

| poner la mesa | *to set the table* |

Words In Use

Te falta un **tenedor**. *You're missing a fork.*

¿Qué tipo de **platos** quiere que ponga? *What type of plates do you want me to use?*

Es una ocasión especial; pongamos la **vajilla fina**. *It's a special occasion, let's use the fine china.*

Yo te ayudo **a poner la mesa**. *I'll help you set the table.*

Tienes una **mesa de comedor** muy grande. *You have a big dining table.*

STORAGE AND CONTAINERS

Almacenamiento y envases

la bolsa	*bag*
la botella	*bottle*
la lata	*can*
el tarro	*jar*
el bote	*jar*
la caja	*box*
la caja de cartón	*carton*
el recipiente	*bin*
el cajón	*crate*
el cubo	*bucket*
el balde	*bucket*
el envase plástico	*plastic container*
el paquete	*packet*
el tubo	*tube*
el archivo	*file*

Words In Use

Tengo que conseguir **cajas** para la mudanza. *I have to find boxes for my move.*

Prefiero los refrescos en **botella**. *I prefer soda out of a bottle.*

Necesito una **lata** de jugo. *I need a can of juice.*

OUTSIDE

En el exterior

OUTSIDE NOUNS

el césped	*lawn*
el patio	*yard*
el arbusto	*bush*
el jardín	*garden*
el camino de entrada	*driveway*
el garaje	*garage*
la valla	*fence*
la cerca	*fence*
la propiedad	*property*
el buzón	*mailbox*

OUTSIDE ADJECTIVES

afuera	*outside*
en el exterior	*outside*

OUTSIDE VERBS

cultivar	*to grow*
crecer	*to grow*
cortar	*to mow*
segar	*to mow*
regar	*to water*
podar	*to prune*
fertilizar	*to fertilize*

NOTE: More words related to the Outside of the House can be found in other categories in this book, such as the Natural World.

Words In Use

Tengo varios tipos de flores en el **jardín**. *I have several types of flowers in my garden.*

Los niños están jugando en el **patio**. *The children are playing in the yard.*

Tengo que **podar** el árbol; está muy alto. *I have to prune that tree, it's too high.*

Voy a poner una valla alrededor del **césped**. *I'm going to put a fence around the lawn.*

CLEANING
La limpieza

CLEANING NOUNS—PRODUCTS

el jabón	*soap*
la lejía	*bleach*
el amoníaco	*ammonia*
el desinfectante	*disinfectant*
el abrasivo	*abrasive*
la cera para pisos	*floor wax*
el ambientador	*air freshener*

CLEANING NOUNS—TOOLS

la aspiradora	*vacuum cleaner*
la escoba	*broom*
la fregona	*mop*
el trapeador	*mop*
la esponja	*sponge*
el cubo	*bucket*
el balde	*bucket*
el trapo	*cloth*
el trapo del polvo	*duster*
el paño	*duster*
la escobilla de goma	*squeegee*
el rodillo de goma	*squeegee*

CLEANING ADJECTIVES

sucio	*dirty*
mugriento	*grimy*
polvoriento	*dusty*
lúgubre	*dingy*
manchado	*soiled*
sucio	*soiled*
limpio	*clean*
reluciente	*shiny*
brillante	*shiny, sparkling*
centelleante	*sparkling*
mojado	*wet*
seco	*dry*
sanitario	*sanitary*

House and Real Estate Terms

Living Room

Bedroom

Bathroom

Attic

Basement

Kitchen

Dining Room

Storage and Containers

Outside/ Cleaning

Tools

Home Decoration

Plumbing and Electricity

antihigiénico	*unsanitary, unhygienic*
insalubre	*unhealthy, unsanitary*

CLEANING VERBS

limpiar	*to clean, to clean up, to wipe*
limpiar a fondo	*to clean out*
lavar	*to wash*
estregar	*to scrub*
restregar	*to scrub*
enjugar	*to wipe*
quitar el polvo	*to dust*
pulir	*to polish*
encerar	*to wax*
airear	*to air out*
orear	*to air out*

Words In Use

¿Sueles **encerar** el piso a menudo? *Do you wax your floors frequently?*

Tengo que **airear** la sala; había varios fumadores. *I have to air out the living room; there were several smokers.*

Ese **desinfectante** tiene un olor muy fuerte. *That disinfectant has a strong smell.*

Contiene **amoníaco**. *It contains ammonia.*

TOOLS

Herramientas

TOOLS NOUNS

el tornillo	*screw*
el clavo	*nail*
el martillo	*hammer*
el mazo	*mallet*
la almádana	*sledgehammer*
el destornillador	*screwdriver*
el taladro	*drill*
la llave inglesa	*wrench*
la llave de tuerca	*spanner*
el alicate	*pliers*
la sierra	*saw*
la sierra de vaivén	*jigsaw*
el torno	*lathe*

el cincel	*chisel*
el nivel	*plane*
la cinta métrica	*measuring tape*
la regla	*ruler*
la palanca	*crowbar*
el soplete	*blowtorch*
el tornillo de banco	*vise grip*
la abrazadera	*clamp*
la caja de las herramientas	*toolbox*
el banco de trabajo	*workbench*
la máscara para soldar	*welding mask*

TOOLS VERBS

martillar	*to hammer*
clavar	*to nail*
atornillar	*to screw*
enroscar	*to screw*
serrar	*to saw*
medir	*to measure*

Words In Use

No puedo encontrar mis **herramientas**. *I can't find my tools.*

¿Dónde pusiste la **llave inglesa**? *Where did you put the wrench?*

Está en la **caja de herramientas**. *It's in the toolbox.*

Tengo que **medir** el largo de la pared. *I have to measure the length of the wall.*

Sí, pero no tengo una **cinta métrica**. *Yes, but I don't have measuring tape.*

HOME DECORATION
Decoración del hogar

HOME DECORATION NOUNS

los muebles	*furniture*
la tapicería	*upholstery*
el tapete	*carpet, area rug*
la alfombra	*carpet, area rug*
la alfombra de pared a pared	*wall-to-wall carpet*
el pasacaminos	*runner*
la alfombra continua	*runner*
el dibujo	*picture*
el marco	*picture frame*

14

House and Real
Estate Terms

Living Room

Bedroom

Bathroom

Attic

Basement

Kitchen

Dining Room

Storage and
Containers

Outside

Cleaning

**Tools/Home
Decoration**

Plumbing and
Electricity

la pintura	*paint, painting*
el cuadro	*painting*
el papel pintado	*wallpaper*
el ribete	*trim*
la vela	*candle*
el jarrón	*vase*
el florero	*vase*
la varilla para colgar las cortinas	*curtain rod*
el trapo del polvo	*dust cloth*

HOME DECORATION ADJECTIVES

decorado	*decorated*
sin decorar	*undecorated*
moderno	*modern*
retro	*retro*
minimalista	*minimalist*
simple	*simple, undecorated*

HOME DECORATION VERBS

renovar	*to renovate*
reamueblar	*to refurnish*
amueblar de nuevo	*to refurnish*
remozar	*to refurbish*
restaurar	*to refurbish*
tapizar	*to upholster*
cubrir	*to cover*
alfombrar	*to carpet/to lay carpet*
colgar	*to hang*
pintar	*to paint*
empapelar	*to wallpaper*
blanquear	*to whitewash*
encalar	*to whitewash*

NOTE: More words related to Home Decoration can be found in the Construction and Architecture section of this book.

Words In Use

Ya es hora de **renovar** este apartamento. *It's time to renovate this apartment.*

Necesitas **amueblarlo de nuevo**. *You need to refurnish it.*

Sí, también pienso **alfombrar** los dormitorios. *Yes, I'm also thinking of carpeting the bedrooms.*

Quiero **muebles modernos**. *I want modern furniture.*

Necesita una nueva mano de **pintura**. *It needs a fresh coat of paint.*

PLUMBING AND ELECTRICITY
Fontanería y electricidad

PLUMBING NOUNS

el grifo	*faucet*
la tubería	*pipe*
el desagüe	*drain*
el drenaje	*drainage*
la gotera	*leak*
el atasco	*clog*
las aguas negras	*sewage*
el limpiador del desagüe	*drain cleaner*

PLUMBING ADJECTIVES

tupido	*clogged*
con un escape	*leaky*

PLUMBING VERBS

llamar a un fontanero	*to call a plumber*
tener un escape	*to leak*

ELECTRICITY NOUNS

la electricidad	*electricity*
la corriente	*current*
el cable	*wire*
la toma	*outlet*
el enchufe	*socket*
el interruptor	*switch*
el cordón de extensión	*extension cord*
el convertidor de electricidad	*power converter*
el transformador	*power converter*
el protector de subida de tensión	*surge protector/power strip*
el fusible	*fuse*
el cajón de fusibles	*fuse box*
el generador	*generator*
la descarga	*shock*

ELECTRICITY VERBS

haber un apagón	to black out
llamar a un electricista	to call an electrician
rehacer la instalación eléctrica	to rewire

Words In Use

Tengo una **gotera** en el **grifo**. *I have a leak in my faucet.*

Tengo la **tubería tupida**. *I have a clogged pipe.*

Deberías **llamar a un fontanero**. *You should call a plumber.*

No es necesario **rehacer la instalación eléctrica** en la habitación. *It's not necessary to rewire the room.*

¿No hay un **enchufe** más cerca? *Is there a nearer socket?*

EXERCISES

I. Match the Spanish word on the left with the English word on the right.

1. el cuchillo		A. *to rent*	
2. la cocina		B. *broker*	
3. la alfombra		C. *auction*	
4. alquilar		D. *nightmare*	
5. el/la agente		E. *carpet*	
6. la subasta		F. *kitchen*	
7. el/la propietario/a		G. *owner*	
8. la silla		H. *sink*	
9. la pesadilla		I. *knife*	
10. el lavabo		J. *chair*	

II. Fill in the blanks with the appropriate Spanish word.

1. Estoy muy _____ (*tired*); me voy a la cama.

2. El carro está muy _____ (*dirty*).

3. Tengo que _____ (*to prepare*) la cena para la fiesta.

4. No me gusta mirar la televisión en el _____ (*bedroom*).

5. Me gusta _____ (*to read*) en la sala.

ANSWERS: I. 1. I, 2. F, 3. E, 4. A, 5. B, 6. C, 7. G, 8. J, 9. D, 10. H
II. 1. ESTOY MUY **CANSADO**; ME VOY A LA CAMA. 2. EL CARRO ESTÁ MUY
SUCIO. 3. TENGO QUE **PREPARAR** LA CENA PARA LA FIESTA. 4. NO ME GUSTA
MIRAR LA TELEVISIÓN EN EL **DORMITORIO**. 5. ME GUSTA **LEER** EN LA SALA.

Around Town— The Town and Daily Town Activities

De paseo por la ciudad: Actividades diarias

TOWN DESCRIPTIONS

Describiendo una ciudad

TOWN DESCRIPTIONS NOUNS

la ciudad	*city, town*
el pueblo	*town*
la zona residencial	*suburb, residential area*
la zona suburbana	*suburb, suburban area*
el suburbio	*suburb*
el campo	*country*
la campiña	*countryside*

TOWN DESCRIPTIONS ADJECTIVES

urbano	*urban*
suburbano	*suburban*
rural	*rural*

Words In Use

Los problemas **urbanos** están afectando mucho a la ciudad. *Urban problems are affecting the city greatly.*

Me gusta más el paisaje **rural**. *I prefer rural landscapes.*

Se mudó a la **zona residencial**. *He moved to a suburban area.*

TOWN FEATURES

Características de una ciudad

TOWN FEATURES NOUNS—BUILDINGS AND PLACES

el ayuntamiento	*town*
la municipalidad	*town hall*
la escuela	*school*

el colegio	*school, college*
la biblioteca	*library*
el museo	*museum*
el zoológico	*zoo*
el correo	*post office*
el hospital	*hospital*
la estación de autobuses	*bus station*
la estación de ferrocarril	*train station*
la iglesia	*church*
la catedral	*cathedral*
el templo	*temple*
la sinagoga	*synagogue*
la mezquita	*mosque*
el cine	*movie theater*
la fábrica	*factory*
la cárcel	*jail*
la prisión	*prison*
el centro para visitantes	*visitor's center*
el centro comunal	*community center*
el área de negocios	*business center*
el centro de oficinas	*business center*
el edificio de oficinas	*office building*
el edificio de apartamentos	*apartment building*
el condominio	*condominium*
el rascacielos	*skyscraper*
la infraestructura	*infrastructure*

TOWN FEATURES NOUNS—STREET FEATURES

la calle	*street*
la calle principal	*main street*
la avenida	*avenue*
la farola	*street light*
el semáforo	*traffic light*
la intersección	*intersection*
el paso de peatones	*crosswalk*
la acera	*sidewalk*
el andén	*sidewalk*
la plaza	*square*
el centro de la ciudad	*city center*

| el parque | *park* |
| el depósito de agua | *water tower* |

TOWN FEATURES NOUNS—PEOPLE

el/la alcalde/alcaldesa	*mayor*
el/la jefe de la policía	*police chief*
el/la alguacil	*sheriff*

NOTE: More words related to Town Features can be found in other categories of this book, such as Transportation and School.

Words In Use

El nuevo **jefe de la policía** es una persona muy respetada. *The new police chief is highly respected.*

El **alcalde** de la ciudad enfrenta problemas económicos difíciles. *The mayor of the city faces difficult economic problems.*

¿En qué **calle** vives? *On what street do you live?*

En la ciudad de Nueva York hay muchos **rascacielos**. *There are many skyscrapers in New York City.*

¿Dónde está el **hospital** más cercano? *Where's the nearest hospital?*

Tengo que ir al **correo** para enviar este paquete. *I have to go to the post office to send this package.*

STORES

Tiendas

el mercado	*market*
el supermercado	*supermarket*
la panadería	*bakery*
la carnicería	*butcher shop*
la charcutería	*deli*
la tienda de alimentos	*deli*
la tienda por departamentos	*department store*
la ferretería	*hardware store*
la tienda de discos	*music store/record shop*
la farmacia	*pharmacy*
la zapatería	*shoe store*
la librería	*bookstore*

Words In Use

El servicio en la **carnicería** no es bueno. *The service is not good at that butcher shop.*

Prefiero ir a la del **supermercado**. *I prefer to go to the one in the supermarket.*

¿Está muy lejos la **farmacia**? *Is the pharmacy very far?*

Está justo al lado de la **ferretería**. *It's right next to the hardware store.*

Esa **librería** se especializa en libros extranjeros. *That bookstore specializes in foreign books.*

SHOPPING
De compras

SHOPPING NOUNS

la tienda	store
la tienda por departamentos	department store
el centro comercial	mall, strip mall
la boutique	boutique
la tienda de ropa fina	boutique
el mercado de las pulgas	flea market
el mercadillo	flea market
la subasta	auction
las antigüedades	antiques
la lista de compras	shopping list
la bolsa de compras	shopping bag
el probador	fitting room
el artículo rebajado	sale item
la ganga	bargain, deal
el buen negocio	good deal
el cupón	coupon
las compras	purchases
el/la cajero/a	cashier
la caja registradora	cash register
la tarjeta de crédito	credit card
el cheque	check
el recibo	receipt
los bienes	goods
el inventario	inventory

SHOPPING ADJECTIVES

nuevo	new, brand new
usado	used
de segunda mano	second-hand
antiguo	antique
barato	cheap
caro	expensive

hecho a mano	*hand-crafted*
bien hecho	*well-made*
rebajado	*on sale*
vendido	*sold*

SHOPPING VERBS

ir de compras	*to shop*
echar un vistazo	*to browse*
comprar	*to buy, to purchase*
comprar al por mayor	*to buy in bulk*
hacer una oferta	*to bid*
hacer un trato	*to deal*
hacer un negocio	*to deal*
arrendar	*to lease*
alquilar	*to lease*
cargarlo a la cuenta	*to charge it*
probarse	*to try on*
quedar bien	*to fit*
separar a plazos	*to put on layaway*

NOTE: More words related to Shopping can be found in other sections of this book, such as Clothing and Money.

Words In Use

Hice una oferta para la casa que me gusta. *I bid on the house that I like.*

No sabía que pensabas **comprarla**. *I didn't know you wanted to purchase it.*

No es demasiado **cara**, ¿verdad? *It's not too expensive, right?*

No tengo tiempo para **probarme** los pantalones. *I have no time to try on the pants.*

Son pantalones de **segunda mano**. *They're second-hand pants.*

Me gusta la ropa **antigua** y **usada**. *I like antique and used clothes.*

RUNNING ERRANDS
Haciendo mandados

RUNNING ERRANDS NOUNS

las cuentas	*bills*
las compras	*groceries*
los comestibles	*groceries*
el lavado en seco	*dry cleaning*
la lavandería	*laundry*

RUNNING ERRANDS VERBS

hacer un mandado	*to run an errand*
pagar las cuentas	*to pay the bills*
hacer mercado	*to go grocery shopping*
hacer la compra	*to go grocery shopping*
mandar a lavar en seco	*to do the dry cleaning*
lavar la ropa	*to do the laundry*
ir al peluquero	*to go to the hairdresser's*
ir al barbero	*to go to the barber's*
recoger a los niños	*to pick up the kids*
devolver los libros de la biblioteca	*to return library books*

EXERCISES

I. Match the Spanish word on the left with the English word on the right.

1. la ciudad		A.	*street*
2. la biblioteca		B.	*city*
3. la calle		C.	*market*
4. la zapatería		D.	*church*
5. rebajado		E.	*bookstore*
6. el mercado		F.	*on sale*
7. el cine		G.	*shoe store*
8. la iglesia		H.	*bakery*
9. la librería		I.	*movie theater*
10. la panadería		J.	*library*

II. Fill in the blanks with the appropriate Spanish word.

1. Hay una excelente exposición de Picasso en el _____ (*museum*).

2. El _____ (*post office*) cierra a las tres de la tarde hoy.

3. Si quieres puedes pagar con _____ (*credit card*).

4. Hay un concierto al aire libre en el _____ (*park*).

5. Antes de volver a casa tengo que ir al _____ (*supermarket*).

ANSWERS: I., 1. B, 2. J, 3. A , 4. G, 5. F, 6. C, 7. I, 8. D, 9. E, 10. H
II. 1. HAY UNA EXCELENTE EXPOSICIÓN DE PICASSO EN EL **MUSEO**.
2. EL **CORREO** CIERRA A LAS TRES DE LA TARDE HOY. 3. SI QUIERES PUEDES
PAGAR CON **TARJETA DE CRÉDITO**. 4. HAY UN CONCIERTO AL AIRE LIBRE EN
EL **PARQUE**. 5. ANTES DE VOLVER A CASA TENGO QUE IR AL
SUPERMERCADO.

Transportation

Transporte

MODES OF TRANSPORTATION

Medios de transporte

el coche	*car*
el carro	*car*
el automóvil	*car*
el auto	*car*
el autobús	*bus*
el bus	*bus*
el ómnibus	*bus*
la guagua	*bus (Cuba)*
la motocicleta	*motorcycle*
la motoneta	*motor scooter*
el tren	*train*
el tranvía	*tram*
el avión	*plane*
el helicóptero	*helicopter*
el barco	*boat*
el buque	*ship*
la embarcación	*ship*
el transbordador	*ferry*
el ferry	*ferry*
la canoa	*canoe*
la bicicleta	*bike*
el funicular	*cable car*
el ascensor	*elevator*
la escalera mecánica	*escalator*
la escalera eléctrica	*escalator*
la cinta móvil	*moving walkway*

Words In Use

El **funicular** llega a la cima de la montaña. *The cable car reaches the top of the mountain.*

La **escalera mecánica** no estaba funcionando. *The escalator was not working properly.*

Transportation Transporte

El **avión** llegó con tres horas de retraso. *The plane arrived with a delay of three hours.*

El viaje en **transbordador** dura sólo una hora. *The ferry trip lasts only one hour.*

Tuve que esperar por el otro **autobús** porque el primero estaba lleno. *I had to wait for the next bus because the first one was full.*

Le compré a mi hijo una **bicicleta** nueva. *I got my son a new bicycle.*

DRIVING
Conducir

DRIVING NOUNS

la calle	street
la carretera	road, highway, public road
la carretera de vía libre	expressway
la autovía	highway
la autopista	turnpike, expressway
la carretera secundaria	side road
la vía lateral	side road
el carril	lane
el callejón	alley
la carretera pavimentada	paved road
el camino de gravilla	gravel road
el camino de tierra	dirt road
el accidente	accident
la avería	break down
el embotellamiento	traffic jam
el trancón	traffic jam
el tranque	traffic jam
el tapón	traffic jam
el atasco	traffic jam
el límite de velocidad	speed limit
el andén	shoulder
el arcén	shoulder
la franja central	median
la señal de tráfico	road sign
la salida	exit
el área de descanso	rest stop
el bache	pothole
el desvío	detour
la bifurcación	fork in the road

el empalme	*merge*
la unión	*merge*
la intersección	*intersection*
el cono señalizador	*traffic cone*
el semáforo	*traffic light*
la ruta panorámica	*scenic route*

DRIVING ADJECTIVES

rápido	*fast, speedy*
veloz	*speedy*
despacio	*slow*
de dos vías	*two-lane*
de tres vías	*three-lane*

DRIVING VERBS

conducir	*to drive*
encender	*to start*
frenar	*to brake*
dar marcha atrás	*to reverse*
llevar el timón	*to steer*
cambiar de marcha	*to shift*
meter el cambio	*to shift*
girar	*to turn*
hacer señas	*to signal*
convertirse en	*to turn into*
ceder el paso	*to yield*
chocar contra	*to run into*
pararse	*to stall*
ahogarse	*to stall*
estacionar	*to park*
aparcar	*to park*
parquear	*to park*
cerrar con llave	*to lock*
abrir	*to open*
descongelar	*to defrost/defog*

Modes of
Transportation

Driving

Cars

Buying a Car

Mechanical and
Maintenance

Flying

Trains and
Subways

Boats

Space Travel

Other Travel
Words

Words In Use

Cuando llegues a la **intersección**, debes **girar** a la izquierda. *When you get to the intersection, you must turn left.*

No puedes **aparcar** si hay línea amarilla. *You can't park if there's a yellow line.*

El **límite de velocidad** aquí es sesenta y cinco millas por hora. *The speed limit here is sixty-five miles per hour.*

El **carril** de la derecha es el más **rápido**. *The right lane is the fastest.*

Encontrarás un **desvío** a dos millas de aquí. *You'll find a detour in two miles.*

CARS

Carros

CAR NOUNS—GENERAL

el automóvil	*automobile*
el aparcamiento	*parking*
el estacionamiento	*parking*
la estación de servicio	*service station*
la gasolinera	*service station*
el garaje	*garage*
el servicio	*service*
la gasolina	*gasoline*
el aceite	*oil*
el combustible	*fuel*
el surtidor	*fuel pump*
la bomba de gasolina	*fuel pump*
los gases de escape	*exhaust*
las millas/los kilómetros por galón	*miles per gallon/kilometers per gallon*
las millas/los kilómetros por hora	*miles per hour/kilometers per hour*

CAR NOUNS—WORKING PARTS

el motor	*engine*
el engranaje	*gear*
el cambio de marcha	*gear shift*
la palanca de cambios	*stick shift*
la transmisión automática	*automatic transmission*
los frenos	*brakes*
el freno de emergencia	*emergency brake*
el freno de mano	*parking brake*
la llave	*key*
el pedal	*pedal*
el capó	*hood*
el baúl	*trunk*

el gato	*jack*
el parachoques	*bumper*
el volante	*steering wheel*
el timón	*steering wheel*
la rueda	*wheel*
la llanta	*tire*
el neumático	*tire*
la rueda de repuesto	*spare tire*
el tapacubos	*hubcap*
la puerta	*door*
la puerta corredera	*sliding door*
la manija	*door handle*
la cerradura	*lock*
la cerradura de la puerta	*door lock*
el parabrisas	*windshield*
el limpiaparabrisas	*windshield wipers*
el desempañador	*windshield wipers*
la ventanilla	*window*
el techo descapotable	*sun roof/moon roof*
el faro delantero	*headlight*
las luces largas	*high beam*
la luz alta/plena	*high beam*
la señal	*signal*
el indicador	*gauge, indicator lights*
las luces direccionales	*indicator lights*
el intermitente	*turn signal, blinker*
la luz direccional	*turn signal*
las luces de emergencia	*hazards, emergency flashers*
la luz trasera	*taillights*
la luz superior	*dome light*
el regulador de intensidad de luz	*dimmer switch*
la consola	*console*
el panel de instrumentos	*instrument panel*
el velocímetro	*speedometer*
el cuentakilómetros	*odometer*
el cuentamillas	*odometer*
el indicador del aceite	*oil gauge*
el indicador del nivel de gasolina	*fuel gauge*
el tanque de gasolina	*fuel tank, gas tank*

16

Modes of
Transportation

Driving

Cars

Buying a Car

Mechanical and
Maintenance

Flying

Trains and
Subways

Boats

Space Travel

Other Travel
Words

el control de crucero	cruise control
el asiento	seat
el asiento del conductor	driver's seat
el asiento de pasajeros	passenger's seat
el asiento delantero	front seat
el asiento trasero	back seat
el asiento de niños	child seat
el cinturón de seguridad	seat belt
la bolsa de aire	air bag
el espejo	mirror
el espejo retrovisor	rear-view mirror
el espejo lateral	side mirror
el espejo interior	vanity mirror
el salpicadero	dashboard
el tablero de mandos	dashboard
la guantera	glove compartment
el portavasos	cup holder
el encendedor	cigarette lighter
el mechero	cigarette lighter
el cenicero	ashtray
el aire acondicionado	air conditioning
la calefacción	heating
el aire para desempañar	defogger
la radio	radio
el sistema de sonido	sound system
la alta fidelidad	sound system
los altoparlantes	speakers
los bafles	speakers
el ruido	noise
la pintura	paint
el adorno del capó	hood ornament

CAR NOUNS—TYPES OF CARS

el vehículo	vehicle
el coche	car
el carro	car
el automóvil	car, automobile
el coche deportivo	sports car
el carro deportivo	sports car

el auto deportivo	*sports car*
el coche compacto	*compact car*
el convertible	*convertible*
el descapotable	*convertible*
el sedán	*sedan*
el cuatro puertas	*sedan*
la furgoneta	*station wagon*
el vagón	*wagon*
el camión	*truck, wagon*
el camión de transporte	*pick-up truck*
el suv	*S.U.V. (sports utility vehicle)*
el vehículo deportivo útil	*S.U.V.*
el todoterreno	*S.U.V.*
la camioneta	*van*
el miniván	*minivan*
el jeep	*jeep*
la limosina	*limousine*
el coche fúnebre	*hearse*
el taxi	*taxi cab*
el gasóleo	*diesel*

16

Modes of
Transportation

Driving

Cars

Buying a Car

Mechanical and
Maintenance

Flying

Trains and
Subways

Boats

Space Travel

Other Travel
Words

CAR ADJECTIVES

de cuatro puertas	*four-door*
de dos puertas	*two-door*
diesel	*diesel*

Words In Use

Abre la **ventanilla** por favor, me encanta el olor de la vegetación. *Please open the window; I love the smell of the vegetation here.*

Su carro nuevo tiene **techo** descapotable. *His new car has a sun roof.*

Me gusta revisar el **aceite** cada tres meses. *I like to check the oil every three months.*

La **cerradura** me está dando problemas. *The lock is giving me problems.*

Siempre he querido tener un carro **descapotable**. *I've always wanted to have a convertible.*

El **asiento trasero** es demasiado incómodo. *The back seat is too uncomfortable.*

BUYING A CAR

Comprando un carro

BUYING A CAR NOUNS

el concesionario de autos	*car dealer*
el terreno	*lot*
la sala de muestras	*showroom*
el precio	*price*
el precio de venta	*price tag*
el diseño	*design*
el/la diseñador/a	*designer*
el terminado	*finish*
el modelo	*model*
el modelo nuevo	*new model*
el cacharro	*piece of junk, lemon*
el automóvil en malas condiciones	*car in bad condition, lemon*

BUYING A CAR ADJECTIVES

en perfectas condiciones	*mint condition*
mandado a pedir	*custom made*

BUYING A CAR VERBS

comprar	*to buy*
alquilar	*to rent, to lease*

Words In Use

Mariela decidió **alquilar** un carro nuevo. *Mariela decided to lease a new car.*

Ella no tenía suficiente dinero para **comprarlo**. *She didn't have enough money to buy one.*

El carro que arrendó está **en perfectas condiciones**. *The one she leased is in mint condition.*

Sí, pero no me gusta mucho ese **modelo**. *Yes, but I don't like the model very much.*

Pienso que es un **diseño** muy elegante. *I think it's a very elegant design.*

MECHANICAL AND MAINTENANCE

Mecánica y mantenimiento

la alfombra	*carpet*
el anticongelante	*antifreeze*
el árbol de levas	*camshaft*

el bloque del motor	*engine block*
la bujía	*spark plug*
la caja de fusible	*fuse box*
el carburador	*carburetor*
la carrocería	*body*
el chasis	*chassis*
el cigüeñal	*crankshaft*
el cilindro	*cylinder*
el cilindro de frenos	*brake cylinder*
el cojinete	*bearing*
el control de emisión	*emissions testing*
el control de gases de escape	*exhaust system*
la correa	*belt*
la correa del ventilador	*fan belt*
el cromo	*chrome*
la culata de cilindro	*cylinder head*
el desplazamiento	*displacement*
el distribuidor	*distributor*
el eje	*axle*
el empaque	*gasket*
el exterior	*exterior*
el freno reforzado	*power brakes*
el freno tipo ABS/antilock	*antilock brakes*
el fusible	*fuse*
el hueco para el motor	*engine cradle*
el interior	*interior*
la junta	*gasket*
el líquido para el limpiaparabrisas	*washer fluid*
el líquido refrigerante	*coolant*
la luz de precaución	*warning light*
el mantenimiento	*maintenance*
el mantenimiento del carro	*car maintenance*
el manual	*manual*
el marco	*frame*
el panel de la carrocería	*body panel*
el panel de puerta	*door panel*
el par	*torque*
el par motor	*torque*
la parte	*part*

la pieza	part
la pieza de refacción	spare part
el pistón	piston
la presión del aceite	oil pressure
el puntal	strut
el radiador	radiator
la rejilla de ventilación	vent
el repuesto	spare part
el respiradero	air vent
el revestimiento de cilindro	cylinder lining
la riostra	strut
el sistema de calefacción	heating system
el sistema de refrigeración	cooling system
el sistema de calefacción y refrigeración	cooling and heating system
la suspensión	suspension
la suspensión trasera	rear suspension
el taller de reparación de motor	machine shop
el taller de reparaciones	body shop, repair shop
la transmisión	transmission
la válvula	valve
las ventanillas automáticas	power windows
el ventilador	fan

Words In Use

Después del accidente tuve que ordenar **repuestos**. *After the accident I had to order spare parts.*

Tuve que llevarlo al **taller de reparaciones**. *I had to take it to the repair shop.*

Me dijeron que tendrían que reemplazar el **radiador**. *They told me they would have to replace the radiator.*

Hubo que cambiarle la **correa de ventilación**. *The fan belt had to be changed.*

Es importante darles buen **mantenimiento** a los carros nuevos. *It's important to give new cars good maintenance.*

El **exterior** de ese carro es muy elegante. *The exterior of this car is very elegant.*

FLYING
En vuelo

FLYING NOUNS—AIRPORT

el aeropuerto	*airport*
la puerta de embarque	*gate*
el eje	*hub*
la base	*hub*
el avión	*plane*
la cabina	*cabin*
la cubierta de vuelo	*flight deck*
la pista	*runway*
la pista de aterrizaje	*landing strip*
el reclamo de equipaje	*baggage claim*
la estera rodante para equipaje	*carousel*
la tarjeta de embarque	*boarding pass*
la aduana	*customs*
la escala	*layover*
el pasaporte	*passport*
la reserva	*reservation*

FLYING NOUNS—PARTS OF THE PLANE

la cola	*tail*
la ovija	*nose cone*
el ala	*wing*
el alerón	*wing flap*
la propulsión a chorro	*jet propeller*
el asiento	*seat*
el cinturón de seguridad	*seat belt*
la mesita plegable	*tray table*
la luz de techo	*overhead light*
el espacio superior para maletas	*overhead storage bins*
la salida de emergencia	*emergency exit*
el salvavida	*flotation device*
el flotador	*flotation device*

FLYING NOUNS—PEOPLE

el/la capitán	*captain*
el/la asistente de vuelo	*flight attendant*
el/la controlador/a aéreo/a	*air traffic controller*

FLYING ADJECTIVES

turbulento	*turbulent*
plano	*smooth, level*
libre de impuestos	*duty free*

FLYING VERBS

despegar	*to take off*
aterrizar	*to land*
rodar por la pista	*to taxi*

Words In Use

El **aeropuerto** está cerca de la ciudad. *The airport is near the city.*

Primero tienes que sacar tu **tarjeta de embarque**. *First you have to get your boarding card.*

¿Estás sentado en la fila de la **salida de emergencia**? *Are you seated on the emergency exit row?*

Después tienes que localizar la **puerta de embarque**. *Then you have to locate your gate.*

Acuérdate de revisar el número de tu **asiento**. *Don't forget to double check your seat number.*

Abróchate el **cinturón de seguridad**. *Buckle your seat belt.*

Vamos a **despegar** pronto. *We'll be taking off soon.*

TRAINS AND SUBWAYS

Trenes y subterráneos

TRAIN AND SUBWAY NOUNS—GENERAL

el ferrocarril	*railroad*
el cruce de ferrocarril	*railroad crossing*
el túnel	*tunnel*
la estación	*station*
el andén	*platform*
la vía	*track*
la próxima parada	*next stop*
el paisaje	*scenery*
la caseta	*booth*
la máquina de picar billete	*ticket punch*
la ficha	*token*
la correspondencia	*transfer*
la transferencia	*transfer*
el billete de excursión	*travel card*

el billete de viaje	*travel card*
el torniquete	*turnstile*
el coche club	*club car*
el coche comedor	*dining car*
el vagón restaurante	*dining car*

TRAIN AND SUBWAY NOUNS—PEOPLE

| el/la conductor/a | *conductor* |
| el/la maquinista | *driver* |

TRAIN AND SUBWAY ADJECTIVES

expreso	*express*
local	*local*
rápido	*express, fast*
lento	*local, slow*

TRAIN AND SUBWAY VERBS

terminar	*to terminate*
transferir	*to transfer*
hacer correspondencia	*to transfer*

TRAIN AND SUBWAY EXPRESSIONS

| No se apoye contra la puerta. | *"Stand clear of the closing doors."* |

Words In Use

¡Qué problema! Nuestra **estación** está cerrada. *What a problem! Our station is closed.*

Tenemos que hacer una **transferencia** en la **próxima parada**. *We have to transfer at the next stop.*

Me gusta sentarme en la ventanilla para ver el **paisaje**. *I like to sit by the window to admire the scenery.*

El **tren** sale del **andén** cinco. *The train leaves out of platform five.*

Vamos al **coche comedor** a tomar algo. *Let's go to the dining car to have something to drink.*

BOATS

Barcos

BOAT NOUNS—GENERAL

el barco	*boat, ship*
la embarcación	*ship*
el transbordador	*ferry, shuttle*

16

Modes of
Transportation

Driving

Cars

Buying a Car

Mechanical and
Maintenance

Flying

**Trains and
Subways/Boats**

Space Travel

Other Travel
Words

el ferry	*ferry*
el transatlántico	*ocean liner*
el barco de vela	*sailboat*
la vela	*sail*
el mástil	*mast*
las sogas	*ropes*
el ancla	*anchor*
el casco	*hull*
la popa	*stern*
el puerto	*port*
el estribor	*starboard*
la cabina	*cabin*
la portilla	*porthole*
la cubierta	*deck*
la sala de máquinas	*engine room*
el bote de remo	*life boat*
el chaleco salvavidas	*life jacket, life preserver*
el crucero	*cruise*
el naufragio	*shipwreck*

BOAT NOUNS—PEOPLE

el/la capitán	*captain*
el/la primer oficial	*first mate*
el camarero	*steward*
la camarera	*stewardess*

BOAT ADJECTIVES

con brisa	*breezy*
ventoso	*windy*
tormentoso	*stormy*
impresionante	*breathtaking*

BOAT VERBS

navegar	*to sail*
flotar	*to float*
ir a la deriva	*to drift*
nadar	*to swim*
arrastrar	*to wash up*

NOTE: More words related to Boats can be found in other sections of this book, such as Ocean and At the Beach.

Words In Use

El **capitán** nos dio la bienvenida a todos. *The captain welcomed all of us.*

La vista desde la **cubierta** era **impresionante**. *The view from the deck was breathtaking.*

Nos bajaremos en el próximo **puerto** para caminar por el pueblo. *We will get off on the next port to take a stroll through the town.*

El tiempo se puso **tormentoso**. *The weather turned stormy.*

Tuvimos que parar de **nadar**. *We had to stop swimming.*

SPACE TRAVEL
Viaje al espacio

SPACE TRAVEL NOUNS

el transbordador	*space shuttle*
el/la astronauta	*astronaut*
la cuenta regresiva	*countdown*
la gravedad	*gravity*
la fuerza de gravedad	*G-force*
la levedad	*antigravity*
el satélite	*satellite*
la estación espacial	*space station*

SPACE TRAVEL VERBS

lanzar	*to launch*
despegar	*to lift off*
caminar en la Luna	*to walk on the moon*
aterrizar	*to land*

NOTE: More words related to Space Travel can be found in the Solar System and Universe sections of this book.

Words In Use

El **transbordador** tuvo un accidente terrible. *The space shuttle was involved in a terrible accident.*

La **estación espacial** llegará a Marte mañana. *The space station will reach Mars tomorrow.*

Es el segundo **viaje al espacio** para este **astronauta**. *It's the second trip to space for this astronaut.*

Armstrong fue el primer hombre que **caminó en la Luna**. *Armstrong was the first man to walk on the moon.*

OTHER TRAVEL WORDS

Otras palabras de viaje

OTHER TRAVEL NOUNS

el viaje	*travel, trip*
el cambio de moneda	*currency exchange*
el día de fiesta	*holiday*
el itinerario	*itinerary*
la travesía	*journey*
la escala	*layover*
la maleta	*suitcase*
el/la agente de viajes	*travel agent*
las vacaciones	*vacation*
la clase ejecutiva	*business class*
la clase turista	*economy class*
la primera clase	*first class*

OTHER TRAVEL ADJECTIVES

reservado	*reserved*
sin reservar	*unreserved*

OTHER TRAVEL VERBS

subir	*to upgrade*
ascender	*to upgrade*
mejorar	*to upgrade*

NOTE: More words related to Travel can be found in other categories of this book, such as Vacation.

Words In Use

Tengo una **escala** de tres horas en Raleigh. *I have a three hour layover in Raleigh.*

Me **subieron** a **clase ejecutiva**. *They upgraded me to business class.*

Tengo un **itinerario** muy cargado para la próxima semana. *My itinerary for next week is quite busy.*

Suelo viajar con una **maleta** solamente. *I normally travel with just one suitcase.*

EXERCISES

I. Match the Spanish word on the left with the English word on the right.

1. el ascensor   A. *truck*

2. dar marcha atrás   B. *mirror*

3. el motor   C. *sail*

4. el día de fiesta   D. *plane*

5. el avión   E. *to reverse*

6. la vela   F. *holiday*

7. el camión   G. *elevator*

8. el espejo   H. *to drive*

9. el parachoques   I. *engine*

10. conducir   J. *bumper*

II. Fill in the blanks with the appropriate Spanish word.

1. Llegué tarde porque hubo un _____ (*traffic jam*) horrible.

2. Al llegar al país tenemos que pasar por _____ (*customs*).

3. Al sentarte en el avión abróchate tu _____ (*seat belt*).

4. Si necesitas algo, avísale al _____ (*flight attendant*).

5. Después de _____ (*to take off*) nos van a servir comida.

ANSWERS: I. 1. G, 2. E, 3. I, 4. F, 5. D, 6. C, 7. A, 8. B, 9. J, 10. H
II. 1. LLEGUÉ TARDE PORQUE HUBO UN **ATASCO** HORRIBLE. 2. AL LLEGAR
AL PAÍS TENEMOS QUE PASAR POR **ADUANAS**. 3. AL SENTARTE EN EL AVIÓN
ABRÓCHATE TU **CINTURÓN DE SEGURIDAD**. 4. SI NECESITAS ALGO, AVÍSALE
AL **ASISTENTE DE VUELO**. 5. DESPUÉS DE **DESPEGAR** NOS VAN A SERVIR
COMIDA.

Modes of
Transportation

Driving

Cars

Buying a Car

Mechanical and
Maintenance

Flying

Trains and
Subways

Boats

Space Travel

**Other Travel
Words**

School

Escuelas y colegios

17

TYPES OF SCHOOLS
Tipos de colegios

el parvulario	pre-school
el preescolar	pre-school
el kínder	kindergarten
el jardín infantil	kindergarten, nursery school
la escuela elemental	elementary school
la escuela primaria	primary school
el centro de enseñanza secundaria	middle school/junior high school
la escuela secundaria	(senior) high school, secondary school
la secundaria	(senior) high school, secondary school
la escuela pública	public school
el colegio privado	private school
el internado	boarding school
el colegio preparatorio	prep(aratory) school
el conservatorio de música	music school/conservatory
la escuela de baile	dance school
la escuela de ballet	ballet school
el colegio alternativo	alternative school
el colegio sin internado	(country) day school
la academia militar	military academy
la escuela de formación profesional	vocational school
la escuela secretarial y de comercio	trade school
el colegio parroquial	parochial school
el colegio de la parroquia	parish school
el seminario	seminary
el catecismo	church school
la catequesis	Sunday school
la escuela dominical	Sunday school
la yeshiva	jeshiva
las clases de verano	summer school

el grupo de juego	playgroup
la guardería	day-care
el distrito escolar	school district
la junta de educación	board of education

Words In Use

Mi sobrina comenzó este año el jardín **infantil**. *My niece started nursery school this year.*

El año que viene empieza en la **escuela primaria**. *Next year she'll be in primary school.*

Por las tardes va a la **escuela de ballet**. *In the afternoon she goes to ballet school.*

El hijo de Ana asiste a la **escuela de verano**. *Ana's son is taking summer school.*

El **colegio parroquial** de este pueblo es muy bueno. *The parochial school in this town is very good.*

Es mejor que el otro **colegio privado**. *It's better than the other private school.*

Cuando era adolescente asistí a una **escuela militar**. *When I was a teenager I attended a military school.*

SCHOOL AREAS
Áreas del colegio

el aula	classroom
el salón de clases	classroom
el salón general	homeroom
el salón de tareas	homeroom
el estudio	art room/studio
el auditorio	auditorium
la cafetería	cafeteria
el laboratorio de ciencias	science lab
el laboratorio de computadoras	computer lab
el laboratorio de lenguas	language lab
el gimnasio	gym
el patio	school yard
el estudio de baile	dance studio
el casillero	lockers
los baños	restrooms
la oficina principal	school office
la sala de la facultad	teacher's lounge

Words In Use

¡No me gusta nada la comida que sirven en la **cafetería**! *I don't like the food from the cafeteria in the least!*

La **oficina principal** está en el tercer nivel. *The school office is on the third floor.*

¿Quién es tu profesor en el **salón de tareas**? *Who is your homeroom teacher?*

El **laboratorio de ciencias** ha sido renovado recientemente. *The science lab was renovated recently.*

¿Tiene aire acondicionado tu **aula**? *Is your classroom air-conditioned?*

La reunión de padres será en el **auditorio**. *The parent meeting will be in the auditorium.*

CLASSROOM AREAS AND OBJECTS

Objetos y áreas del aula

la silla	*chair*
el pupitre	*chair, student desk/table*
el escritorio	*teacher's desk*
el área de lectura	*reading area*
el rincón de lectura	*reading corner*
la pizarra	*blackboard/chalkboard*
el pizarrón	*blackboard/chalkboard*
la pizarra de fieltro	*felt board*
la pizarra de corcho	*push board*
la pizarra seca	*dry board*
la tiza	*chalk*
el rotulador seco	*dry board marker*
el borrador	*eraser*
los objetos reales	*realia*
la ayuda visual	*visual aid*
el lavabo	*sink*

Words In Use

No puedo ver la **pizarra** desde la parte de atrás del aula. *I can't see the blackboard from the back of the classroom.*

¿Por qué no te cambias de **pupitre**? *Why don't you change desks?*

No me gusta sentarme delante del **escritorio** del maestro. *I don't like to sit in front of the teacher's desk.*

El color de la **tiza** es muy claro; no puedo verlo bien. *The color of the chalk is too light; I can't read what's on the board.*

SCHOOL PEOPLE
Gente en el colegio

STUDENTS

el/la estudiante	*student*
el/la alumno/a de escuela	*schoolchild*
el alumno	*pupil, schoolboy*
la alumna	*pupil, schoolgirl*
el colegial	*schoolboy*
la colegiala	*schoolgirl*
el/la estudiante de primer año	*freshman*
el/la estudiante de segundo año	*sophomore*
el/la estudiante de penúltimo año	*junior*
el/la estudiante de último año	*senior*
el/la estudiante de kínder	*kindergartener*
el/la preescolar	*preschooler*
el/la alumno/a que pronuncia el discurso de despedida	*valedictorian*
el/la prodigio	*prodigy, gifted child*
el/la estudiante prodigio	*wunderkind*
el/la mentecato/a	*geek*
el/la pazguato/a	*geek*
el/la ratón de biblioteca	*bookworm*
el/la preferido/a del profesor	*teacher's pet*
el/la que siempre logra éxitos	*overachiever*
el/la estudiante que no rinde	*underachiever*
el/la estudiante de educación especial	*special ed student*
el/la estudiante de intercambio	*exchange student*
el/la estudiante nuevo	*transfer student, new student*
el/la estudiante que se transfiere	*transfer student*
el grupo de lectura	*reading group*

FACULTY

el director de escuela	*headmaster*
la directora de escuela	*headmistress*
el/la directora/a	*principal*
el/la maestro/a	*teacher*
el/la maestro/a de escuela	*schoolteacher*
el/la profesor/a	*teacher*
el/la estudiante de magisterio	*student teacher*

el/la ayudante del profesor	*teacher's aid*
el/la instructor	*instructor*
el/la tutor/a	*tutor*
el/la pedagogo/a	*educator*
el/la consejero/a estudiantil	*student advisor*
el/la consejero/a	*college counselor*
el/la conserje	*janitor*
el/la entrenador/a	*coach*

Words In Use

La nueva **directora** de la escuela me dio muy buena impresión. *I was impressed with the new principal.*

Los **profesores** están muy contentos con ella. *The teachers are very happy with her.*

Dice que va a implementar un **grupo de lectura**. *She says she wants to implement a reading group.*

También piensa crear una clase avanzada para los **estudiantes de segundo año**. *She also wants to create an advanced group for the sophomore class.*

Los **estudiantes de primer año** ya tienen una clase avanzada. *The freshman class already has an advanced group.*

SCHOOL SOCIAL LIFE
La vida social en el colegio

SOCIAL LIFE NOUNS

el club	*club*
los compañeros de clase	*peer group*
la presión ejercida por los compañeros de clase	*peer pressure*
el grupo popular	*popular group*
el deportista	*jock*
el/la pazguato/a	*geek*
el paria	*outcast*

SOCIAL LIFE VERBS

| socializar | *to socialize* |
| gastar novatadas | *to haze* |

Words In Use

Los adolescentes se pasan mucho tiempo **socializando**. *Teenagers spend a long time socializing.*

La **vida social en el colegio** parece ser lo más importante para ellos. *School social life seems to be the most important thing for them.*

De joven nunca pertenecí al **grupo** más **popular**. *As a teenager I never belonged to the most popular group.*

Siempre fui miembro del **club** de idiomas. *I was always a member of the foreign language club.*

SCHOOL ACTIVITIES
Actividades escolares

SCHOOL ACTIVITIES NOUNS—IN-SCHOOL

la clase	*class*
la asignatura	*subject*
el plan de estudios	*curriculum/course of study*
el curso	*course*
la sesión	*session*
el tema	*subject*
el plan de la lección	*lesson plan*
el contenido de la lección	*lesson plan*
la asignación	*assignment*
la tarea	*assignment*
el trabajo	*paper*
la lección	*lesson*
el libro de texto	*textbook*
el cuaderno de trabajo	*workbook*
el ejercicio	*exercise*
los ejercicios de repetición	*drills, exercises*
la prueba corta	*quiz*
el examen	*exam/examination, test*
el examen de aptitud	*achievement test*
la evaluación	*assessment*
el examen de evaluación	*assessment test*
la investigación	*research*
el informe	*report*
el proyecto	*project*
el laboratorio	*lab*
el experimento	*lab (assignment)*
el informe de laboratorio	*lab report*
el portafolio	*portfolio*
la calificación	*grade, mark*
la nota	*grade, mark*
la nota media	*grade point average (GPA)*
el promedio	*grade point average (GPA)*

el período de calificaciones	*grading period, marking period*
el período de evaluación	*assessment period*
la tarjeta de notas	*report card*
la prueba estandarizada	*standardized test*
la clase de nivel avanzado	*AP (advance placement) class*
la clase de honor	*honors class*
el cuadro de honor	*honor roll*
el año académico	*academic year*
el grupo de estudio	*study group*
la graduación	*graduation*
el anuario	*yearbook*
las recomendaciones	*recommendations*

SCHOOL ACTIVITIES NOUNS—EXTRACURRICULARS

los deberes	*homework*
la tarea	*homework*
las actividades extraescolares	*extracurricular activities*
el club	*club*
el receso	*recess*
la excursión	*field trip*
la excursión con la escuela	*school trip*
la reunión	*reunion*

SCHOOL ACTIVITIES VERBS

enseñar	*to teach*
explicar	*to explain*
aprender	*to learn*
entender	*to understand*
estudiar	*to study*
memorizar	*to memorize*
escribir	*to write*
leer	*to read*
discutir	*to discuss*
debatir	*to debate*
analizar	*to analyze*
hacer ejercicios de repetición	*to drill*
evaluar	*to evaluate*
calificar	*to grade*
pasar	*to pass*
aprobar	*to pass*

desaprobar	*to fail*
reprobar	*to fail, to flunk*
suspender	*to flunk, to fail*
graduar	*to graduate*
faltar a clase	*to skip (classes)*
cortar a clase	*to skip (classes)*
recomendar	*to recommend*
dar de comer a cucharaditas	*to spoon-feed*
gastar novatadas	*to haze*

Words In Use

El **año académico** comienza en septiembre y termina en junio. *The academic year starts in September and ends in June.*

Me sentí muy mal cuando **reprobé** el **examen** de biología. *I felt horrible when I failed the biology exam.*

Para el siguiente me pasé semanas **estudiando**. *For the next one I spent weeks studying.*

Lo **aprobé** con muy buena **nota**. *I passed it with a very good grade.*

Mi **promedio** subió después del **examen**. *My GPA went up after the test.*

Tengo que pedirles **recomendaciones** a mis profesores. *I have to ask my teachers for some recommendations.*

Dicen que el **curso** del Sr. Montero es muy difícil. *They say that Mr. Montero's class is very difficult.*

Vas a tener que **escribir** dos **informes** por semana. *You'll have to write two reports per week.*

Tendrás que **leer** un capítulo por día. *You will have to read a chapter per day.*

También tendrás que hacer mucha **investigación**. *You will also have to do a lot of research.*

Para su clase no es bueno **memorizar** la materia sin **analizar**. *In his class it's not good to memorize the facts without analyzing them.*

SCHOOL ADJECTIVES
Adjetivos escolares

de edad escolar	*school age*
listo	*smart*
inteligente	*intelligent*
superdotado	*gifted*
talentoso	*talented, gifted*
torpe	*slow*
lento	*slow*

educación especial	special ed(ucation)
estricto	strict
extraescolar	extracurricular

Words In Use

Roberto es un estudiante muy **talentoso**. *Roberto is a very talented student.*

Siempre actúa de una manera **inteligente**. *He always acts in a very intelligent way.*

Participa en muchas actividades **extraescolares**. *He participates in many extracurricular activities.*

Sus hermanos son muy **listos** también. *His siblings are also very smart.*

SCHOOL SUBJECTS
Materias del colegio

los estudios sociales	social studies
la historia	history
la clase de lenguaje	language class
el español	Spanish
el castellano	Spanish (Castilian)
el inglés	English
el arte	art
la actuación	drama
la música	music
las matemáticas	math
las ciencias	science
la biología	biology
la química	chemistry
la física	physics
las computadoras	computers
la tecnología	technology
la educación física	phys(ical) ed(ucation)
la clase avanzada	AP class
la clase de honor	honors class
el curso obligatorio	required course
la actividad extraescolar	extracurricular activity
el club	club
el consejo estudiantil	student government
el servicio comunitario	community service

Words In Use

No tenemos clases de **computadoras** este año. *We don't have computer classes this year.*

Mi hijo es miembro del **consejo estudiantil**. *My son is a member of the student government.*

Mi clase de **ciencias** favorita es la **biología**. *My favorite science class is biology.*

Te recomiendo que tomes **música** con la Sra. Padilla. *I suggest you take music with Mrs. Padilla.*

UNIVERSITY
La universidad

el curso	course
la especialización	major
la asignatura secundaria	minor
el/la profesor/a	professor
la investigación	research
el trabajo	paper
el informe	paper

Words In Use

Todavía no he declarado cuál es mi **especialización**. *I have not declared my major yet.*

¿Cuántos **cursos** te faltan? *How many courses do you have left?*

Me falta el semestre de **investigación**. *I have to do my research this semester.*

TYPES OF COLLEGES
Universidades y estudios superiores

el mundo académico	academia
la educación superior	higher education
la educación después de secundaria	postsecondary education
la universidad	university
la escuela universitaria pública	public college
la escuela universitaria del estado	state college
la escuela universitaria privada	private college
la escuela profesional superior	professional school
la facultad de derecho	law school
la facultad de medicina	medical school
el instituto de educación comunitaria	community college

el instituto de preparación de dos años	two-year college
la escuela universitaria de cuatro años	four-year college
la escuela de Bellas Artes	art school
el conservatorio de música	conservatory/music school
el instituto teológico	divinity school
el seminario	seminary
el seminario teológico	theological seminary
el instituto de investigación	research institute
la universidad de investigación	research university
el instituto de enseñanza para adultos	school of continuing education
el instituto de ciencias para la educación	teachers college

Words In Use

Harvard es una **universidad** muy prestigiosa. *Harvard is a very prestigious university.*

Las **escuelas universitarias del estado** suelen ser menos costosas. *State colleges are usually less expensive.*

Él fue aceptado a la **facultad de derecho** de Columbia. *He was accepted to Columbia law school.*

La Universidad de Nueva York es una **escuela universitaria privada**. *New York University is a private college.*

Puedes tomar clases de bienes raíces en el **instituto de enseñanza para adultos**. *You can take real estate classes in the school for continuing education.*

COLLEGE AREAS
Áreas de la universidad

la ciudad universitaria	campus
el aula	classroom, lecture hall
la sala de conferencias	lecture hall
el auditorio	auditorium
la librería	college bookstore
la biblioteca	college library
el departamento	department
la facultad	department
el edificio de la facultad	department building
la oficina del decano	dean's office
la oficina de becas y ayuda económica	financial aid office

la oficina de asuntos estudiantiles	office of student affairs
la oficina del secretario del registro	registrar's office
la escuela de artes	art center
el polideportivo	sports center
el centro de deportes	sports center
el campo de fútbol americano	football field
el campo de fútbol	soccer field
el centro de recursos para estudiantes	student center
la residencia estudiantil	dormitory, dorm
la cafetería	cafeteria

Words In Use

Tengo que buscar un cheque en la **oficina de becas y ayuda económica**. *I have to pick up a check in the financial aid office.*

¿Dónde es la **librería**? *Where's the bookstore?*

Está detrás de la **cafetería**. *It's behind the cafeteria.*

Mis amigos viven en la **residencia estudiantil**. *My friends live in the dorm.*

Yo prefiero vivir fuera de la **ciudad universitaria**. *I prefer to live off campus.*

Cualquier estudiante puede usar el **polideportivo**. *Any student can use the sports center.*

COLLEGE-RELATED ACTIVITIES
Actividades relacionadas con la universidad

el plazo	term
el semestre	semester
el trimestre	quarter, term, trimester
la clase	lecture
la conferencia	lecture
la presentación	presentation
la charla	talk
el artículo	paper
el ensayo	paper
la tesis	thesis
el estudio	study
el estudio de campo	field study
la investigación	research

la investigación del estudio de campo	field research
la investigación del experimento	experimental research
la investigación teórica	theoretical research
el proyecto de investigación	research project
los datos	data
la recogida de datos	data collection
el análisis	analysis
el análisis estadístico	statistical analysis
la síntesis	synthesis
el experimento	experiment
el examen	exam, examination
el examen oral	oral examination
la asamblea	assembly, convocation
la convocatoria	convocation
la graduación	graduation
el comité	committee
el comité de búsqueda	search committee
el comité de disertación	dissertation committee
la disertación doctoral	doctoral dissertation
la defensa	defense
la beca	grant
el puesto vitalicio	tenure
la tenencia	tenure
la reunión de la facultad	faculty meeting

Words In Use

Ella se pasó dos años trabajando en la **investigación**. *She spent two years working on her research.*

El último **trimestre** fue el más difícil para ella. *The last trimester was the most difficult for her.*

Tuvo que presentar una **monografía** de doscientas páginas. *She had to present a two-hundred page monograph.*

Sólo le falta la **disertación doctoral**. *She only has her doctoral dissertation to go.*

Su **graduación** será en junio. *Her graduation will be in June.*

COLLEGE/UNIVERSITY PEOPLE
Gente en la universidad

el/la estudiante	student
el/la estudiante de primer año	freshman

el/la estudiante de segundo año	*sophomore*
el/la estudiante de tercer año	*junior*
el/la estudiante de último año	*senior*
el/la estudiante de pregrado	*undergraduate student*
el/la estudiante graduado/a	*graduate student*
el/la candidato/a al doctorado	*doctoral candidate*
el/la ex alumno/a	*alumnus*
los ex alumnos	*alumni*
las ex alumnas	*alumnae*
la facultad	*faculty*
el cuerpo docente	*staff*
el/la presidente/a de la universidad	*college/university president*
el/la decano/a	*dean*
el/la asistente del decano	*assistant dean*
el/la asistente del profesor	*teaching assistant*
el/la asistente graduado/a	*graduate assistant*
el/la profesor/a	*professor*
el/la profesor/a de tiempo completo	*full professor*
el/la profesor/a emérito/a	*professor emeritus*
el/la profesor/a permanente	*tenured professor*
el/la profesor/a asociado/a	*associate professor*
el/la profesor/a asistente	*assistant professor*
el/la profesor/a adjunto/a	*adjunct professor*
el/la catedrático/a	*lecturer*
el/la conferenciante	*lecturer*
el/la conferencista	*lecturer*
el/la instructor/a	*instructor*
el/la investigador	*researcher*
el/la investigador/a asistente	*research assistant*
el/la presidente/a	*chair/chairperson*
el/la experto/a	*scholar*

Words In Use

Los ex alumnos de esta universidad hacen muchas donaciones económicas. *The alumni of this university make good economic donations.*

El **cuerpo docente** está muy bien calificado. *The staff is very well qualified.*

Los **estudiantes de último año** se preparan para las entrevistas de trabajo. *Seniors are getting ready for job interviews.*

El nuevo **decano** de la universidad fue escogido entre docenas de candidatos. *The new dean was chosen from dozens of candidates.*

Estoy casi seguro de que Luis es **estudiante de segundo año**. *I'm almost sure that Luis is a sophomore.*

UNIVERSITY ADJECTIVES
Adjetivos universitarios

académico	*academic*
predoctorado	*predoctoral*
postdoctorado	*postdoctoral*
completo	*full*
asociado	*associate*
asistente	*assistant*
permanente (puesto)	*tenured*
vitalicio (puesto)	*tenured*
en camino a ser permanente	*tenure-track*
en camino a ser vitalicio	*tenure-track*
acreditado	*accredited*

Words In Use

El colegio privado de tu hija está muy bien **acreditado**. *Your daughter's private school is very well accredited.*

¡Felicitaciones! Por fin tienes un **puesto permanente**. *Congratulations! You're finally tenured.*

DEGREES
Diplomas

el título	*degree*
el diploma	*degree, diploma, certificate*
la licenciatura en filosofía y letras	*bachelor's/bachelor of arts degree (B.A.)*
la maestría (máster) en filosofía y letras	*master's/master of arts degree (M.A.)*
la maestría (máster) en ciencias	*master of science degree (M.S.)*
el doctorado en filosofía	*doctor's degree/doctorate (Ph.D.)*
el doctorado en teología	*doctor of theology degree (D.Th.)*
el doctorado en derecho	*doctor of laws degree (LL.D.)*
el bachillerato	*advanced degree*
la licenciatura	*associate degree*
el certificado	*certificate*

Words In Use

Este año Miguel termina su **doctorado**. *Miguel finishes his doctorate this year.*

Ya tenía una **maestría en ciencias**. *He already has a Master of Science degree.*

Su **licenciatura** es en biología. *He has a B.A. in biology.*

SUBJECTS
Asignaturas

la concentración	*major, concentration*
la especialización	*major, specialization*
la asignatura secundaria	*minor*
la concentración secundaria	*minor*
las asignaturas	*subjects*
las materias	*subjects*
la literatura comparada	*comparative literature*
la literatura inglesa	*English literature*
la lingüística	*linguistics*
las lenguas extranjeras	*foreign languages*
la música	*music*
el arte	*art*
la historia del arte	*art history*
la filología	*philology*
la filosofía	*philosophy*
las ciencias políticas	*political science*
la historia	*history*
la antropología	*anthropology*
la sociología	*sociology*
la medicina	*medicine*
la preparatoria para la facultad de medicina	*premed*
la biología	*biology*
la bioquímica	*bio-chemistry*
la química	*chemistry*
la física	*physics*
las matemáticas	*mathematics*
la economía	*economics*
los negocios	*business*
el comercio	*business*
la educación	*education*

Words In Use

Siempre fui muy bueno en **biología**. *I was always good in biology.*

No me gusta mucho la clase de **matemáticas**. *I don't like my math class too much.*

Mi clase favorita es la de **historia del arte**. *My favorite class is art history.*

También me gusta mucho la clase de **antropología**. *I also enjoy anthropology.*

He tomado cinco clases de **historia**. *I've already taken five history courses.*

EXERCISES

I. Match the Spanish word on the left with the English word on the right.

1. la química	A. *homework*
2. el/la estudiante de tercer año	B. *chalk*
3. la escuela universitaria del estado	C. *economics*
4. aprender	D. *chemistry*
5. la tarea	E. *strict*
6. el aula	F. *junior*
7. el colegio privado	G. *to learn*
8. la tiza	H. *state college*
9. estricto	I. *classroom*
10. la economía	J. *private school*

II. Fill in the blanks with the appropriate Spanish word.

1. Él tiene un _____ (*degree*) en historia del arte.

2. Mi hijo vive en la _____ (*dorm*).

3. Su _____ (*major*) es en economía.

4. No le gusta mucho la clase de _____ (*math*).

5. ¿Me puedes _____ (*to explain*) este problema?

ANSWERS: I. 1. D, 2. F, 3. H, 4. G, 5. A, 6. I, 7. J, 8. B, 9. E, 10. C
II. 1. ÉL TIENE UN TÍTULO EN HISTORIA DEL ARTE. 2. MI HIJO VIVE EN LA **RESIDENCIA ESTUDIANTIL**. 3. SU **ESPECIALIZACIÓN** ES EN ECONOMÍA. 4. NO LE GUSTA MUCHO LA CLASE DE **MATEMÁTICAS**. 5. ¿ME PUEDES **EXPLICAR** ESTE PROBLEMA?

Work

Trabajo

PROFESSIONS

Profesiones

el/la abogado/a*	attorney, lawyer
el/la acomodador/a	usher
el actor	actor
la actriz	actress
el/la administrador/a	administrator
el/la agente	agent
el/la agente de bolsa	stockbroker
el/la agente de capital-riesgo	venture capitalist
el/la agente de casting	talent agent
el/la agente de prensa	press agent
el/la agente de viajes	travel agent
el/la agente immobiliario/a	real estate broker
el/la agricultor/a	farmer
el/la agrimensor/a	surveyor
el/la albañil	bricklayer, mason, stonemason
el/la alfarero/a	ceramicist
el ama de casa	homemaker, housewife
el ama de llaves	housekeeper
el/la analista	analyst
la anfitriona	hostess
el/la antropólogo/a	anthropologist
el/la apiculturista	beekeeper
el/la archivero/a	archivist
el/la arqueólogo/a	archaeologist
el/la arquitecto/a	architect
el/la artesano/a	artisan
el/la artista	artist, entertainer
la asistenta	housecleaner
el/la asistente de vuelo	flight attendant

* For the most part, professions are listed in both male and female forms. There are several cases, however, where a profession is usually attributed to one gender in Spanish, and, therefore, only one form is listed here.

el/la astrólogo/a	astrologer
el/la astronauta	astronaut
el/la astrónomo/a	astronomer
el/la atleta	athlete
la au pair	au pair
el/la auditor/a	auditor
el/la autor/a	author
la babysitter	babysitter
el bailarín	dancer (male)
la bailarina	dancer (female)
la bailarina de ballet	ballerina
el/la banquero/a de inversiones	investment banker
el/la banquero/a	banker
el/la barbero/a	barber
el barrendero	street sweeper
el basurero	garbageman
el/la bibliotecario/a	librarian
el/la biólogo/a	biologist
el/la bioquímico/a	biochemist
el bombero	firefighter
el/la botánico/a	botanist
el botones	bellboy, bellhop
el/la cajero/a de banco	bank teller
el/la cajero/a	cashier, teller
el/la cajista	typesetter
la camarera	hostess, waitress
el camarero	waiter, bartender
el camillero	orderly
el camionero	trucker, truck driver
la canguro	babysitter
el/la cantante	singer
el/la cantante de ópera	opera singer
el cantero	stonecutter, stonemason
el/la cantinero/a	bartender
el capitán de barco	ship's captain
el carnicero	butcher
el carpintero	carpenter, woodworker
el/la cartero/a	mailman
el/la cartógrafo/a	cartographer

el cazador	*hunter, trapper*
el/la celador/a	*warden*
el/la ceramista/a	*potter, ceramicist*
el cerrajero	*locksmith*
el/la chef	*chef*
el/la chófer	*chauffeur*
el/la cinematógrafo/a	*cinematographer*
el/la cirujano/a	*surgeon*
el/la cocinero/a	*chef, cook*
la comadrona	*midwife*
el/la comerciante	*trader*
el/la comerciante de arte	*art dealer*
el/la compositor/a	*composer*
el/la conductor/a	*driver, conductor, chauffeur*
el/la conductor/a de autobús	*bus driver*
el conductor de tren	*train conductor, railroad conductor*
el/la confitero/a	*confectioner*
el/la consejero/a	*adviser, counselor*
el/la consejero/a de orientación profesional	*vocational therapist*
el/la conserje	*janitor*
el/la conservador/a	*curator*
el/la constructor/a	*builder*
el/la cónsul	*consul*
el/la consultor/a	*consultant*
el/la contable	*bookkeeper*
el/la contador/a	*accountant*
el/la contralor/a	*comptroller*
el contratista	*contractor*
el/la controlador/a aéreo/a	*air traffic controller*
el/la coreógrafo/a	*choreographer*
el/la corrector/a	*copyeditor*
el/la corrector/a de pruebas	*proofreader*
el/la corredor/a de bolsa	*stockbroker, broker*
el/la cortador/a de piedras preciosas	*gem cutter*
el/la cosmetólogo/a	*beautician*
la costurera	*seamstress*
el costurero	*machinist*
la criada	*housecleaner, maid*

el/la crítico/a	*critic*
el custodio	*custodian*
el/la decorador/a	*decorator*
el/la demandante	*prosecutor*
el demoledor	*wrecker*
el/la dentista	*dentist*
el/la dependiente/a	*salesperson, sales clerk, shopkeeper*
el deshollinador	*chimney sweep*
el/la detective privado/a	*private investigator*
el/la detective	*detective*
el/la dietista	*dietitian*
el/la diplomático/a	*diplomat*
el/la director/a	*director*
el/la director/a de cine	*filmmaker*
el/la director/a de funeraria	*undertaker*
el/la discjockey	*disc jockey*
el/la diseñador/a	*designer*
el/la diseñador/a de interiores	*interior designer*
el/la diseñador/a de modas	*fashion designer*
el/la diseñador/a de patrones	*patternmaker*
el/la diseñador/a gráfico/a	*graphic artist, graphic designer*
el/la distribuidor/a	*distributor*
el/la doble	*stunt man*
el/la doctor/a	*doctor*
el/la dramaturgo/a	*playwright*
el/la ecólogo/a	*ecologist*
el/la economista	*economist*
el/la editor/a	*editor, publisher*
el/la educador/a	*educator*
el electricista	*electrician*
el embajador	*ambassador*
la embajadora	*ambassadress*
el/la empresario/a	*entrepreneur*
la enfermera	*female nurse*
el enfermero	*male nurse, orderly*
el/la entrenador/a	*trainer*
el/la escritor/a	*writer*
el/la escultor/a	*sculptor*
el/la estadístico/a	*statistician*

el/la estanquero/a	*tobacconist*
el/la esteticista	*beautician*
el estibador	*longshoreman, stevedore*
el/la estilista	*stylist*
el/la estudiante	*student*
el/la evangelista	*evangelist*
el/la experto/a en ciencias políticas	*political scientist*
el/la extra	*extra (film)*
el/la fabricante	*manufacturer*
el/la fabricante de cerveza	*brewer*
el/la fabricante de muebles	*furniture maker*
el/la farmacéutico/a	*pharmacist*
el/la filósofa/a	*philosopher*
el/la fiscal	*prosecutor*
el/la físico/a	*physicist*
el/la fisiólogo/a	*physiologist*
el/la fisioterapeuta	*physical therapist*
el fontanero	*plumber*
el/la fotógrafo/a	*photographer*
el fumigador	*pest control worker*
el/la funcionario/a civil	*civil service employee*
el/la funcionario/a de correos	*postal clerk*
el fundidor	*foundryman*
el ganadero	*rancher*
el gaucho	*cowboy*
el/la geneticista	*geneticist*
el/la geógrafo/a	*geographer*
el/la geólogo/a	*geologist*
el/la ginecólogo/a	*gynecologist*
el gorila	*bouncer*
el/la gramático/a	*grammarian*
el/la granjero/a	*farmer*
el/la guardia/ana	*guard, police officer*
el/la guardia/ana de seguridad	*security guard*
el/la guardia/ana de un correccional	*correctional officer*
el/la guardia/ana de un reformatorio	*correctional officer*
el guardián del zoológico	*zookeeper*

18

Professions

Office People

Office Areas

Office Activities

Job Search

Office Objects

Business Practices

Telecommunications

Mail

Company Departments

Accounting

Manufacturing and Operations

Advertising, Marketing, Public Relations, and Sales

Human Resources

Industries

Agriculture

Construction and Architecture

Building Materials

Mining

el/la guía	guide
el/la guía turístico/a	tour guide
el/la guionista	screenwriter
el/la gurú	guru
el herrero	blacksmith
el/la higienista dental	dental technician
el/la hilandero	spinner
el/la historiador/a	historian
el hojalatero	tinsmith
el hombre de negocios	businessman
el/la ilustrador/a	illustrator
el/la impresor/a	printer
el/la industrial	industrialist
el/la ingeniero/a	engineer
el/la inspector/a	inspector
la institutriz	governess
el/la interno/a	intern
el/la intérprete	interpreter
el/la interventor/a	comptroller
el/la inversionista	investor
el/la investigador/a	investigator, researcher
el/la jardinero/a	gardener
el/la jornalero/a	farm hand
el/la joyero/a	jeweler
el/la juez	judge, justice
la jueza	judge, justice (female)
el/la jurado	juror
el/la lavaplatos	dishwasher
el/la legislador/a	legislator
el leñador	logger, lumberjack
el/la lexicógrafo/a	lexicographer
el/la lingüista	linguist
el/la locutor/a	broadcaster, newscaster
el/la locutor/a de radio	radio commentator
el/la logopeda	speech pathologist
el/la maestro/a	teacher
el/la mago/a	magician
el/la malabarista	juggler
el maletero	porter

el mampostero	*mason*
la manicurista	*manicurist*
el manitas	*handyman*
el/la marchante/a de arte	*art dealer*
el marinero	*marine, sailor*
el/la mariscal/a	*marshal*
el/la masajista	*masseur, masseuse*
el/la matemático/a	*mathematician*
el mayordomo	*butler*
el/la mayorista	*wholesaler*
el/la mecánico/a	*mechanic*
el/la mecanógrafo/a	*typist*
el/la médico/a	*doctor, physician*
el/la médico/a forense	*coroner*
el/la mensajero/a	*courier, messenger*
el/la metalúrgica	*metallurgist*
el/la metereólogo/a	*meteorologist, weatherman/woman*
el minero	*miner*
el/la ministro/a	*minister*
el/la modelo	*model*
la mucama	*maid*
la mujer de negocios	*businesswoman*
el/la músico/a	*musician*
la niñera	*babysitter, nanny*
el/la novelista	*novelist*
el/la nutricionista	*nutritionist*
el/la obrero/a de construcción	*construction worker*
el/la obrero/a migratorio/a	*migrant worker*
el/la obstetra	*obstetrician*
el/la oficial de navegación	*navigator*
el/la oficinista	*clerk*
los oficios	*professions*
el/la oftalmólogo/a	*ophthalmologist*
el/la operario/a	*machinist*
el/la óptico/a	*optician*
el/la orfebre	*goldsmith*
el/la ortopedista	*orthopedist*
el/la paleontólogo/a	*paleontologist*
el/la panadero/a	*baker*

la partera	*midwife*
el/la payaso/a	*clown*
el/la peluquero/a	*hairdresser*
el peón	*laborer*
el/la periodista	*journalist*
el pescador	*fisherman*
el/la piloto	*pilot*
el/la pincha discos	*disc jockey*
el/la pintor/a	*painter*
el/la platero/a	*silversmith*
el poeta	*poet*
la poetisa	*poetess*
el/la policía	*police officer*
el/la policía de tráfico	*traffic officer*
el/la político/a	*politician*
el/la portero/a	*doorman*
el presidente	*chairman, president*
la presidenta	*chairwoman, president*
el/la procurador/a	*solicitor*
el/la productor/a	*producer*
las profesiones	*professions*
el/la profesor/a	*professor, teacher*
el/la profesor/a particular	*tutor*
el/la programador/a de computadoras	*computer programmer*
el/la proveedor/a para banquetes y fiestas	*caterer*
el/la publicista	*publicist*
el/la químico/a	*chemist*
el/la quiropráctico/a	*chiropractor*
el rabino	*rabbi*
el ranchero	*rancher*
el/la recaudador/a de peaje	*toll taker*
el/la recepcionista	*receptionist*
el/la redactor/a	*copyeditor, editor*
el/la redactor/a publicitario/a	*copywriter*
el relojero	*clockmaker*
el reparador	*repairman*
el reparador de autos	*auto repairman*
el reparador de techos	*roofer*

el sacerdote	*clergyman, priest*
el sastre	*tailor*
la sastra	*tailor*
el/la secretario/a legal	*legal secretary*
el sepulturero	*gravedigger*
el/la sicoanalista	*psychoanalyst*
el/la sicólogo/a	*psychologist*
el/la sicoterapista	*psychoterapist*
el/la sindicalista	*trade unionist*
el/la siquiatra	*psychiatrist*
el sirviente	*servant*
el/la sociólogo/a	*sociologist*
el/la soldado	*soldier*
el soldador	*welder*
el/la sombrerero/a	*hat maker*
el soplador de vidrio	*glassblower*
el/la subastador/a	*auctioneer*
el/la subcontratista	*subcontractor*
el/la tabaquero/a	*tobacconist*
el/la tabernero/a	*bartender*
el/la tapicero/a	*upholsterer*
el/la taquígrafo/a	*stenographer*
el/la tasador/a	*appraiser*
el/la taxista	*cabdriver, taxi driver*
el/la técnico/a	*technician*
el/la técnico/a de laboratorio	*lab technician*
el/la técnico/a dental	*dental technician*
el/la tejedor/a	*weaver*
el/la tejedor/a de punto	*knitter*
el/la tendero/a	*shopkeeper*
el/la tenedor/a de libros	*bookkeeper*
el/la terapeuta ocupacional	*occupational therapist*
el/la topógrafo/a	*surveyor*
el/la trabajador/a	*laborer*
el trabajador de astillero	*rigger*
el/la trabajador/a de cera	*waxer*
el/la empleado/a de correos	*mailroom worker*
el/la trabajador/a de empresa naviera	*shipper*

Professions

Office People

Office Areas

Office Activities

Job Search

Office Objects

Business
Practices

Telecommunica-
tions

Mail

Company
Departments

Accounting

Manufacturing
and Operations

Advertising,
Marketing,
Public Relations,
and Sales

Human
Resources

Industries

Agriculture

Construction and
Architecture

Building
Materials

Mining

el/la trabajador/a de la industria automovilística	auto worker
el trabajador del estaño	tinner
el trabajador del metal	metalworker
el/la trabajador/a social	social worker
el/la traductor/a	translator
el trampero	trapper
el/la transportista	trucker
el/la tutor/a	tutor
el ujier	usher
el/la urbanista	urban planner
el vaquero	cowboy
el/la vendedor/a	vendor, salesperson
el/la vendedor/a de piedras preciosas	gem dealer
el/la veterinario/a	veterinarian
el viajante	traveling salesman
el/la vinatero/a	winemaker
el yesero	plasterer
el zapatero	cobbler, shoemaker
el/la zoólogo/a	zoologist
desempleado	unemployed

Words In Use

Tengo que conseguir un buen **profesor particular** para mi hija. *I have to get my daughter a good tutor.*

Tuve que esperar mucho porque sólo había un **cajero** en el banco. *I had to wait a long time at the bank because there was only one teller.*

Además de ser **pintor**, Picasso trabajó como **escultor**. *In addition to being a painter, Picasso worked as a sculptor.*

Al **crítico** del periódico no le gustó la película. *The critic of the newspaper did not like the movie.*

Mi prima trabaja como **cantante** de comerciales. *My cousin works as a singer for commercials.*

El **rabino** de mi sinagoga es muy buen **consejero**. *The rabbi of my synagogue is a great counselor.*

La **recepcionista** me dijo que esperara aquí. *The receptionist told me to wait here.*

¿Ya pasó el **cartero** por la casa? *Did the mailman stop by the house?*

Jorge es el mejor **abogado** que hay en el pueblo. *Jorge is the best lawyer in town.*

La línea aérea está contratando **asistentes de vuelos**. *The airline is hiring flight attendants.*

OFFICE PEOPLE
La gente en la oficina

el/la empleado/a	*employee*
el patrón	*employer (male)*
la patrona	*employer (female)*
el/la presidente/a	*president*
el/la vicepresidente/a	*vice president*
el/la jefe/a	*boss*
el/la gerente	*manager*
el/la directora/a	*director*
el/la supervisor/a	*supervisor*
el/la asistente	*assistant*
el/la trabajador/a de tiempo completo	*full-time worker*
el/la trabajador/a de medio tiempo	*part-time worker*
el/la trabajador/a de tiempo parcial	*part-time worker*
el/la trabajador/a por cuenta propia	*freelancer*
el/la colega	*colleague*
el/la compañero/a	*peer*
el/la mentor/a	*mentor*
el/la oficinista	*clerk*
el/la aprendiz	*trainee*
el/la que trabaja bien en equipo	*team player*
el/la competidor/a	*competitor*

Words In Use

El **gerente** del edificio es un hombre muy dinámico. *The manager of the building is a very dynamic man.*

Mi **supervisor** es un hombre muy justo. *My supervisor is a very fair man.*

Me llevo bien con todos mis **compañeros**. *I get along with all my peers.*

¿Te llevas bien con tu **jefe**? *Do you get along with your boss?*

El **director** de la empresa está en viaje de negocios. *The director of the company is on a business trip.*

OFFICE AREAS
Áreas de la oficina

la oficina	*office*
la oficina ejecutiva	*executive office*

el cubículo	cubicle
la oficina de la junta directiva	boardroom
la sala de conferencias	conference room
la sala de entrenamiento	training room
la sala de fotocopias	copy room
la cafetería	cafeteria
los ascensores	elevators
las escaleras	staircase
los lavabos	restrooms
los baños	restrooms
el baño para caballeros	men's room
el baño para damas	ladies' room
la fábrica	factory, plant
la planta	plant
el almacén	warehouse
la bodega	warehouse
el centro de coordinación	operations
la informática	data processing
el procesamiento de datos	data processing
los productos nuevos	new products
el control de producto	product control
el control de calidad	product control, quality control
las relaciones públicas	public relations
las compras	purchasing

Words In Use

Disculpe, ¿dónde están los **baños**? *Excuse me, where are the restrooms?*

En este piso no hay **baño para caballeros**. *There's no men's room on this floor.*

La **oficina ejecutiva** está en el quinto piso. *The executive office is on the fifth floor.*

Tuvieron que mudar la **fábrica** a México. *They had to move the plant to Mexico.*

Los **ascensores** no están funcionando. *The elevators are not working.*

OFFICE ACTIVITIES

Actividades en la oficina

OFFICE ACTIVITIES NOUNS

la reunión	meeting
la presentación	presentation

la fusión	*merger*
la negociación	*negotiation*
la puesta en común	*brainstorming*
el brainstorming	*brainstorming*
la conversación telefónica	*telephone conversation*
la llamada local	*local call*
la llamada de larga distancia	*long-distance call*
la llamada internacional	*international call*
la llamada de conferencia	*conference call*
el chismorreo de oficina	*office gossip*
el cotilleo de oficina	*office gossip*
la política interna de oficina	*office politics*
el establecimiento de contactos	*networking*
la reestructuración	*restructuring*
la asesoría	*consulting*
la jerarquía	*hierarchy*
el nepotismo	*nepotism*

OFFICE ACTIVITIES VERBS

consultar	*to consult*
discutir	*to discuss*
convencer	*to convince*
decidir	*to decide*
hacer puesta en común	*to brainstorm*
negociar	*to negotiate*
dirigir desde arriba	*to manage up*
dirigir desde abajo	*to manage down*
hacer una llamada	*to make a call*
no dar con alguien	*to miss a call*
devolver la llamada	*to return a call*
dejar un mensaje	*to leave a message*
recibir un mensaje	*to get a message*
grabar un mensaje	*to record a message*
grabar un saludo	*to record a greeting*
borrar un mensaje	*to erase a message*
avanzar en la carrera	*to advance in a career*
ser promovido	*to be promoted*
obtener una bonificación	*to get a bonus*
recibir un aumento	*to get a raise*
renunciar al trabajo	*to quit a job*

18

Professions

Office People

Office Areas

Office Activities

Job Search

Office Objects

Business
Practices

Telecommunica-
tions

Mail

Company
Departments

Accounting

Manufacturing
and Operations

Advertising,
Marketing,
Public Relations,
and Sales

Human
Resources

Industries

Agriculture

Construction and
Architecture

Building
Materials

Mining

dimitir del trabajo	*to resign from a job*
renunciar a un trabajo	*to resign from a job*
despedir	*to fire*
ser suspendido	*to be fired, to be laid off*
ser despedido	*to be fired, to be laid off*
llamar para decir que se está enfermo	*to call in sick*
tomarse un día de vacaciones	*to take a vacation/a personal day*
pedir vacaciones	*to ask for a vacation*
volver de vacaciones	*to be back from a vacation*
quejarse	*to complain*
chismorrear	*to gossip*
cotillear	*to gossip*
dar coba a alguien	*to suck up*
enjabonar	*to suck up*
dar otra oportunidad	*to give another chance*

Words In Use

Siempre es difícil **despedir** a alguien. *It's always difficult to fire someone.*

Decidimos **darle otra oportunidad**. *We decided to give him another chance.*

Tuvimos que **consultar** con el jefe de personal. *We had to consult with the personnel director.*

No creo que quiera **dimitir del trabajo**. *I don't think he wants to resign from his job.*

Hace cuatro años que no **recibe un aumento**. *He hasn't gotten a raise in four years.*

JOB SEARCH

Buscando trabajo

JOB SEARCH NOUNS—GENERAL

la carrera	*career*
la búsqueda laboral	*job search*
el mercado laboral	*job market*
la demanda de trabajo	*job demand*
la disponibilidad de trabajo	*job availability*
la tasa de empleo	*employment rate*

JOB SEARCH NOUNS—APPLICATION

la carta de explicación	*cover letter*
la carta de interés	*letter of interest*
la carta de solicitud	*application letter*

la carta para indagar	*letter of inquiry*
el curriculum vitae	*curriculum vitae, resume*
la hoja de vida	*curriculum vitae, resume*
las metas profesionales	*career goals/plans*
los objetivos profesionales	*(career) objective*
los logros profesionales	*professional achievements*
los conocimientos profesionales	*professional expertise*
la pericia	*professional expertise*
el interés especial	*special interest*
la experiencia laboral	*work experience*
la formación educativa	*educational background*
las destrezas	*skills*
las destrezas adicionales	*additional skills*
el trabajo comunitario	*community work*
la información personal	*personal information*

JOB SEARCH NOUNS—INTERVIEW

la entrevista	*interview*
la primera entrevista	*first interview*
la segunda entrevista	*second interview*
la entrevista introductoria	*introductory interview*
la entrevista buena	*good interview*
la entrevista exitosa	*successful interview*
la entrevista mala	*bad interview*
la entrevista larga	*long interview*
la entrevista rápida	*quick interview*
el/la entrevistador/a	*interviewer*
la oferta	*offer*
las referencias	*references*

JOB SEARCH NOUNS—WAGES

el sueldo	*wage*
los honorarios	*fee*
el salario	*salary*
los requisitos salariales	*salary requirement*
el sueldo mínimo	*minimum wage*
el ascenso	*promotion*
el ascenso en la carrera	*career advancement*
las posibilidades de ascenso	*advancement possibilities*
el aumento	*raise*

18

Professions

Office People

Office Areas

Office Activities

Job Search

Office Objects

Business
Practices

Telecommunications

Mail

Company
Departments

Accounting

Manufacturing
and Operations

Advertising,
Marketing,
Public Relations,
and Sales

Human
Resources

Industries

Agriculture

Construction and
Architecture

Building
Materials

Mining

| el aumento de sueldo | *wage increase* |
| la bonificación de fin de año | *(yearly/end-of-the-year) bonus* |

JOB SEARCH NOUNS—BENEFITS

los beneficios	*benefits*
el seguro de vida	*life insurance*
el seguro médico	*medical insurance*
los beneficios de jubilación	*retirement benefits*
el plan de jubilación 401-K	*401-K plan*
el plan de jubilación	*pension/retirement plan*
la contribución	*personal contribution*
el pago	*compensation*
la licencia por maternidad	*maternity leave*
la licencia por paternidad	*paternity leave*
las vacaciones	*vacation*
el día libre	*day off*
el día para asuntos personales	*personal day*
el día por enfermedad	*sick day*
el entrenamiento en el trabajo	*on-the-job training*

JOB SEARCH NOUNS—TYPES OF COMPANIES

la oficina	*office*
la organización	*organization*
la compañía	*company*
el instituto	*institute*
la corporación	*corporation*
la empresa grande	*big corporation*
la corporación de tamaño medio	*mid-size corporation*
la corporación pequeña	*small corporation*
la cultura corporativa	*corporate culture*
la jerarquía corporativa	*corporate hierarchy*
la jerga corporativa	*corporate jargon/language*
la política corporativa	*corporate policies*
la vida corporativa	*corporate life*

JOB SEARCH NOUNS—POSITIONS

el puesto	*position*
la posición gerencial	*managerial position*
la posición importante	*high-level position*
la posición ejecutiva	*executive position*

el trabajo de nueve a cinco	*nine-to-five job*
el trabajo de tiempo completo	*full-time work/job*
el trabajo de tiempo parcial	*part-time work/job*
el trabajo de medio tiempo	*part-time work/job*
el trabajo por cuenta propia	*freelance work/job*
el/la empleado/a de medio tiempo	*part-time worker*
el/la empleado/a de tiempo parcial	*part-time worker*
el horario de tiempo parcial	*part-time schedule*
el departamento	*department*

JOB SEARCH NOUNS—UNEMPLOYMENT

el desempleo	*unemployment*
los beneficios de desempleo	*unemployment benefits*
la oficina del desempleo	*unemployment office*

JOB SEARCH ADJECTIVES

de tiempo completo	*full-time*
de medio tiempo	*part-time*
de tiempo parcial	*part-time*
de nueve a cinco	*nine-to-five*
por cuenta propia	*freelance*

JOB SEARCH VERBS

buscar un trabajo	*to search for a job*
buscar trabajo	*to look for work*
investigar una empresa	*to research a company*
escribir un currículum	*to write a resume/curriculum vitae*
escribir una hoja de vida	*to write a resume/curriculum vitae*
solicitar un puesto de trabajo	*to apply for a job*
solicitar un empleo	*to apply for a job*
enviar una solicitud de empleo	*to send an application for a job*
ser invitado a hacer una entrevista	*to be invited for an interview*
hacer una cita para una entrevista	*to schedule an interview*
tener una entrevista con	*to get an interview with*
hacer una entrevista de trabajo	*to interview for a job*
hacer entrevistas introductorias	*to do introductory interviews*
entrevistar a alguien	*to interview someone*
conducir una entrevista	*to conduct an interview*
recibir una oferta	*to get an offer*

recibir una oferta de trabajo	*to be offered a job*
considerar un puesto	*to think about a job*
decidirse por un trabajo	*to decide on a job*
rechazar un trabajo	*to refuse a job*
aceptar un puesto	*to take a job*
aceptar una oferta de trabajo	*to accept a job*
tener trabajo	*to get a job*
trabajar de tiempo completo	*to work full-time*
estar de tiempo completo	*to be full-time*
trabajar de medio tiempo	*to work part-time*
estar de medio tiempo	*to be part-time*
trabajar de tiempo parcial	*to work part-time*
estar de tiempo parcial	*to be part-time*
trabajar por cuenta propia	*to freelance*
ganar dinero	*to make money*
ganar lo adecuado	*to make decent money*
ganar mucho dinero	*to make a lot of money*
ganar poco dinero	*to make very little money*
hacer contactos	*to network*
buscar desarrollo profesional	*to look for professional development*
no llevarse bien con el jefe	*to not get along well with your boss*
no llevarse bien con los compañeros	*to not get along well with your peers*
no ser retado	*to not be challenged*
sentirse atascado con un trabajo	*to be stuck in a position*
perder un trabajo	*to lose a job*
estar desempleado	*to be unemployed*
estar sin trabajo	*to be out of work*
enlistarse en la oficina del desempleo	*to register with the unemployment office*
solicitar beneficios de desempleo	*to apply for unemployment benefits*

NOTE: More words related to Job Search can be found in the Human Resources section of this book.

Words In Use

¿Perdiste el trabajo? *Did you lose your job?*

Sí, **estoy sin trabajo** ahora. *Yes, I'm without a job now.*

Estoy **buscando trabajo** en otra empresa. *I'm looking for a job in another company.*

Con tus **logros profesionales** no tendrás problemas. *With your professional achievements you will have no problem.*

¿Ya escribiste tu **currículum**? *Did you write your resume?*

Sí, pero tengo que escribir un listado de **referencias**. *Yes, but I have to write a list with my references.*

Tengo una **entrevista** mañana. *I have an interview tomorrow.*

¿Vas a **trabajar de tiempo completo**? *Are you going to work full time?*

No, prefiero **trabajar de tiempo parcial**. *No, I prefer to work part time.*

En esa compañía los **beneficios** son muy buenos. *That company offers good benefits.*

OFFICE OBJECTS
Objetos de oficina

OFFICE OBJECT NOUNS—WRITING TOOLS

la pluma	*pen*
la pluma de escribir	*writing pen*
la pluma estilográfica	*ink pen*
la pluma retractable	*retractable pen*
el bolígrafo	*ballpoint pen*
el marcador	*marker*
el lápiz	*pencil*
el lápiz de madera	*wood pencil*
el lápiz mecánico	*mechanical pencil*
el borrador	*eraser*
el líquido corrector	*correction fluid*
la almohadilla de entintar	*ink pad*
el resaltador	*highlighter*
el grafito	*lead*
la máquina de escribir	*typewriter*
la cinta de máquina de escribir	*typewriter ribbon*
el sacapuntas	*pencil sharpener*

OFFICE OBJECT NOUNS—PAPER

el papel	*paper*
la papelería con membrete	*business stationery*
la libreta	*notebook*
el libro de citas	*appointment book*
la cartulina	*construction paper*
el cuaderno para informes	*reporter notebook*
el bloc borrador	*scratch pad*
el bloc con rayas	*ruled writing pad*
el bloc de mensajes	*message pad*

el bloc de notas	*note pad, writing pad*
el bloc estenográfico	*steno pad*
la cubierta para informes	*report cover*
el formulario	*form*
el membrete	*letterhead*
las notas post-it	*post-it® notes*
el papel de computadora	*computer paper*
el papel de ordenador	*computer paper*
el papel de copiadora	*copier paper*
el papel de fax	*fax paper*
el papel de gráficas	*graph paper*
el sobre	*envelope*
el sobre comercial grande	*large business envelope*
la etiqueta	*label*

OFFICE OBJECT NOUNS—ORGANIZATIONAL

la bandeja	*tray*
la bandeja apilable de cartas	*stacking letter tray*
la canasta	*basket tray*
la cesta	*basket tray*
la cesta de recibo/envío	*in/out box*
el organizador de escritorio	*desk organizer*
el organizador vertical	*vertical holder*
el archivo	*file cabinet*
el armario de almacenaje	*storage cabinet*
el armario de metal	*steel cabinet*
el archivo de carpetas	*file folder*
el archivo colgante	*hanging file holder*
el archivo vertical	*vertical file*
la carpeta	*binder, folder*
la tarjeta de visita	*business card*
el portador de tarjetas de visita	*business card holder*
el tarjetero Rolodex	*Rolodex® card file*
el tarjetero	*business card file*

OFFICE OBJECT NOUNS—ADHESIVES

la cinta	*tape, ribbon*
la cinta adhesiva protectora	*masking tape*
la cinta adhesiva scotch	*scotch® tape*

la cinta de conductos	duct tape
la cinta de embalaje	shipping tape
el dispensador de cinta adhesiva	tape dispenser
la liga de goma	rubber band
la banda elástica	rubber band
la grapadora	stapler
la presilladora	stapler
el pegamento	glue
el sujetapapeles	paper clip

OFFICE OBJECTS NOUNS—OTHER SUPPLIES

la regla	ruler
la cortadora de papel	paper cutter
las tijeras	scissors
la perforadora triple	three-hole punch
el sacagrapas	staple remover
la tablilla con sujetapapeles	clipboard

OFFICE OBJECT NOUNS—ELECTRONICS

la impresora	printer
el fax	fax
el chorro de tinta	inkjet
el cartucho	cartridge
el cartucho de repuesto	replacement cartridge
el cartucho de tinta en polvo	toner cartridge
el cable	cable
el cordón de extensión	extension cord
el cordón eléctrico	power cord
la linterna	flashlight
la pantalla de proyección	projection screen
la batería	battery
la pila	battery
el protector contra subida de voltaje	surge protector
el monitor	monitor
el teclado	keyboard
el ratón	mouse
la unidad de disco Zip	Zip® drive
la grabadora de CD	CD burner
el disco	diskette or floppy disk

el adaptador	*adapter*
la alfombrilla para ratón	*mouse pad*
el descansador de muñeca	*wrist rest*

OFFICE OBJECT NOUNS—POST

la balanza postal	*postal scale*
el sello	*stamp*
el contador postal	*postal meter*
el humedecedor de sellos	*stamp moistener*
el abridor de cartas	*letter opener*

OFFICE OBJECT NOUNS—CHAIRS

la silla apilable	*stacking chair*
la silla de cuero	*leather chair*
la silla de gerente	*manager chair*
la silla ejecutiva	*executive chair*
la silla ergonómica	*ergonomic chair*
la silla giratoria	*swivel chair*
la silla lateral	*side chair*
la mesa plegable	*folding chair*

OFFICE OBJECT NOUNS—TABLES

el escritorio	*desk*
el escritorio de computadora	*computer desk*
el escritorio de computadora	*computer desk*
la mesa de computadora	*computer table*
la mesa de ordenador	*computer table*
la mesa de conferencias	*conference table*
la mesa de dibujantes	*drafting/artist table*
el caballete	*easel*
la mesita para el café	*coffee table*
la mesita para el fax	*fax stand*
la mesita para la impresora	*printer stand*
el carrito de almacenaje	*storage cart*
el carrito para computadoras	*computer cart*
el carrito para el correo	*mail cart*
el carrito para libros	*book cart*
el carrito para ordenadores	*computer cart*

OFFICE OBJECT NOUNS—SHELVES

el estante	*book shelf*
la estantería	*bookcase*
el sujetalibros	*bookend*

OFFICE OBJECT NOUNS—BOARDS

la pizarra	*chalk board*
el tablón de anuncios	*bulletin board*
las tachuelas	*tacks*
las chinchetas	*tacks*
los alfileres marcadores	*push pin*

OFFICE OBJECT NOUNS—ACCENTS

la caja fuerte	*safe*
la cerradura	*lock*
el calendario	*calendar*
el planificador	*planner*
la cuña	*door stop, door jam*
el estante de revistas	*magazine rack*
la foto	*picture, photograph*
el cuadro	*picture*
el marco	*frame*
el gancho para abrigos	*coat hook/rack*
la lámpara de escritorio	*desk lamp*
la lámpara de suelo	*floor lamp*
la percha	*coat hook/rack*
el ventilador	*fan*
la taza	*cup*
la alfombra	*floor mat*
el reloj	*clock*
la guía telefónica	*telephone book*

OFFICE OBJECT NOUNS—CLEANING AND MAINTENANCE

los productos de limpieza	*cleaning supplies*
la papelera	*waste basket*
la bolsa para la basura	*trash/garbage bag*
la escoba	*broom*
el paño de limpiar	*cleaning cloth*
el paño	*duster*

el trapo del polvo	*duster*
la bombilla	*light bulb*

Words In Use

Es bonita tu **silla de cuero**. *Your leather chair is very nice.*

No es cómoda; necesito una **silla ergonómica**. *It's not comfortable, I need an ergonomic chair.*

El **reloj** tiene cinco minutos de retraso. *The clock is five minutes late.*

No te olvides de comprar **sellos**. *Don't forget to buy stamps.*

También hay que cambiar la **bombilla**. *We also have to change the light bulb.*

La **impresora** está sin papel. *The printer is out of paper.*

Como el aire acondicionado no es muy fuerte, encendí el **ventilador**. *Because the air conditioning is not very strong, I had to turn on the fan.*

Tengo que llenar este **formulario** a máquina. *I have to type the information on this form.*

En esta oficina no tenemos **máquinas de escribir**. *There are no typewriters in this office.*

¿Ya archivaste las **carpetas**? *Did you file the binders?*

Envía el documento por **fax**. *You can send the document via fax.*

BUSINESS PRACTICES
Prácticas comerciales

la corporación	*corporation*
la organización	*organization*
la asociación	*association*
el instituto	*institute*
el conglomerado	*conglomerate*
el comercio	*trade*
la consultoría	*consulting*
los bienes raíces	*real estate*
la inmobiliaria	*real estate*
el seguro	*insurance*
la banca	*banking*
la contabilidad	*accounting*
la empresa naviera	*shipping*
la fabricación	*manufacturing*
la sede mundial	*corporate/world headquarters*
la oficina central	*central office*
la oficina principal	*main office*

| la sucursal | *branch office* |
| la oficina corporativa | *corporate offices* |

Words In Use

Es una **organización** con alcance internacional. *The organization has an international reach.*

Es un **conglomerado** con muchas divisiones. *It's a conglomerate with many different divisions.*

Sus dos áreas principales son la **contabilidad** y la **consultoría**. *Its two main fields are accounting and consulting.*

La **sede mundial** está en Londres. *The world headquarters is in London.*

El **comercio** entre Argentina y Brasil ha subido. *There's been an increase in trade between Argentina and Brazil.*

TELECOMMUNICATIONS

Telecomunicaciones

TELECOMMUNICATIONS NOUNS—GENERAL

las telecomunicaciones	*telecommunications*
la línea	*line*
la línea de fibra óptica	*fiber optical line*
la red	*network*
la seguridad	*security*
el inalámbrico	*wireless*
el cable	*cable*
la transmisión de datos	*data transmission*
la transmisión	*transmission*

TELECOMMUNICATIONS NOUNS—PHONES

el teléfono	*telephone*
la línea telefónica	*phone line*
el correo de voz	*voice mail*
la llamada de larga distancia	*long distance call*
la llamada local	*local call*
el móvil	*cellular*
el celular	*cellular*
el teléfono celular	*cellular phone, mobile phone*
el teléfono móvil	*mobile phone, cellular phone*
el satélite	*satellite*

18

Professions

Office People

Office Areas

Office Activities

Job Search

Office Objects

Business Practices/ Telecommunications

Mail

Company Departments

Accounting

Manufacturing and Operations

Advertising, Marketing, Public Relations, and Sales

Human Resources

Industries

Agriculture

Construction and Architecture

Building Materials

Mining

TELECOMMUNICATIONS NOUNS— E-MAIL AND THE INTERNET

el/la Internet *	*internet*
el/la intranet *	*intranet*
el correo electrónico	*e-mail*
la web mundial	*world wide web*
la web	*web*
la página web	*web page*
el sitio web	*web site*
el enlace	*link*
el servidor	*server*
el módem	*modem*
los datos	*data*
la alta velocidad	*high speed*
el comercio electrónico	*e-commerce*
la computadora de bolsillo	*palmtop computer*
el teclado	*keyboard, keypad*

TELECOMMUNICATIONS NOUNS—OTHER DEVICES

el fax	*fax/facsimile*
el telégrafo	*telegraph*
el telegrama	*telegram*
el código de Morse	*Morse code*
la conferencia por vídeo	*video conferencing*
la asistente personal digital	*personal digital assistant (pda)*

TELECOMMUNICATIONS VERBS

llamar	*to call*
transmitir	*to transmit*
conectarse	*to connect, to log on*

NOTE: More words related to Telecommunications can be found in the Computers and Internet category.

Words In Use

Tu conexión de **Internet** es muy rápida. *Your internet connection is very fast.*

Necesito enviar un **correo electrónico**. *I need to send an e-mail.*

¿Puedo **conectarme** con el **Internet**? *Can I get on the Internet?*

¿Cuánto cuesta un **fax** a los Estados Unidos? *How much is a fax to the United States?*

* *The terms* Internet *and* intranet *are used most of the time without an article, but on occasion some writers use them preceded by the articles* el *or* la.

MAIL

El Correo

MAIL NOUNS—GENERAL

la entrega	*delivery*
la dirección	*address*
el destino	*destination*
el/la destinatario/a	*addressee*
la estampilla	*stamp*
el sello	*stamp*
el sobre	*envelope*
el paquete	*package*
la expedición	*forwarding*
el pedido	*order*
la ruta	*route*

MAIL NOUNS—SERVICES

el servicio	*service*
el/la portador/a	*carrier*
el transportador	*carrier*
el transportador de carga	*freight carrier*
el transporte a granel	*bulk carrier*
el correo aéreo	*air mail*
el correo por tierra	*surface mail*
la recogida	*pickup*
el tiempo de entrega	*delivery time*
la fecha de llegada garantizada	*guaranteed arrival date*
el cargador	*loader*
la capacidad de carga	*load capacity*
el certificado	*certificate*
el consignador	*consignor*
el elevador de carga	*fork lift*
el elevador de horquilla	*fork lift*
el fletador	*shipper*
el manifiesto	*manifest*

MAIL NOUNS—CONTAINERS

la caja	*box*
el contenedor	*container*
el embalaje de tablas	*crate*

el empaque	packaging
el envase	small container
el guacal	crate
la refrigeración	refrigeration
el barco mercantil	merchant ship

MAIL NOUNS—ITEMS

los bienes	goods
la mercancía	goods
el flete	freight
la carga	cargo, freight, load
los lotes	lots
los materiales peligrosos	hazardous materials

MAIL NOUNS—COSTS

el costo	cost
el seguro	insurance
el estimado	estimate
la factura	bill
el impuesto	duty
el seguro y el flete	cif (costs, insurance, and freight)
los costos	cif (costs, insurance, and freight)

MAIL NOUNS—PLACES

el puerto	port
el muelle	dock
el almacén	depot
la aduana	customs
la central de mensajes	message center

MAIL ADJECTIVES

por avión	by air
aéreo	by air
por mar	by sea
marítimo	by sea
por tierra	by land
terrestre	by land
frágil	fragile

MAIL VERBS

enviar por correo	*to mail*
entregar	*to deliver*
transportar	*to transport*
remitir	*to forward*
embarcar	*to ship*
llevar	*to truck*
empacar	*to package*
embalar	*to package*
empaquetar	*to package*
dirigir	*to address*
poner la dirección	*to address*
recoger	*to pick up*
ordenar (pedir)	*to order*
facturar	*to bill*
asegurar	*to insure*
seguir la pista	*to track, to follow the trail*
rastrear	*to track*
fletar	*to charter*
atracar	*to dock*
combinar	*to combine*
despachar	*to dispatch*
cargar	*to load*
descargar	*to unload*
refrigerar	*to refrigerate*
fijar el itinerario	*to route*

Words In Use

Tengo que **enviar** las cartas **por correo** hoy. *I have to mail these letters today.*

Se equivocaron; me **facturaron** por el artículo equivocado. *They made a mistake; they billed me for the wrong item.*

¿Cuándo **ordenaste** los pantalones? *When did you order the pants?*

Se supone que los **entreguen** mañana. *They're supposed to be delivered tomorrow.*

El **tiempo de entrega** es muy corto. *The delivery time is very short.*

COMPANY DEPARTMENTS

Departamentos de una empresa

el marketing	*marketing*
el mercadeo	*marketing*
la mercadotecnia	*marketing*
las ventas	*sales*
el departamento de fabricación	*manufacturing*
las operaciones	*operations*
el departamento de informática	*IT*
el departamento legal	*legal*
la contabilidad	*accounting*
las finanzas	*finance*
el departamento de correo	*mail room*

Words In Use

El **departamento legal** está en el quinto piso. *The legal department is on the fifth floor.*

Está enfrente del departamento de **ventas**. *It's directly across from the sales department.*

Ha habido una reestructuración en el departamento de **finanzas**. *There's been some restructuring in the finance department.*

Consuelo trabaja en el departamento de **contabilidad**. *Consuelo works in the accounting department.*

ACCOUNTING

Contabilidad

ACCOUNTING NOUNS

la cuenta	*account*
el/la contable	*accountant*
los activos	*assets*
la auditoría	*audit*
el balance general	*balance sheet*
la bancarrota	*bankruptcy*
los registros de facturación	*billing records*
las cuentas	*bills*
el presupuesto	*budget*
el año natural	*calendar year*
el capital	*capital*
el presupuesto capital	*capital budget*
las mejoras de capital	*capital improvements*

el efectivo	cash
el flujo de efectivo	cash flow
el costo	cost
la contabilidad de costos	cost accounting
el crédito	credit
el débito	debit
la deuda	debt
la falta de pago	default
la depreciación	depreciation
el desembolso	disbursement
los dividendos	dividends
la equidad	equity
el/la analista financiero/a	financial analyst
el estado financiero	financial statement
el año fiscal	fiscal year
el ingreso bruto	gross income
las ventas brutas	gross sales
el ingreso	income
el estado de ingresos	income statement
el interés	interest
el inventario	inventory
la factura	invoice
el libro mayor	ledger
las obligaciones	liabilities
el activo disponible	liquid asset
el activo realizable	liquid asset
el margen	margin
el valor comercial	market value
el precio de mercado	market value
los beneficios netos	net earnings
las utilidades líquidas	net earnings
el activo neto	net worth
el patrimonio líquido	net worth
los gastos de operación	operating expenses
los gastos generales	overhead expenses
la nómina	payroll
el por día	per diem
la ganancia	profit
el estado de ganancias y pérdidas	profit and loss statement

la petición	requisition
el rendimiento de la inversión	return on investment
las ventas	sales
el estado de flujo de efectivo	statement of cash flows
las acciones	stock
el comprobante	voucher
los salarios	wages

ACCOUNTING VERBS

contar	to count
tener ingresos y gastos iguales	to break even

NOTE: More words related to Accounting can be found in the Money section of this book.

Words In Use

Las **ganancias** este trimestre han subido mucho. *This quarter's profits are way up.*

Se espera que las **ventas** sigan en ascenso. *They expect sales to continue to improve.*

Las **acciones** de la compañía reflejan este aumento. *The company's stock reflects this increase.*

Los **analistas financieros** lo estaban esperando. *The financial analysts were expecting it.*

Han aumentado el **presupuesto** para el año que viene. *They've increased the budget for next year.*

Nuestro **año fiscal** termina en julio. *Our fiscal year ends in July.*

MANUFACTURING AND OPERATIONS

Fabricación y operaciones

MANUFACTURING AND OPERATIONS NOUNS—GENERAL

la fábrica	factory
el almacén	warehouse
la bodega	warehouse
el piso	floor
la planta	floor, plant
la planta de fábrica	factory floor
el tanque	tank, vat
la tinaja	vat
el ferrocarril	railroad
la línea de ensamblaje	assembly line
la maquinaria	machinery
la materia prima	raw materials

el modelo	*model*
el inventario	*inventory*
la calidad	*quality*
el control de calidad	*quality control*
las compras	*purchasing*
los controles	*controls*
el elevador de carga	*fork lift*
el elevador de horquilla	*fork lift*
el envío	*shipping*
las especificaciones	*specifications*
el horario	*schedule, scheduling*
las operaciones	*operations*
el sindicato	*union*
el contrato laboral	*union contract*

MANUFACTURING AND OPERATIONS NOUNS—SAFETY

la seguridad	*safety*
las gafas protectoras	*safety goggles*
los tapones para los oídos	*ear plugs*
el accidente	*accident*

MANUFACTURING AND OPERATIONS NOUNS—PEOPLE

el/la ingeniero/a	*engineer*
el capataz	*foreman*
el/la supervisor/a	*supervisor*
el/la gerente de planta	*plant manager*
el/la trabajador/a	*worker*
el/la obrero/a	*worker*
el turno	*shift*
el primer turno	*first shift*
el segundo turno	*second shift*
el tercer turno	*third shift*
el productor	*manufacturer*
el proveedor	*supplier*
los distribuidores	*distributors*

MANUFACTURING AND OPERATIONS VERBS

manufacturar	*to manufacture*
elaborar	*to manufacture*
operar	*to operate*

18

Professions

Office People

Office Areas

Office Activities

Job Search

Office Objects

Business
Practices

Telecommunica-
tions

Mail

Company
Departments

Accounting

**Manufacturing
and Operations**

Advertising,
Marketing,
Public Relations,
and Sales

Human
Resources

Industries

Agriculture

Construction and
Architecture

Building
Materials

Mining

fabricar	to fabricate
diseñar	to engineer
manejar	to engineer
planear	to engineer
programar	to schedule
comprar	to purchase
enviar	to ship

Words In Use

El nuevo **almacén** tiene el doble de capacidad. *The new warehouse has double capacity.*

Enviamos directamente desde el almacén hasta los **distribuidores**. *We ship directly from the warehouse to the distributors.*

La **materia prima** viene directamente desde la **fábrica**. *The raw materials come directly from the factory.*

Por razones económicas se ha tenido que reducir el **inventario**. *For economic reasons, they had to reduce inventory.*

La **línea de ensamblaje** consta de treinta y cinco personas. *The assembly line consists of thirty-five people.*

ADVERTISING, MARKETING, PUBLIC RELATIONS, AND SALES

Publicidad, mercadeo relaciones públicas y ventas

ADVERTISING NOUNS—GENERAL

el anuncio	ad, advertisement
el anuncio publicitario	ad, advertisement
el aviso	ad, advertisement
la campaña	campaign
la campaña publicitaria	ad campaign
la estrategia	strategy
el estilo del anuncio	ad style
la estrategia publicitaria	advertising strategy
la publicidad	advertising, publicity
la publicidad de boca en boca	word-of-mouth advertising
la publicidad de gancho	bait and switch advertising
la publicidad subliminal	subliminal advertising
el presupuesto publicitario	advertising budget
la repetición	repetition
el incentivo	incentive
los medios de comunicación	media

los medios de comunicación en masa	*mass media*
la publicación	*publication*
el periódico	*newspaper, periodical*
la revista	*magazine*
la circulación	*circulation*
la circular	*circular*
el encarte	*insert*
la valla publicitaria	*billboard*
el tiempo del anuncio	*ad time*
el anuncio (radio y televisión)	*spot (radio and TV)*
el anuncio publicitario	*commercial*
el comercial	*commercial*
el comercial informativo	*infomercial*
la canción publicitaria	*jingle*
el cartel	*banner ad*
el análisis de opinión	*opinion research*
la agencia	*agency*
la agencia de publicidad	*ad agency*
la cuenta	*account*
la creatividad	*creativity*
el estilo de vida	*lifestyle*
la efectividad	*effectiveness*
el patrocinador	*sponsor*
el patrocinio	*sponsorship*
el endoso	*endorsement*
el eslogan	*slogan*
el lema	*slogan*
la etiqueta	*label*
la exposición	*exposure*
el guión	*storyboard*
el nombre de marca	*brand name*
la imagen	*image*
el logotipo	*logo*
la marca	*brand*
el material gráfico	*artwork*
el diseño de un producto	*product design*
el diseño gráfico	*graphic design*
el diseño	*layout*

la composición	*layout*
la copia	*copy*
el empaque	*packaging*
la presentación	*packaging, presentation*

ADVERTISING NOUNS—PEOPLE

el/la agente	*agent*
el/la agente de publicidad	*media agent*
el/la ejecutivo/a contable	*account executive*
el/la director/a artístico/a	*art director*
el/la director/a creativo/a	*creative director*
el/la consumidor/a	*consumer*
la audiencia	*audience*
el público	*audience*
el público al que se quiere llegar	*target audience*
la composición demográfica	*demographics*
el grupo al que se quiere llegar	*target group*
el grupo de enfoque	*focus group*
el grupo de prueba	*test group*
los oyentes	*listenership*
la audiencia	*listenership*

ADVERTISING VERBS

anunciar	*to advertise*
llegar	*to reach*
auspiciar	*to sponsor*
patrocinar	*to sponsor*
enfocarse en un grupo	*to target*
tener un grupo como objetivo	*to target*
emitir	*to air/to broadcast*
transmitir	*to air/to broadcast*

MARKETING NOUNS—GENERAL

el mercadeo	*marketing*
el plan de mercadeo	*marketing plan*
el mercadeo directo	*direct marketing*
el mercadeo en masa	*mass marketing*
el mercadeo global	*global marketing*
el mercadeo de nicho	*niche marketing*
el nicho	*niche*

la posición	niche
la posición en el mercado	market niche
la investigación del mercado	market research
el mensaje	message
el mercado al que se quiere llegar	target market
el mercado cautivo	captive market
el mercado de prueba	test market
el mercado	market
la penetración en el mercado	market penetration
el perfil de la audiencia	audience profile
la composición demográfica	demographics
la encuesta	survey
la encuesta de opinión	opinion research
la efectividad	effectiveness
el presupuesto para el mercadeo	marketing budget
el telemercadeo	telemarketing
el correo directo	direct mail
la lista de direcciones	mailing list
los medios de comunicación	media
los medios de comunicación en masa	mass media
la publicación	publication
el periódico	newspaper, periodical
la revista	magazine
la circulación	circulation
la comercialización	merchandising
la competencia	competition
la cultura	culture
la cuota	market share
el desarrollo de nuevos productos	new product development
la lealtad a una marca	brand loyalty
la feria comercial	trade show
la inserción	insert
la introducción de un producto	rollout
la investigación	research
la investigación de consumo	consumer research
la parte	share
la parte del mercado	market share
el sitio web	web site

MARKETING NOUNS—PEOPLE

el/la director/a de mercadeo	*marketing director*
el/la gerente de mercadeo	*marketing manager*
la audiencia	*audience*
el público	*audience*
el público al que se quiere llegar	*target audience*
el grupo al que se quiere llegar	*target group*
el grupo de enfoque	*focus group*
el grupo de prueba	*test group*

MARKETING VERBS

poner a la venta	*to market*
distribuir	*to market*
comercializar	*to market, to merchandise*
promover la venta de	*to merchandise*
situar en una posición conveniente	*to position*
poner en una posición conveniente	*to position*
promover	*to promote*
llegar	*to reach*
enfocarse en un grupo	*to target*
tener un grupo como objetivo	*to target*

PUBLIC RELATIONS NOUNS—GENERAL

el comunicado de prensa	*news release, press release*
la conferencia de prensa	*news conference*
los medios de comunicación	*media*
los medios de comunicación en masa	*mass media*
la publicación	*publication*
el periódico	*newspaper, periodical*
la revista	*magazine*
la circulación	*circulation*
las relaciones públicas	*public relations*
la información sobre un producto	*product information*
el plan de publicidad	*media plan*

PUBLIC RELATIONS NOUNS—PEOPLE

el/la funcionario/a de prensa	*press officer*
el/la periodista	*journalist*
los oyentes	*listenership*

la audiencia	*listenership*
los lectores	*readership*

PUBLIC RELATIONS VERBS

enfocarse en un grupo	*to target*
tener un grupo como objetivo	*to target*
llegar	*to reach*
auspiciar	*to sponsor*
patrocinar	*to sponsor*
emitir	*to air/to broadcast*
transmitir	*to air/to broadcast, to transmit*

SALES NOUNS—GENERAL

el almacén	*warehouse*
la fijación de precios	*pricing*
el formulario de pedidos	*order form*
el folleto	*brochure, insert, leaflet*
el catálogo	*catalog*
la compra por impulso	*impulse buying*
la demanda	*demand*
el cupón	*coupon*
el descuento	*discount*
las devoluciones y las concesiones	*returns and allowances*
la distribución	*distribution*
la prima	*premium*
el producto	*product, commodity*
la promoción de ventas	*sales promotion*
la promoción	*promotion*
la propaganda por correo	*junk mail*
el proveedor	*supplier*
el precio	*price*
la predicción	*forecast*
el personal de ventas	*sales force*
la llamada sin previo aviso	*cold call*
el informe de ventas	*sales report*
la oferta de introducción	*trial offer*
la oferta especial	*special offer*
la oferta y la demanda	*supply and demand*
las necesidades	*needs, wants*
el pedido por correo	*mail order*

18

Professions

Office People

Office Areas

Office Activities

Job Search

Office Objects

Business
Practices

Telecommunica-
tions

Mail

Company
Departments

Accounting

Manufacturing
and Operations

**Advertising,
Marketing,
Public Relations,
and Sales**

Human
Resources

Industries

Agriculture

Construction and
Architecture

Building
Materials

Mining

la mercancía	*merchandise*
la muestra	*sample*
el período de prueba	*trial*
la tarifa	*rate(s)*
la retirada	*recall*
la satisfacción del cliente	*customer satisfaction*
el servicio al cliente	*customer service*
las ventas	*sales*
la visita sin previo aviso	*cold call*
las quejas de los clientes	*customer complaints*
la reacción	*response*
la rebaja	*rebate*
el registro	*licensing*
el permiso	*licensing, permissions*

SALES NOUNS—PEOPLE

el/la gerente de ventas	*sales manager*
el/la gerente general de ventas	*general sales manager*
el/la representante de ventas	*sales representative*
el/la vendedor/a	*salesperson, vendor*
el/la cliente/a	*customer*
el/la comprador/a	*buyer*

SALES VERBS

vender	*to sell*
fijar el precio	*to price*

Words In Use

La **encuesta** reveló unos resultados asombrosos. *The survey showed some surprising results.*

El **público al que se quiere llegar** no respondió favorablemente. *The target audience didn't respond favorably.*

Ellos van a tener que cambiar la **campaña publicitaria**. *They'll have to change the ad campaign.*

La **reacción** del público fue negativa. *The public's response was negative.*

La percepción es que el **precio** es muy alto. *The perception is that the price is too high.*

La **presentación** del producto no es la adecuada. *The presentation of the product is not adequate.*

El **director creativo** renunció a su trabajo. *The creative director quit his job.*

HUMAN RESOURCES

Departamento de personal

HUMAN RESOURCES NOUNS—GENERAL

el departamento de personal	*personnel (department), human resources*
los recursos humanos	*human resources*
las relaciones personales	*human relations*
la entrevista	*interview*
el trabajo	*job*
el puesto	*job, position*
la descripción del puesto	*job description*
el listado de oportunidades de empleo	*job listing*
las habilidades de trabajo	*job skills*
la carrera	*career*
los antecedentes	*background*
el relevo	*turnover*
el relevo de los empleados	*employee turnover*
el empleo	*employment*
el nepotismo	*nepotism*
la organización	*organization*
el personal	*personnel*
el cargo	*position*
el/la reclutador/a	*recruiter*
la hoja de vida	*resume*
el currículum	*resume, C.V.*
las destrezas	*skills*
el desempleo	*unemployment*

HUMAN RESOURCES NOUNS—SALARY AND BENEFITS

el salario	*salary*
el nivel del salario	*salary grade*
la encuesta de salario	*salary survey*
el sueldo	*wages*
el cheque de paga	*paycheck*
la promoción	*promotion*
el plan de jubilación	*retirement plan*
la pensión	*pension*
los beneficios de los empleados	*employee benefits*

las vacaciones	*vacation*
el tiempo flexible	*flextime*
los beneficios laborales	*fringe benefits*
el seguro de salud	*health insurance*
el seguro de vida	*life insurance*
la opción de comprar acciones	*stock options*
el/la actuario/a	*actuary*
el/la beneficiario/a	*beneficiary*
la bonificación	*bonus*
el pago	*compensation*
la incapacidad	*disability*

HUMAN RESOURCES NOUNS—MANAGEMENT

la administración	*management*
el adiestramiento de administración	*management training*
la cultura corporativa	*corporate culture*
el asesoramiento	*counseling*
la consejería	*counseling*
la moral	*morale*
la motivación	*motivation*
la evaluación personal	*performance appraisal*
el traslado	*relocation*
la antigüedad	*seniority*
el/la supervisor/a	*supervisor*
el entrenamiento	*training*

HUMAN RESOURCES ADJECTIVES

| ausente | *absent* |

HUMAN RESOURCES VERBS

asesorar	*to counsel*
entrevistar	*to interview*
anunciar un puesto de trabajo	*to advertise a position/job*
administrar	*to manage*
microadministrar	*to micromanage*
supervisar	*to supervise*
evaluar a un/a empleado/a	*to appraise job performance*
reestructurar	*to restructure*
entrenar	*to train*

| promover | *to promote* |
| jubilarse | *to retire* |

NOTE: More words related to Human Resources can be found in the Job Search section of this book.

Words In Use

En esta compañía el **salario** lo determina la **antigüedad**. *In this company the salary is determined by seniority.*

En mi compañía el **salario** depende de las **destrezas** particulares del empleado. *In my company the salary depends on the employee's skills.*

A Miguel le acaban de dar una **promoción**. *Miguel just got a promotion.*

Le van a dar una **bonificación** bastante alta a fines de año. *He's getting a very high bonus at the end of the year.*

El **entrenamiento** durará el mes completo. *The training will take the whole month.*

Todavía no he empezado a contribuir a mi **plan de jubilación**. *I haven't started contributing to my retirement plan.*

INDUSTRIES
La industria

INDUSTRY NOUNS

la publicidad	*advertising*
las relaciones públicas	*public relations*
la industria automotriz	*automotive*
la banca	*banking*
las finanzas	*finance*
el entretenimiento	*entertainment*
los medios publicitarios	*media*
la moda	*fashion*
la industria alimenticia	*food service*
el gobierno	*government*
los seguros	*insurance*
la industria médica	*medical*
los bienes raíces	*real estate*
el embarque y la distribución	*shipping and distribution*
las telecomunicaciones	*telecommunications*

INDUSTRY ADJECTIVES

dental	*dental*
farmacéutica	*pharmaceutical*
editorial	*publishing*
inmobiliaria	*real estate*
textil	*textiles*

Words In Use

La **industria automotriz** está sufriendo un bajón. *The automobile industry is suffering a slump.*

Gracias a los intereses bajos, la **inmobiliaria** está muy bien equilibrada. *Because of low interest rates, real estate is poised for a rebound.*

Las **telecomunicaciones** tuvieron mucho éxito en la década de los noventa. *The telecommunications industry had a boom in the nineties.*

Ha habido muchas fusiones en la **industria farmacéutica**. *There have been a lot of mergers in the pharmaceutical industry.*

La **banca** también ha reportado muchas ganancias. *The banking industry has reported good profits.*

AGRICULTURE

Industria agrícola

AGRICULTURE NOUNS — GENERAL

el cultivo	farming, cultivation
la agronomía	agronomy
la granja	farm
el/la agricultor/a	farmer, agriculturalist
el/la granjero/a	farmer
el terreno	land
el campo	field
la tierra	soil
el granero	barn
el cubo	bin
el balde	bin, grain bin
el silo	silo
la tienda	store
la maquinaria	machinery
la labranza	husbandry
el ganado	livestock
el forraje	feedstock
el pienso	feedstock
la irrigación	irrigation
las semillas	seeds
el fertilizante	fertilizer(s)
los pesticidas	pesticides
el insecticida	insecticide
la sequía	drought
el área	area
el acre	acre

AGRICULTURE NOUNS—CROPS

la cosecha	*crop, harvest*
la fruta	*fruit*
la planta	*plant*
el tabaco	*tobacco*
los vegetales	*vegetables*
las verduras	*vegetables*
el trigo	*wheat*

AGRICULTURE NOUNS—BUSINESS

la producción	*production*
el rendimiento	*yield*
el precio	*price*
el subsidio	*subsidy*
el excedente	*surplus*
la exportación	*export*
la tarifa	*tariff*

AGRICULTURE ADJECTIVES

árido	*arid*
fértil	*fertile*

AGRICULTURE VERBS

labrar	*to farm, to till*
cultivar	*to cultivate, to grow, to farm*
sembrar	*to plant, to seed*
plantar	*to plant*
arrojar la semilla	*to seed*
irrigar	*to irrigate*
arar	*to plow*
producir	*to produce*
cosechar	*to harvest*
fertilizar	*to fertilize*

NOTE: More words related to Agriculture can be found in the Farm Animals section of this book.

Words In Use

Esta **sequía** ha sido devastadora para la industria. *This drought has been devastating for the industry.*

Los **agricultores** están sufriendo los estragos. *The farmers are suffering the effects.*

Han tenido que usar nuevos métodos de **irrigación**. *They've had to use new irrigation methods.*

La **producción** de **trigo** ha bajado muchísimo. *Wheat production has decreased significantly.*

El **precio** de las frutas está por las nubes. *The price of fruit has gone through the roof.*

La **cosecha** de manzanas de este año va a ser muy escasa. *This year's apple harvest will be very scarce.*

CONSTRUCTION AND ARCHITECTURE
Construcción y arquitectura

ARCHITECTURE NOUNS

el diseño	*design*
el plano	*blueprint*
los planos	*plans*
el borrador	*draft*
el bosquejo	*draft*
el dibujo	*drawing*
el esbozo	*drafting*
el diseño computarizado	*computer design*
el edificio	*building*
el diseño de oficina	*office layout*
la estructura	*structure*
el modelo	*model*
el terreno	*land*

CONSTRUCTION NOUNS

la construcción	*construction*
la encuesta	*survey*
el estudio	*survey*
la excavación	*excavation*
la fundición	*ironworks*
la grúa	*crane*
la máquina excavadora	*bulldozer*
la motoniveladora	*bulldozer*

CONSTRUCTION AND ARCHITECTURE NOUNS—PEOPLE

el/la arquitecto/a	*architect*
el/la diseñador/a	*designer*
el/la ingeniero/a	*engineer*
el capataz	*foreman*
el/la constructor	*builder*

el/la agrimensor/a	surveyor
el/la urbanizador/a	developer
el mampostero	mason
el/la albañil	bricklayer, mason
el carpintero	carpenter
el carpintero jefe	master carpenter
el aprendiz de carpintero	apprentice carpenter
el carpintero	joiner
el/la soldador/a	welder
el fontanero	plumber
el yesero	plasterer
el/la pintor/a	painter

CONSTRUCTION AND ARCHITECTURE NOUNS— PARTS OF A BUILDING

el techo	ceiling, roof
la viga	beam, joist
la junta	joint
el piso	floor
la ventana	window
el alféizar	windowsill
la entrada	doorway
el portal	doorway
las escaleras	stairs
la fachada	façade
la columna	column
el elevador	elevator
el ascensor	elevator
la iluminación	lighting
la luz	light
la instalación fija	fixture
el calor	heat
la calefacción y la ventilación	heating and ventilation
el arte	art
el parqueadero	parking
el estacionamiento	parking
el aparcamiento	parking
el material	material
los materiales de construcción	building materials
el azulejo	tile

18

Professions

Office People

Office Areas

Office Activities

Job Search

Office Objects

Business
Practices

Telecommunica-
tions

Mail

Company
Departments

Accounting

Manufacturing
and Operations

Advertising,
Marketing,
Public Relations,
and Sales

Human
Resources

Industries

Agriculture

**Construction and
Architecture**

Building
Materials

Mining

la baldosa	*tile*
el bloque de ceniza	*cinder blocks*
el ladrillo	*brick*
la pintura	*paint*

CONSTRUCTION AND ARCHITECTURE ADJECTIVES

erguido	*erected*
construido	*built*
demolido	*demolished*

CONSTRUCTION AND ARCHITECTURE VERBS

construir	*to construct, to build*
diseñar	*to design*
esbozar	*to draft*
dibujar	*to draw*
planificar	*to plan*
estudiar	*to survey*
sondear	*to survey*
medir	*to measure*
desarrollar	*to develop*
cavar	*to dig*
excavar	*to excavate*
colocar	*to lay*
erigir	*to erect*
completar	*to complete*
implementar	*to implement*
destruir	*to destroy*
demoler	*to demolish*
arreglar	*to fix*
reparar	*to repair*
reemplazar	*to replace*
renovar	*to renovate*
restaurar	*to refurbish*
reforzar	*to reinforce*
pintar	*to paint*
electrificar	*to wire*
hacer la instalación eléctrica	*to wire*
calentar	*to heat*
refrescar	*to cool*

embaldosar	to tile
azulejar	to tile

NOTE: More words related to Construction and Architecture can be found in other sections of the book, such as Around the House.

Words In Use

Tengo que **arreglar** el baño. *I have to have the bathroom fixed.*

Te puedo recomendar un buen **fontanero**. *I can recommend a good plumber.*

¿Sabe él **reemplazar** lavabos? *Does he know how to replace sinks?*

Sí, pero tendrás que **demoler** la pared. *Yes, but you would have to demolish the wall.*

¿Qué tipo de **pintura** vas a usar? *What type of paint are you going to use?*

Depende de las **baldosas** que decida poner. *It depends on the type of tiles that I get.*

BUILDING MATERIALS
Materiales de construcción

BUILDING MATERIALS—METAL

el metal	metal
el hierro	iron
el acero	steel
el aluminio	aluminum

BUILDING MATERIALS—STONE

la piedra	stone, rock
la roca	rock
el ladrillo	brick
la grava	gravel
el azulejo	tile, ceramic tile
la baldosa	tile
la baldosa de cerámica	ceramic tile
el cemento	cement
el concreto	concrete
la argamasa	mortar
el asfalto	asphalt

BUILDING MATERIALS—GLASS

el vidrio	glass
el vidrio de seguridad	safety glass

el vidrio escarchado	frosted glass
el cristal	glass
el cristal aislado	insulated glass
el cristal de seguridad	safety glass
el cristal escarchado	frosted glass

BUILDING MATERIALS—WOOD

la madera	wood
el pino	pine
el roble	oak
la madera de secoya	redwood
el ébano	ebony
la caoba	mahogany
el cedro	cedar
el bambú	bamboo

BUILDING MATERIALS—MAN-MADE

el plástico	plastic
el polímero sintético	manmade polymer

Words In Use

¿De qué **madera** están hechos tus muebles? *What type of wood is your furniture?*

Son muebles de **pino**. *They're made of pine wood.*

Prefiero la **secoya**. *I prefer redwood.*

Quizás la **caoba** combine mejor con este tipo de decoración. *Mahogany might go better with this type of decoration.*

Sí, va muy bien con la pared de **ladrillos**. *Yes, it matches with the brick wall.*

MINING

Minería

MINING NOUNS—RESOURCES

los recursos	resources
los recursos naturales	natural resources
el metal	metal
el mineral	mineral, ore
la gema	gem
la piedra semipreciosa	gem
el químico	chemical
el gas	gas

el gas natural	natural gas
el oro	gold
la plata	silver
el hierro	iron
el plomo	lead
el estaño	tin
el cobre	copper
el uranio	uranium
el aceite	oil
el cristal	crystal
el diamante	diamond
el carbón	coal
el zinc	zinc
la fuerza	power
la energía	energy, power
el desperdicio	waste
el agua	water
la compuerta	sluice
la tonelada	ton

MINING NOUNS—PROCESSES

la ingeniería	engineering
la excavación	excavating
la acción de cavar	digging
el dragado	dredging
la perforación	drilling
el despojamiento de minas	strip mining
el corte transversal	crosscut
la voladura	blasting
la explosión	blasting
la apertura de una compuerta	sluicing
el bombeo	pumping
la extracción	extraction
la fundición	smelting
la refrigeración	cooling
el procesamiento	processing

MINING NOUNS—AREAS AND EQUIPMENT

la tierra	earth
el depósito	deposit

la vena	vein
la mina	mine
el fuste	shaft
el túnel	tunnel
el pozo	well
la fosa	pit
la fosa abierta	open-pit
la cantera	quarry
la refinería	refinery
el afloramiento	outcrop
la plataforma	platform
la superficie	surface
la seguridad	safety
la correa	conveyor
la trituradora	crusher
la bomba	pump
el camión	truck

MINING NOUNS—PEOPLE

el/la geólogo/a	geologist
el/la ingeniero/a	engineer

MINING ADJECTIVES

hidráulico	hydraulic

MINING VERBS

minar	to mine
extraer	to mine
excavar	to dig
cavar un túnel	to tunnel
dragar	to dredge
extraer de la cantera	to quarry
bombear	to pump
triturar	to crush
refinar	to refine

NOTE: More words related to Mining can be found in the Natural World category.

Words In Use

Los habitantes del pueblo están en contra de la construcción de la nueva **refinería**. *The people in the town are against building a new refinery.*

El precio de la **plata** está muy por debajo del precio del **oro**. *The price of silver is well below the price of gold.*

Los ladrones escaparon con los **diamantes** en la bolsa. *The thieves escaped with the diamonds in the bag.*

Hay gran necesidad de encontrar nuevas formas de **energía**. *There is great need to find new forms of energy.*

Para llegar al **depósito** tuvieron que **excavar** durante muchos días. *To get to the deposit they had to dig for many days.*

EXERCISES

I. Match the Spanish word on the left with the English word on the right.

1. el/la camarero/a		A. *scissors*	
2. las tijeras		B. *harvest*	
3. la seguridad		C. *magazine*	
4. jubilarse		D. *journalist*	
5. la revista		E. *tile*	
6. la baldosa		F. *to deliver*	
7. la cosecha		G. *waiter*	
8. facturar		H. *safety*	
9. entregar		I. *to retire*	
10. el/la periodista		J. *to bill*	

II. Fill in the blanks with the appropriate Spanish word.

1. La fila de _____ (*customs*) en el aeropuerto era muy larga.

2. El _____ (*training*) será en Miami y durará tres días.

3. Tengo que enviar mi _____ (*application*) de trabajo.

4. He recibido una _____ (*offer*) de trabajo muy buena.

5. El _____ (*trade*) entre los dos países ha crecido mucho.

ANSWERS: I. 1. G, 2. A, 3. H, 4. I, 5. C, 6. E, 7. B, 8. J, 9. F, 10. D
II. 1. LA FILA DE **ADUANAS** EN EL AEROPUERTO ERA MUY LARGA.
2. EL **ENTRENAMIENTO** SERÁ EN MIAMI Y DURARÁ TRES DÍAS. 3. TENGO
QUE ENVIAR MI **SOLICITUD** DE TRABAJO. 4. HE RECIBIDO UNA **OFERTA**
DE TRABAJO MUY BUENA. 5. EL **COMERCIO** ENTRE LOS DOS PAÍSES HA
CRECIDO MUCHO.

Computers & The Internet

Computadoras e Internet

COMPUTER TERMINOLOGY

Terminología de computación

COMPUTER NOUNS—HARDWARE

el hardware	*hardware*
el ordenador*	*computer*
la computadora*	*computer*
la computadora de bolsillo	*palmtop computer*
la computadora de mesa	*desktop computer*
la computadora personal	*pc (personal computer)*
la computadora portátil	*laptop/notebook computer*
el procesador de textos	*word processor*
el monitor	*monitor*
la pantalla	*screen*
la pantalla LCD	*LCD screen*
la pantalla plana	*flat screen*
el disco duro	*hard drive*
la unidad de discos	*disk drive*
el disco	*disk*
el disco flexible	*diskette*
el disco zip	*zip® disk*
el CD-ROM	*CD(-ROM)*
el lector de CD-ROM	*CD-ROM drive*
la unidad de disco zip	*zip® drive*
el grabador de CD	*CD burner*
el DVD	*DVD*
la unidad central de proceso	*central processing unit (cpu)*
la unidad central	*mainframe*
el motor	*engine*

* *The term* ordenador *for the most part is used only in Spain. In Latin America,* computadora *is the preferred term.*

el puerto de comunicaciones	*communications port*
el puerto paralelo	*parallel port*
el puerto serie	*serial port*
el chip	*chip*
la microprocesadora	*microprocessor*
el circuito integrado	*integrated circuit*
la impresora	*printer*
la impresora láser	*laser printer*
el digitalizador de imágenes	*scanner*
el escáner	*scanner*
los altavoces	*speakers*
los bafles	*speakers*
el ratón	*mouse*
la almohadilla del ratón	*mouse pad*
la célula	*cell*
la memoria	*memory*
el baudio	*baud*
el octeto	*byte*
el byte	*byte*
el gigabyte	*gigabyte*
el hertzio	*hertz*
el megaciclo	*megahertz*

COMPUTER NOUNS—SOFTWARE

el software	*software*
el sistema	*system*
el sistema operativo	*operating system*
la aplicación	*application*
el archivo	*file*
el archivo comprimido	*compressed file*
la carpeta	*folder*
el documento	*document*
el programa	*program*
el programa beta	*beta program*
la prueba beta	*beta test*
el idioma	*language*
el lenguaje básico	*basic language*
el lenguaje cobol	*cobol language*
el lenguaje fortrán	*fortran language*
la base de datos	*data base*

el bug, el fallo lógico	*bug*
la búsqueda	*search*
el campo	*field*
la autoedición	*desktop publishing*
la maquetación	*desktop publishing*
el corrector de texto	*spell checker*
la copia	*copy*
el hipertexto	*hypertext*
el cursor	*cursor*
la línea de mandatos	*prompt*
el mandato	*command*
los datos	*data*
el icono	*icon*
los diseños genéricos	*clip art*
los gráficos	*graphics*
las instrucciones	*instructions*
el mensaje de error	*error message*
el menú	*menu*
la página	*page*
el reconocimiento de voz	*voice recognition*
el registro	*record*
el servidor	*server*
el tipo de letra	*font*
la ventana de diálogo	*dialog box*

COMPUTER NOUNS—KEYBOARDS

el teclado	*keyboard*
la tecla de entrada	*enter key*
la tecla de borrar	*delete key*
la tecla de retroceder	*backspace key*
la tecla de control	*control (ctrl) key*
la tecla de mayúsculas	*shift key*
el tabulador	*tab key*
la tecla alternativa	*alt key*
la tecla de escape	*escape (esc) key*
la barra espaciadora	*space bar*
la raya vertical delantera	*forward slash*
la raya vertical posterior	*back slash*
la contrabarra	*back slash*

COMPUTER NOUNS—OTHER NOUNS

el usuario	*user*
el asesoramiento técnico	*technical support*
el/la programador/a	*programmer*
el código de acceso	*access code*
el virus	*virus*
el fallo del sistema	*crash*

COMPUTER ADJECTIVES

compatible	*compatible*
compatible con IBM	*IBM-compatible*
fácil de usar	*user-friendly*
análogico	*analog*
digital	*digital*

COMPUTER VERBS

arrancar	*to boot*
guardar	*to save*
borrar	*to delete*
cargar	*to load*
abrir	*to open*
cerrar	*to close*
entrar	*to enter, to key*
introducir	*to key*
oprimir un botón	*to press a button*
maximizar	*to maximize*
minimizar	*to minimize*
cortar	*to cut*
copiar	*to copy*
pegar	*to paste*
insertar	*to insert*
examinar	*to screen*
desplazarse	*to scroll*
bajar la página	*to page down*
subir la página	*to page up*
buscar	*to search*
ordenar	*to sort*
pulsar	*to click*
hacer doble clic	*to double-click*
arrastrar y soltar	*to drag and drop*

pulsar el botón izquierdo	*to left click*
pulsar el botón derecho	*to right click*
imprimir	*to print*
programar	*to program*
depurar	*to debug*
limpiar	*to debug*
instalar	*to install*
escanear	*to scan*
digitalizar	*to scan*
corregir el texto	*to spell check*
usar	*to use*

Words In Use

¿Me dejas **imprimir** este **documento** en tu **computadora**? *Would you let me print this document on your computer?*

He hecho una **búsqueda** y no he encontrado nada. *I did a search but could not find anything.*

No te olvides de **guardar** tus **documentos** con regularidad. *Don't forget to save your documents regularly.*

Debes hacer una **copia** en tu **disco duro**. *You should make a copy on your hard drive.*

Me he comprado un **programa** para ayudarme con los impuestos. *I bought a program that will help me with my income taxes.*

Necesito ayuda para **instalarlo**. *I need help installing it.*

ONLINE TERMINOLOGY

Terminología de Internet

ONLINE NOUNS

Internet*	*Internet*
intranet*	*intranet*
el correo electrónico	*e-mail*
la web	*web*
el navegador de web	*web browser*
la página web	*web page*
el sitio web	*web site*
la web mundial	*world wide web (www)*
la red	*network*
el proveedor de servicios de Internet	*isp (Internet service provider)*

* Internet *and* intranet *are most often used in Spanish without an article; occasionally you may see them preceded by an article, either* el *or* la.

el servidor	host
el módem	modem
la conexión	connection
la dirección de Internet	Internet address
la contraseña	password
el motor de búsqueda	search engine
el navegador	browser
la banda ancha	broadband
la arroba	at sign (@)
el adjunto	attachment
la fusión postal	mail merge
el comercio electrónico	e-commerce
las compañías de comercio electrónico	e-commerce companies
la publicidad de Internet	Internet advertising
el anuncio cartel	banner ad
el pirata informático	hacker

ONLINE ADJECTIVES

en línea	online
inalámbrico	wireless

ONLINE VERBS

comenzar la conexión	to log on
terminar la conexión	to log off
conectarse	to go online
conseguir acceso a Internet	to access the Internet
navegar	to browse
navegar por Internet	to surf the Internet
hojear	to browse
descargar	to download
enviar un correo electrónico	to e-mail
pasar un correo electrónico	to forward an e-mail
adjuntar un archivo	to attach a file e-mail
servir	to host

Words In Use

Me pasé dos horas **navegando por el Internet**. *I spent two hours surfing the Internet.*

¿A qué hora sueles **conectarte**? *At what time do you normally go online?*

Mi **conexión** es rápida porque tengo **banda ancha**. *My connection is very fast because I have broadband.*

Nunca le des la **contraseña** a nadie. *Never share your password with anyone.*

Cuando llegues a París me **envias un correo electrónico**. *Send me an email when you get to Paris.*

EXERCISES

I. Match the Spanish word on the left with the English word on the right.

1. el mandato	A. *to close*
2. la pantalla plana	B. *to paste*
3. pegar	C. *host*
4. corregir el texto	D. *keyboard*
5. el adjunto	E. *delete key*
6. rastrear	F. *attachment*
7. el servidor	G. *command*
8. cerrar	H. *to spell check*
9. el teclado	I. *flat screen*
10. la tecla de borrar	J. *to browse*

II. Fill in the blanks with the appropriate Spanish word.

1. Hice una _____ (*search*) investigativa en Internet.

2. Es importante _____ (*to save*) el trabajo para que no lo pierdas.

3. No puedo acordarme de mi _____ (*password*).

4. Tengo que ir a la oficina para _____ (*to print*) los documentos.

5. El _____ (*program*) me ha ayudado mucho con el presupuesto.

ANSWERS: I. 1. G, 2. I, 3. B, 4. H, 5. F, 6. J, 7. C, 8. A, 9. D, 10. E
II. 1. HICE UNA **BÚSQUEDA** INVESTIGATIVA EN INTERNET.
2. ES IMPORTANTE **GUARDAR** EL TRABAJO PARA QUE NO LO PIERDAS.
3. NO PUEDO ACORDARME DE MI **CONTRASEÑA**. 4. TENGO QUE IR A LA OFICINA PARA **IMPRIMIR** LOS DOCUMENTOS. 5. EL **PROGRAMA** ME HA AYUDADO MUCHO CON EL PRESUPUESTO.

Sports & Leisure

Deportes y diversión

SPORTS

Deportes

SPORTS NOUNS—GENERAL

el juego	*game*
el partido	*match, game*
el período	*period*
el set	*set*
el medio tiempo	*half time*
el tiempo completo	*full time*
el campeonato	*championship*
el torneo	*tournament*
la copa	*cup*
el trofeo	*trophy*
el primer lugar	*first place*
el segundo lugar	*second place*
el tercer lugar	*third place*
el último lugar	*last place*
el penalti	*penalty*

SPORTS NOUNS—PLACES

el estadio	*stadium, arena*
el terreno	*ground*
el campo	*field, pitch*

SPORTS NOUNS—PEOPLE

el/la jugador/a	*player*
el equipo	*team*
el/la entrenador/a	*coach*
el/la árbitro/a	*referee*
el/la aficionado/a	*fan*
el/la animador/a	*cheerleader*
el/la campeón/campeona	*champion*

SPORTS VERBS

jugar	*to play*
ganar tantos	*to score*
tantear	*to keep score*
ganar	*to win*
perder	*to lose*
empatar	*to tie*

Words In Use

El **juego** de ayer fue el más emocionante de la serie. *Yesterday's game was the most exciting in the series.*

Ahora el **equipo** se encuentra en el **segundo lugar**. *The team is now in second place.*

El **estadio** estaba lleno a capacidad. *The stadium was full to capacity.*

El **torneo** termina la semana que viene. *The tournament ends next week.*

El **campeonato** se lleva a cabo cada cuatro años. *The championship takes place every four years.*

El **equipo** brasileño **ganó** el **trofeo** el año pasado. *The Brazilian team won the trophy last year.*

SOCCER

Fútbol

SOCCER NOUNS—GENERAL

el terreno	*ground*
el campo	*pitch*
el gol	*goal*
el travesaño	*crossbar*
el larguero	*crossbar*
la red	*net*
el balón	*ball*
la raya de la meta	*goal line*
el área de la meta	*penalty area*
el tiro	*kick, shot*
el inicio del partido	*kick off*
el puntapié	*kick off*
el saque de esquina	*corner kick*
el saque de banda	*throw-in*
el corner	*corner*
la internada	*tackle*
el tiro penal	*penalty kick*

el tiro libre	*free kick*
la tarjeta roja	*red card*
la tarjeta amarilla	*yellow card*
el medio tiempo	*half time*
el tiempo completo	*full time*
el descuento	*injury time*
el tiempo extra	*overtime*
el resultado final	*final score*

SOCCER NOUNS—PEOPLE

el/la jugador/a	*player*
el/la delantero/a	*striker*
el/la delantero/a	*forward*
el/la centrocampista	*midfield player*
el defensor	*defender*
el/la portero/a	*goalkeeper*
el equipo	*team*
el/la entrenador/a	*coach*
el/la árbitro/a	*referee*
el juez de línea	*linesman*
la defensa	*defense*
el gamberro	*hooligan*
la liga	*league*

SOCCER ADJECTIVES

| fuera de lugar | *off-side* |

SOCCER VERBS

dar una patada	*to kick*
cabecear	*to head*
lanzar	*to throw*
sacar	*to throw-in*
pasar	*to pass*
expulsar a un/a jugador/a	*to send a player off*

SOCCER EXPRESSIONS

| ¡Mano! | *Handball!* |
| ¡Pásame! | *Pass it to me!* |

Words In Use

El **fútbol** es muy popular en Sudamérica y Europa. *Soccer is very popular in South America and Europe.*

El primer **gol** ocurrió en los primeros cinco minutos de juego. *The first goal happened within the first five minutes of the game.*

El **portero** interceptó el balón. *The goalkeeper blocked the ball.*

BASEBALL
Béisbol

BASEBALL NOUNS—GENERAL

la pelota	ball
el bate	bat
el guante	glove
el casco	helmet
el cuadro	infield
los jardines	outfield
la base	base
la plancha de la base	home plate
la primera base	first base
la segunda base	second base
la tercera base	third base
el strike	strike
la carrera	run
el jonrón	home run
la entrada	inning
el refugio	dugout
los cacahuetes	peanuts

BASEBALL NOUNS—PEOPLE

el/la bateador/a	batter
el/la lanzador/a	pitcher
el/la receptor/a	catcher
el/la shortstop	shortstop
el/la primera base	first baseman
el/la segunda base	second baseman
el/la tercera base	third baseman
el/la jardinero/a derecho/a	right-fielder
el/la jardinero/a centro/a	center-fielder
el/la jardinero/a izquierdo/a	left-fielder

BASEBALL ADJECTIVES

fuera de juego	*out*
a salvo	*safe*
nulo	*foul*

BASEBALL VERBS

batear	*to bat*
pegar	*to hit*
poncharse	*to strike out*
lanzar	*to pitch*
tirar	*to throw*
coger*	*to catch*
agarrar	*to catch*
dar una vuelta a las bases	*to round the bases*
seguir a alguien	*to tag*

Words In Use

El **béisbol** es un juego muy americano. *Baseball is a very American game.*

El jugador estrella tuvo dos **jonrones** en el mismo juego. *The star player had two homeruns in the same game.*

Le **pegó** tan duro a la pelota que rompió el **bate**. *He hit the ball so hard that he broke the bat.*

Tenían las **bases** llenas. *They had all bases full.*

FOOTBALL (AMERICAN)
Fútbol americano

FOOTBALL NOUNS

el gol de campo	*field goal*
el puntapié de gol	*goal kick*
el ensayo	*touchdown*
la yarda	*yard*
el/la mariscal de campo	*quarterback*
el/la esquinero/a	*cornerback*
el/la apoyador/a	*linebacker*
los/las receptores/as	*receivers*

FOOTBALL VERBS

dar una patada	*to kick*
pasear en batea	*to punt*

* Coger *has a vulgar meaning in some Latin American countries.*

lanzar	to throw
tirar	to toss
ir detrás	to tailgate

Words In Use

A ella no le gusta el **fútbol americano**; le parece violento. *She doesn't like American football, she thinks it's violent.*

Fue derribado en las últimas **yardas**. *He was knocked down on the last few yards.*

El **mariscal de campo** pesa doscientas cincuenta libras. *The quarterback weighs two hundred and fifty pounds.*

BASKETBALL

Baloncesto

BASKETBALL NOUNS

la canasta	basket
la red	net
el balón	ball
la cancha	court
el/la pívot	center
el/la escolta	guard
el/la alero	forward
el tiro libre	free-throw
la línea de tiros libres	free-throw line
la línea de tres puntos	three-point line
el rebote	rebound
la asistencia	assist

BASKETBALL VERBS

rebotar	to bounce
driblar	to dribble
lanzar	to shoot
saltar	to jump
correr con la pelota	to travel

Words In Use

El **baloncesto** es mi deporte favorito. *Basketball is my favorite sport.*

Tengo que practicar a **lanzar** el balón. *I have to practice shooting the ball.*

La **canasta** está muy alta para el niño. *The basket is too high for the boy.*

GOLF
Golf

GOLF NOUNS

las pelotas de golf	*balls*
el caddie	*caddy*
los palos	*clubs*
la bandera	*flag*
el campo de golf	*golf course*
el prado	*green*
el hoyo	*hole*
el hierro	*iron*

GOLF VERBS

conducir	*to drive*
golpear la pelota	*to putt*
dar el primer golpe	*to tee off*

Words In Use

Le voy a comprar a mi padre un **palo de golf**. *I'm getting my father a new golf club.*

Ese centro turístico tiene un **campo de golf** estupendo. *That resort has a wonderful golf course.*

TENNIS AND PING-PONG
Tenis y tenis de mesa

TENNIS AND PING-PONG NOUNS

el revés	*backhand*
el drive	*forehand*
el globo	*lob*
el lob	*lob*
el cero	*love*
la red	*net*
la raqueta	*racket, paddle*
el intercambio	*rally*
la servida de pelota	*serve*
la volea	*volley*
la pelota	*ping-pong ball*
el tenis de mesa	*ping-pong*
el ping-pong	*ping-pong*
la mesa	*table*

TENNIS AND PING-PONG VERBS

bolear por alto	*to lob*
lanzar un globo	*to lob*
intercambiar	*to rally*
servir la bola	*to serve*
volear	*to volley*

Words In Use

Ella lleva jugando al **tenis** desde que era niña. *She's been playing tennis since she was a young girl.*

Su mejor destreza es la **servida de la pelota**. *Her best skill is her serve.*

En la sala de juegos tengo una **mesa** de **ping-pong**. *I have a ping-pong table in the family room.*

Tengo que comprarme una **raqueta** nueva. *I have to buy a new paddle.*

VOLLEYBALL

Voleibol

VOLLEYBALL NOUNS

la red	*net*
el balón	*ball*

VOLLEYBALL VERBS

sacar	*to serve*
dar vueltas	*to rotate*
clavar	*to spike*
poner	*to set, to place*
colocar	*to set*
chocar	*to bump*

Words In Use

Siempre que vamos a la playa jugamos **voleibol**. *Everytime we go to the beach, we play volleyball.*

¿A quién le toca **sacar**? *Whose turn is it to serve?*

HOCKEY

Hockey

HOCKEY NOUNS

la mascarilla	*facemask*
la red	*net*
el período	*period*

el puck	*puck*
el disco	*puck*
los patines	*skates*
el palo	*stick*

HOCKEY VERBS

jugar bruscamente	*to play rough*
lanzar	*to shoot*

Words In Use

¿Cuál es tu equipo de **hockey** favorito? *What's your favorite hockey team?*

Lanzó el **disco** a una velocidad increíble. *He shot the puck at an incredible speed.*

¿Hace falta un tipo especial de **patines** para jugar al **hockey**? *Do you need a special type of skates to play hockey?*

ICE-SKATING

Patinaje sobre hielo

ICE-SKATING NOUNS

el hielo	*ice*
la pista de hielo	*rink*
los patines de hielo	*ice skates*
la rutina	*routine*
los pares	*pairs*
la vuelta	*spin*
la espiral	*spiral*
la música	*music*
el disfraz	*costume*
el traje	*costume*
los jueces	*judges*

ICE-SKATING VERBS

patinar sobre hielo	*to ice-skate*
girar	*to spin*

Words In Use

Los **jueces** no vieron la perfección de su **rutina**. *The judges didn't see how perfect their routine was.*

La **música** que usaron fue muy apropiada. *The music that they used was very appropriate.*

SWIMMING AND DIVING

Natación y salto de trampolín

SWIMMING AND DIVING NOUNS

el estilo libre	*freestyle*
la brazada de espalda	*backstroke*
la brazada de pecho	*breaststroke*
la brazada de mariposa	*butterfly*
la brazada de perro	*doggy paddle*
la piscina olímpica	*olympic size pool*
la piscina	*swimming pool*
el salto de trampolín	*diving*
el clavado	*diving*
el trampolín	*diving board*
el coletazo	*flip*
la pica	*pike*
la salpicadura	*splash*
el pliegue	*tuck*

SWIMMING AND DIVING VERBS

nadar	*to swim*
rebotar	*to bounce*
dar vueltas	*to flip*

Words In Use

La **natación** es un deporte muy completo. *Swimming is a very thorough sport.*

Hay una **piscina olímpica** cerca de mi casa. *There's an olympic sized pool close to my house.*

Me gusta mucho mirar el **salto de trampolín** por televisión. *I like to watch diving on television.*

El **trampolín** de mi piscina no es muy alto. *The diving board in my pool is not too high.*

TRACK AND FIELD

Atletismo

TRACK AND FIELD NOUNS

la carrera	*race*
el maratón	*marathon*
la carrera de relevos	*relay race*
la batuta	*baton*

la valla	hurdle
el obstáculo	hurdle
el salto largo	long jump
el salto alto	high jump
el salto de pértiga	pole vault
el lanzamiento de pesas	shot put
el disco	discus
la jabalina	javelin

TRACK AND FIELD VERBS

correr	to run
esprintar	to sprint
correr a toda velocidad	to sprint
saltar los obstáculos	to hurdle
saltar	to jump
pasar	to pass
tirar	to throw
arrojar	to throw

Words In Use

El **maratón** de la ciudad de Nueva York se celebra en noviembre. *The New York City marathon is in November.*

Mi hermano era campeón universitario de **salto largo**. *My brother was a college champion in long jump.*

GYMNASTICS
Gimnasia

GYMNASTICS NOUNS

la voltereta	tumble
la voltereta sobre las manos	handspring
la voltereta lateral	cartwheel
la rueda	cartwheel
la voltereta en el aire	flip
las anillas	rings
la barra fija	balance beam
el curling	curling

GYMNASTICS VERBS

dar volteretas	to tumble
dar la vuelta	to flip
mantener el equilibrio	to balance

Words In Use

Es muy difícil **mantener el equilibrio** en la **barra fija**. *It's difficult to maintain balance on the balance beam.*

Mi ejercicio favorito de **gimnasia** son las **anillas**. *My favorite exercise in gymnastics is the rings.*

HORSEBACK RIDING AND HORSE RACING

Equitación e hípica

HOREBACK RIDING AND HORSE RACING NOUNS

el caballo	*horse*
la hípica	*horse racing*
la equitación	*horseback riding*
el/la jockey	*jockey*
el/la jinete/ta	*rider*
la carrera	*race*
la pista	*track*
el hipódromo	*course*
la silla de montar	*saddle*
el estribo	*stirrup*
las espuelas	*spurs*
la brida	*bridle*
la rienda	*rein*
el freno	*bit*
las anteojeras	*blinders*
el látigo	*whip*

HORSEBACK RIDING AND HORSE RACING VERBS

trotar	*to trot*
ir al trote	*to trot*
ir a medio galope	*to canter*
galopar	*to gallop*
saltar	*to jump*
mostrar un caballo	*to show a horse*

Words In Use

Mi padre es un gran aficionado de la **hípica**. *My father is a big horse racing fan.*

Los domingos le gusta mucho ver las **carreras**. *On Sundays he likes to go see the races.*

Su **caballo** favorito ha sido campeón desde hace dos años. *His favorite horse has been a champion for two years.*

EXTREME SPORTS
Deportes arriesgados

los deportes arriesgados	*extreme sports*
los deportes extremos	*extreme sports*
el patinaje en línea	*rollerblading*
el monopatinaje	*skateboarding*
el snowboarding	*snowboarding*
el salto elástico	*bungee jumping*
el alpinismo	*mountain climbing (in the Alps)*
el andinismo	*mountain climbing (in the Andes)*
la espeleología	*spelunking*
el parasailing	*parasailing*
el esquí con paracaídas	*parasailing*
el paracaidismo	*skydiving*

Words In Use

En el verano me gusta mucho hacer **alpinismo**. *I like to go mountain climbing in the summer.*

Nunca he practicado el **paracaidismo**; me daría mucho miedo. *I've never done skydiving; I would be very scared.*

En el parque hay muchos jóvenes practicando el **patinaje en línea**. *There are many young people rollerblading in the park.*

OUTDOOR ACTIVITIES
Actividades al aire libre

OUTDOOR ACTIVITY NOUNS

la piragua	*canoe*
la canoa	*canoe*
el piragüismo	*canoeing*
el balsismo	*rafting*
la pesca	*fishing*
el sedal	*fishing line*
la caña de pescar	*fishing rod*
el anzuelo	*bait, hook*
la caza	*hunting, game*
los animales de caza	*game*
la pistola	*gun*
el rifle	*rifle*
la trampa	*trap*
la observación de aves	*bird watching*

OUTDOOR ACTIVITY VERBS

hacer piragüismo	*to canoe*
remar con canalete	*to paddle*
ir en balsa	*to raft*
pescar	*to fish*
ir de pesca	*to go fishing, to fish*
cazar	*to hunt*
poner trampas	*to trap*
atrapar	*to trap*

Words In Use

Vamos a **ir de pesca** en el yate de mi primo. *We're going fishing on my cousin's yacht.*

Me gusta mucho **pescar** en el Caribe. *I like to go fishing in the Caribbean.*

Me acabo de comprar una nueva **caña de pescar**. *I just bought a new fishing rod.*

¿Tienes los **anzuelos** listos? *Do you have the bait ready?*

SPORTS EQUIPMENT
Equipo deportivo

la pelota	*ball*
el balón	*ball*
el bate	*bat*
la tabla	*board*
el monopatín	*skateboard*
el snowboard	*snowboard*
la tablanieve	*snowboard*
la tabla de surf	*surfboard*
la copa	*cup*
la argolla	*hoop*
el aro	*hoop*
la red	*net*
el paracaídas	*parachute*
el puck	*puck*
el disco	*puck*
la cuerda	*rope*
el casco protector	*helmet*
las almohadillas	*pads*
la hombrera	*shoulder pads*

la codera	*elbow pads*
el protector de codos	*elbow pads*
la rodillera	*knee pads*
el protector de rodilla	*knee pads*
la espinillera	*shin guards*
el suspensorio	*jock strap*

Words In Use

Si vas a patinar, debes usar **rodilleras**. *If you're going skating you should wear your knee pads.*

Ten cuidado cuando patines sin **coderas**. *Be careful when you skate without your elbow pads.*

El **paracaídas** abrió enseguida. *The parachute opened rather quickly.*

¿Ya pusiste la **red** para jugar voleibol? *Did you put up the net for our volleyball game?*

SPORTS ADJECTIVES
Adjetivos deportivos

amistoso	*friendly*
amateur	*amateur*
aficionado	*amateur*
profesional	*professional*
atlético	*athletic*
brusco	*rough*
nulo	*foul*
sucio	*foul*
fuera de juego	*out*
fresco	*fresh*
fuerte	*strong*
alto	*tall*
ágil	*agile*
móvil	*mobile*
grácil	*graceful*
elegante	*graceful*
ligero	*quick*
rápido	*fast, quick*
desafiante	*challenging*
motivado	*motivated*
desmotivado	*unmotivated*

| con falta de motivación | *unmotivated* |
| perezoso | *lazy* |

NOTE: More adjectives related to Sports can be found in the General Descriptive Words category.

Words In Use

Es uno de los jugadores más **ágiles** del equipo. *He's one of the most agile players in the team.*

Es **elegante** y **grácil** en la pista. *He's graceful and fast on the field.*

Siempre fue un niño muy **atlético**. *He was always a very athletic child.*

Pienso que va a convertirse en un deportista **profesional** cuando crezca. *I think he'll be a professional player when he grows up.*

EXERCISE

Ejercicio

EXERCISE NOUNS—GENERAL

el gimnasio	*gym*
los abdominales	*sit-ups*
las flexiones de pecho	*push-ups*
las flexiones	*pull-ups*
la estera	*treadmill*
la bicicleta estacionaria	*stationary bicycle*
el entrenamiento con pesas	*strength training*
los aeróbicos	*aerobics*
la clase de baile	*dance class*
el yoga	*yoga*
el pilates	*pilates*
el vestuario	*locker room*

EXERCISE NOUNS—MUSCLES

los abdominales	*abdominals*
los bíceps	*biceps*
los tríceps	*triceps*
el tendón de la corva	*hamstring*
los pectorales	*pecs*
los glúteos	*glutes*

EXERCISE ADJECTIVES

sano	*in shape*
musculoso	*muscular*
sudado	*sweaty*

EXERCISE VERBS

hacer ejercicio	*to work out*
estar en forma	*to be fit, to be in shape*
trotar	*to jog*
hacer jogging	*to jog, to go jogging*
levantar pesas	*to lift weights*
sudar	*to sweat*
irse a la ducha	*to hit the showers*

Words In Use

Si haces ejercicio de la manera correcta, vas a **sudar** mucho. *If you work out correctly, you'll end up sweating.*

¿Haces **abdominales** después o antes del **aeróbico**? *Do you work your abdominals before or after doing aerobics?*

Él se ha puesto muy **musculoso** después de tanto **entrenamiento con pesas**. *He's gotten very muscular from all the strength training.*

Sí, pero siempre ha **estado en forma**. *Yes, but he's always been fit.*

HOBBIES, INTERESTS, AND GAMES
Pasatiempos, intereses y juegos

HOBBIES AND GAMES NOUNS

el tiempo libre	*free time*
los juegos de mesa	*board game*
las damas	*checkers*
el ajedrez	*chess*
los dados	*dice*
el póker	*poker*
las trivialidades	*trivia*
la payasada	*charades*
la farsa	*charades*
el escondite	*hide and seek*
el tejido	*knitting*
la pesca	*fishing*

HOBBIES AND GAMES ADJECTIVES

correcto	*correct*
incorrecto	*wrong/incorrect*

HOBBIES AND GAMES VERBS

jugar	*to play*
tirar los dados	*to roll the dice*

moverse	*to move*
dibujar	*to draw, to sketch*
hacer una pregunta	*to ask a question*
contestar una pregunta	*to answer a question*
ganar	*to win*
perder	*to lose*
atar	*to tie*
divertirse	*to have fun*

Words In Use

Para jugar al **ajedrez** es importante la buena concentración. *It's important to have concentration when playing chess.*

Esta noche nos vamos a reunir en casa de Marcos para **jugar juegos de mesa**. *We're meeting tonight in Mark's house to play board games.*

Siempre **gano** cuando **juego** con Elena. *I always win when I play with Elena.*

CARDS

Naipes

CARD NOUNS

el rey	*king*
la reina	*queen*
la sota	*jack*
el as	*ace*
la espada	*spade*
la mano	*hand*
la partida	*hand*
el palo	*suit*
la espada	*spade*
el corazón	*heart*
el trébol	*club*
el diamante	*diamond*
el póker	*poker*
el juego de flush	*flush*
el juego de flux	*flush*
el juego de full house	*full house*
el juego de vientiuna	*black jack*

CARD VERBS

repartir	*to deal*
rendirse	*to fold*
hacer trampa	*to cheat*

Words In Use

¡No **hagas trampa**! ¡Viste el **naipe**! *Don't cheat! You saw the card!*

Me queda todavía un **as** en esta **mano**. *I have an ace left in this hand.*

Tienes que sacar otro **naipe** del mismo **palo**. *You have to draw another card from the same suit.*

EXERCISES

I. Match the Spanish word on the left with the English word on the right.

1. el/la entrenador/a	A. *track*
2. lanzar	B. *to jump*
3. la pista de hielo	C. *swimming pool*
4. la pista	D. *match*
5. las damas	E. *coach*
6. la piscina	F. *goalkeeper*
7. saltar	G. *ice rink*
8. la cancha	H. *to pitch*
9. el partido	I. *court*
10. el/la portero/a	J. *checkers*

II. Fill in the blanks with the appropriate Spanish word.

1. Fue el _____ (*player*) más valioso dos años seguidos.

2. El _____ (*soccer*) es el deporte más popular en España, Argentina y Colombia.

3. Me tengo que comprar una _____ (*racket*) nueva.

4. Voy a poner la _____ (*net*) para poder jugar voleibol.

5. La _____ (*gymnastics*) es mi deporte favorito.

ANSWERS: I. 1. E, 2. H, 3. G, 4. A, 5. J, 6. C, 7. B, 8. I, 9. D, 10. F
II. 1. FUE EL **JUGADOR** MÁS VALIOSO DOS AÑOS SEGUIDOS. 2. EL **FÚTBOL** ES EL DEPORTE MÁS POPULAR EN ESPAÑA, ARGENTINA Y COLOMBIA. 3. ME TENGO QUE COMPRAR UNA **RAQUETA** NUEVA. 4. VOY A PONER LA **RED** PARA PODER JUGAR VOLEIBOL. 5. LA **GIMNASIA** ES MI DEPORTE FAVORITO.

Entertainment & Media

Entretenimiento y medios de comunicación

FILM AND THEATER

Cine y teatro

FILM AND THEATER NOUNS—GENERAL

la producción	*production*
la representación	*performance*
la función	*performance*
los billetes	*tickets*
los boletos	*tickets*
las entradas	*tickets*
la crítica	*review, critique*
la reseña	*review*
el tema	*theme*
la música	*music*
el musical	*musical*
la partitura	*score*
la iluminación	*lighting*
el plató	*set*
el decorado	*set, decoration*
el foro	*set*

FILM AND THEATER NOUNS—PEOPLE

el/la director/a	*director*
el/la escritor/a	*writer*
el/la productor/a	*producer*
el/la operador/a de cámara	*cinematographer*
el actor	*actor*
la actriz	*actress*
el/la músico/a	*musician*
el/la bailarín/bailarina	*dancer*

el/la coreógrafo/a	*choreographer*
el/la director/a de iluminación	*lighting director*
el/la ingeniero/a de sonido	*sound engineer*
el equipo técnico	*technical team*

FILM NOUNS

el cine	*cinema*
la película	*film, movie*
la filmación	*filming*
el rodaje	*filming*
el guión	*screenplay, script*
la película extranjera	*foreign film*
los subtítulos	*subtitles*

THEATER NOUNS

el teatro	*theater*
el escenario	*set, stage*
los bastidores	*wings*
el techo	*rafters*
la unión de las columnas y los soportes del techo	*rafters*
el telón	*curtain*
la dirección escénica	*stage direction*
el ensayo	*rehearsal*
el monólogo	*monologue*
el soliloquio	*soliloquy*

FILM AND THEATER ADJECTIVES

cinemático	*cinematic*
dramático	*dramatic*
melodramático	*melodramatic*
cómico	*comedic*
extranjero	*foreign*

FILM AND THEATER VERBS

tocar	*to perform*
actuar	*to act, to perform*
dirigir (una orquesta)	*to conduct (an orchestra)*
cantar	*to sing*
bailar	*to dance*
dirigir	*to direct*

causar una emoción	*to emote*
meterse en un personaje	*to get into character*
rodar	*to film*
filmar	*to film*
proyectar	*to project*

Words In Use

Después de muchos años de ser **actor**, ha decidido **dirigir** su primera **película**. *After being an actor for many years, he decided to direct his first film.*

El **rodaje** comienza la semana que viene en Toronto. *Filming begins next week in Toronto.*

Él ha conseguido reunir un **equipo técnico** de primera clase. *He managed to get a first class technical team.*

El **guión** fue escrito por su mejor amigo. *The screenplay was written by his best friend.*

Disfruto mucho viendo **películas extranjeras**. *I enjoy watching foreign films.*

Yo también, pero no voy mucho porque a mi marido no le gusta leer **subtítulos**. *Me too, but I don't go very often because my husband doesn't like to read subtitles.*

MUSIC

Música

MUSIC NOUNS—GENERAL

la música	*music*
la canción	*song*
la canción	*tune*
la partitura	*score*
la nota	*note*
la voz	*voice*
el ensayo	*rehearsal*
el concierto	*concert*
la representación	*performance*
la actuación	*performance*
la grabación	*recording*
la producción	*production*
la posproducción	*post-production*

MUSIC NOUNS—PEOPLE

| el/la músico/a | *musician* |
| la soprano | *soprano* |

el alto	*alto*
el contralto	*contralto*
el tenor	*tenor*
el bajo	*bass*
el/la cantante de cámara	*chamber singer*
el coro	*choir, chorus*
el/la bailarín/bailarina	*dancer*
el/la coreógrafo/a	*choreographer*
el/la director/a	*conductor*
el/la guitarrista	*guitarist*
el/la productor/a	*producer*

Film and Theater

Music

Musical
Instruments

Literature

Art

Television

Radio

Newspapers and
Magazines

MUSIC NOUNS—TYPES OF MUSIC

el pop	*pop*
el rock	*rock*
la música country	*country*
el hip-hop	*hip-hop*
el rap	*rap*
el jazz	*jazz*
la música clásica	*classical*
la ópera	*opera*
el musical	*musical*

MUSIC VERBS

tocar	*to perform, to play*
interpretar	*to perform*
componer	*to compose*
afinar	*to tune*
cantar	*to sing*
hacer rap	*to rap*
grabar	*to record*

NOTE: More words related to Music can be found in the Hearing section of this book.

Words In Use

La música **hip-hop** ha tenido mucha popularidad en los últimos años. *Hip-hop has gained a lot of popularity in the last few years.*

La **cantante** tiene una **voz** inconfundible. *The singer has a distinctive voice.*

Empezó como **cantante** de **música western**, pero ahora **canta** música **pop**. *She started as a country singer but now she sings mostly pop.*

Sus **canciones** suelen ser muy pegajosas. *Her songs are usually very catchy.*

También **grabó** un disco de música **jazz**. *She also recorded a jazz album.*

Nunca le ha interesado el **rap** o el **hip-hop**. *She was never interested in rap or hip-hop.*

MUSICAL INSTRUMENTS
Instrumentos musicales

STRING

el violín	*violin*
la viola	*viola*
el violoncelo	*cello*
el bajo de cuerdas	*string bass*
la guitarra	*guitar*
la guitarra eléctrica	*electric guitar*
la guitarra acústica	*acoustic guitar*
el bajo eléctrico	*electric bass*
el arpa	*harp*

STRING/PERCUSSION

el piano	*piano*
el clavicémbalo	*harpsichord*

WIND

la flauta	*flute*
el oboe	*oboe*
el clarinete	*clarinet*
el bajón	*bassoon*

BRASS

la trompeta	*trumpet*
el corno francés	*French horn*
el trombón	*trombone*
la tuba	*tuba*

PERCUSSION

los tambores	*drums*
la batería	*drums*
el tambor con bordón	*snare*
los timbales	*timpani*
el bombo	*bass drum*

el címbalo	*cymbals*
los platillos	*cymbals*
el xilófono	*xylophone*

OTHER

el acordeón	*accordion*
la filarmónica	*accordion (Mexico)*
la armónica	*harmonica*
el sintetizador	*synthesizer*

Words In Use

Mi abuela siempre quiso que yo aprendiera a tocar el **piano**. *My grandmother always wanted me to play the piano.*

Mi mayor interés era aprender a tocar la **guitarra**. *My main interest was to learn how to play the guitar.*

Tengo boletos para un concierto de **violines** en el Carnegie Hall. *I have tickets for a violin concert in Carnegie Hall.*

La canción mejoró mucho con el sonido de la **trompeta**. *The song improved a lot when they added trumpets.*

El uso de **sintetizadores** le da un aire contemporáneo a la composición. *The synthesizers give the song a very contemporary feel.*

LITERATURE
Literatura

LITERATURE NOUNS—GENERAL

el libro	*book*
el título	*title*
la cubierta	*cover*
la cubierta de libro	*book jacket*
la sobrecubierta	*jacket*
el libro de tapa dura	*hard cover*
el libro de bolsillo	*paperback*
el libro en rústica	*paperback*
la trama	*plot*
la exposición	*exposition*
el desenlace	*denouement*
el personaje	*character*
el bloqueo mental al tratar de escribir	*writer's block*
el contenido	*contents*
el preámbulo	*foreword*
el prefacio	*preface*

el prólogo	prologue
la introducción	introduction
el capítulo	chapter
el cuerpo	body
la nota al calce	footnote
el apéndice	appendix
el glosario	glossary
el índice	index
las páginas finales	end papers
el texto	text
la fundición	font
el tipo de letra	typeface
la negrita	bold type
la cursiva	italics
la bastardilla	italics
el párrafo	paragraph
la oración	sentence
el arte	art
la ilustración	illustration
los márgenes	margins
la página	page
el número de página	page number

LITERATURE NOUNS—GENRES

la ficción	fiction
la literatura no novelesca	non-fiction
la prosa	prose
la poesía	poetry
el poema	poem
el verso	verse
la novela	novel
el cuento corto	short story
el clásico	classic
el misterio	mystery
el horror	horror
el romance	romance
la literatura barata	pulp fiction
la ciencia ficción	science fiction
la literatura de guerra	war fiction
la epopeya	epic

LITERATURE NOUNS—PUBLISHING

la industria editorial	publishing
el manuscrito	manuscript
la lista delantera	front-list
el catálogo antiguo	backlist
el éxito de ventas	best-seller
el best-seller	best-seller
el exitazo	blockbuster
el éxito de taquilla	blockbuster
la librería	book store
la impresión	printing, imprint
los derechos de autor	copyright
el copyright	copyright
la edición	edition
la encuadernación	binding
el tamaño reducido	trim size
la propaganda	blurb
el anuncio posterior	back ad
el isbn	ISBN
el número de identificación internacional	international standard book number (ISBN)

LITERATURE NOUNS—PEOPLE

el/la autor/a	author
el/la escritor/a	writer
el/la redactor/a	editor
la editorial	publisher
el/la traductor/a	translator
el/la ilustrador/a	illustrator

LITERATURE ADJECTIVES

épico	epic
basura	pulp

LITERATURE VERBS

escribir	to write
redactar	to edit
corregir pruebas	to proofread
traducir	to translate
publicar	to publish

imprimir	to print
dedicar	to dedicate

Words In Use

La **novela** tiene más de seiscientas **páginas**. *The novel is over six hundred pages long.*

El **prólogo** da un trasfondo histórico de la **trama**. *The prologue gives a historical background to the plot.*

El **libro** fue el mayor **éxito de ventas** del año pasado. *The book was last year's best-seller.*

La **editorial** no esperaba que iba a tener tanto éxito. *The publisher was not expecting it to be such a major success.*

El libro ya va por su tercera **edición**. *The book already has three editions.*

Lo están **traduciendo** en cuatro idiomas. *It's being translated into four languages.*

Piensan que va a ser un **exitazo** mundial. *They expect it to be a world-wide blockbuster.*

ART

Arte

ART NOUNS—GENERAL

la pintura	paint
los óleos	oils
la tinta	ink
los pasteles	pastels
la pluma	pen
el bolígrafo	pen
el lápiz	pencil
el pincel	paintbrush
el cuadro	painting
el lienzo	canvas
el caballete	easel
la escultura	sculpture
la instalación	installation
la fotografía	photography
el arte en vídeo	video art
la puesta en escena	performance art
la colección	collection
la crítica	review

ART NOUNS—PLACES

el museo	*museum*
el museo de arte	*art museum*
la galería de arte	*art gallery*
la subasta	*auction*
la exhibición	*exhibition*

ART NOUNS—PEOPLE

el/la artista	*artist*
el/la pintor/a	*painter*
el/la fotógrafo/a	*photographer*

ART NOUNS—STYLES

el realismo	*realism*
el surrealismo	*surrealism*
el bodegón	*still life*
el romanticismo	*romanticism*
el expresionismo	*expressionism*
el impresionismo	*impressionism*
el modernismo	*modernism*
el posmodernismo	*post-modernism*

ART ADJECTIVES

artístico	*artistic*
bello	*beautiful*

ART VERBS

pintar	*to paint*
esculpir	*to sculpt*
tallar	*to carve*
fotografiar	*to photograph*
exponer	*to exhibit*
subastar	*to auction*
modelar	*to model*

NOTE: More words related to Art can be found in the Sight section of this book.

Words In Use

El **cuadro** de Van Gogh fue **subastado** por diez millones de dólares. *Van Gogh's painting was auctioned for ten million dollars.*

El **pintor** tiene muchos seguidores en todo el mundo. *The painter has many fans around the world.*

El **Museo** Metropolitano de Nueva York está planificando una **exhibición** de Cèzanne. *The Metropolitan Museum of New York is planning a Cèzanne exhibit.*

El **Museo** de Orsay tiene una impresionante **colección** de **impresionismo**. *The Orsay Museum has an impressive collection of impressionism.*

La **exhibición** del MOMA recibió buena **crítica**, pero poco público. *The exhibit at the MOMA got very good reviews but few people.*

TELEVISION

Televisión

TELEVISION NOUNS — GENERAL

el televisor	*television*
la televisión	*television*
el canal	*channel*
el control remoto	*remote control*
el mando a distancia	*remote control*
la recepción	*reception*
la antena	*antenna*
el cable	*cable*
el satélite	*satellite*
la estática	*static*
la cámara	*camera*
la producción	*production*
la posproducción	*post-production*

TELEVISION NOUNS — TYPES OF SHOWS

el programa	*program*
la comedia	*sitcom*
las telenovelas	*soap operas*
los culebrones	*soap operas*
el drama	*drama*
las noticias	*news*
el reportaje central	*feature story*
el documental	*documentary*
el programa de juegos	*game show*
los dibujos animados	*cartoon*
el comercial	*commercial*
la publicidad	*commercial*
el programa grabado	*pre-recorded program*

TELEVISION NOUNS—PEOPLE

el/la directora/a	*director*
el/la productor/a	*producer*
el actor	*actor*
la actriz	*actress*
el anfitrión	*host*
la anfitriona	*hostess*
el/la presentador/a	*anchor*
el/la periodista	*reporter*
el/la reportero/a	*reporter*
el/la corresponsal	*correspondent*
el/la escritor/a	*writer*
el/la técnico/a	*technician*
la programadora	*broadcaster*

21

Film and Theater

Music

Musical
Instruments

Literature

Art

Television

Radio

Newspapers and
Magazines

TELEVISION ADJECTIVES

divertidísimo	*hilarious*
graciosísimo	*hilarious*
melodramático	*melodramatic*
triste	*sad*
en vivo	*live*
en directo	*live*

TELEVISION VERBS

mirar	*to watch*
transmitir	*to broadcast*

Words In Use

No te debes perder el **documental** acerca de la Guerra Civil. *You can't miss that documentary on the Civil War.*

Lo van a volver a **transmitir** el martes por la noche. *It will be broadcast again on Tuesday night.*

¿Qué tipo de **programa** de televisión prefieres? *What's your favorite type of television program?*

Me gusta mucho ver las **comedias** con mi familia. *I love to watch sitcoms with my family.*

El **corresponsal** está **transmitiendo en vivo** desde el campo de batalla. *The correspondent is broadcasting live from the battlefield.*

RADIO

Radio

RADIO NOUNS—GENERAL

la radio	*radio*
la estación de radio	*radio station*
la antena	*antenna*
el dial	*dial*
el receptor	*receiver*
la recepción	*reception*
la estática	*static*
la interferencia	*interference*
la música	*music*
la lista de canciones	*playlist*
la rotación	*rotation*
la lista de éxitos	*charts*
los diez éxitos principales	*top ten*
las noticias	*news*
el comentario	*commentary*
la llamada telefónica	*phone-in*
la dedicatoria	*dedication*
la producción	*production*
los efectos especiales	*sound effect*

RADIO NOUNS—TYPES OF BROADCASTS

la radio de difusión pública	*public radio*
la estación de comentarios y opiniones	*talk radio*
los clásicos	*oldies*
la música suave	*easy listening*
la música suave	*light*
la onda larga	*long wave*
la onda corta	*short wave*
la emisión de radio	*radio play*

RADIO NOUNS—PEOPLE

el/la productor/a	*producer*
el/la discjockey	*disc jockey (DJ)*
el/la pinchadiscos	*disc jockey (DJ)*
el/la orador/a	*speaker*
el/la invitado/a especial	*speaker*

el/la corresponsal	*correspondent*
el/la técnico/a	*technician*
la programadora	*broadcaster*

RADIO ADJECTIVES

AM	*AM*
FM	*FM*
fácil de escuchar	*easy listening*

RADIO VERBS

escuchar	*to listen*
pedir	*to request*
sintonizar	*to tune in*

NOTE: More words related to Radio can be found in the Music and Hearing sections of this book.

Words In Use

Cuando estoy conduciendo me gusta escuchar **música suave**. *I like to listen to light music when I'm driving.*

Yo oigo **radio de difusión pública** porque las **noticias** son muy interesantes. *I like to listen to public radio because they have interesting news stories.*

Esta noche tienen un **invitado** especial para discutir finanzas. *They're bringing a guest speaker tonight to talk about personal finances.*

Nunca he **pedido** una canción por la **radio**. *I've never called to request a song on the radio.*

NEWSPAPERS AND MAGAZINES
Periódicos y revistas

NEWSPAPER AND MAGAZINE NOUNS—GENERAL

el periodismo	*journalism*
el periódico	*newspaper*
el periódico dominical	*Sunday paper*
el periódico ancho	*broadsheet newspaper*
la prensa amarilla	*tabloid*
la revista	*magazine*
el artículo	*article, piece, story*
la fecha límite	*deadline*
la fecha tope	*deadline*
la inspección de datos	*fact check*
la edición	*editing*
la redacción	*editing*

21

Film and Theater

Music

Musical Instruments

Literature

Art

Television

Radio/ Newspapers and Magazines

la sección de arte	*arts section*
la sección de estilo	*style section*
la sección de bienes raíces	*real estate section*
la sección de inmobiliaria	*real estate section*
las tiras cómicas	*comics*
el quiosco de periódicos y revistas	*newsstand*
la suscripción	*subscription*
la tirada	*circulation*
la circulación	*circulation*

NEWSPAPER AND MAGAZINE NOUNS—LAYOUT

el diseño	*layout*
la mancheta	*masthead*
el titular	*caption, headline*
el subtítulo	*byline*
el título	*caption*
la clave	*legend*
la leyenda	*legend*
el artículo de doble página	*double-page spread*
la portada	*cover*
la plantilla	*template*
el margen	*margin*
la columna	*column*
el borde	*border*
el recuadro	*box*
el color	*color*
la foto a colores	*color photo*
los puntos por pulgada	*dots per inch*
el cuerpo	*body*
el párrafo	*paragraph*
la oración	*sentence*
el texto	*text*
el tipo de letra	*font*
el tipo de letra	*typeface*
la negrita	*bold type*
la cursiva	*italics*
la bastardilla	*italics*
la cruz	*dagger*

la cruz doble	*double dagger*
los puntos	*bullet points*
las mayúsculas	*caps (capital letters)*
la minúscula	*lowercase*
la página	*page*
el número de página	*page number*

NEWSPAPER AND MAGAZINE NOUNS—PEOPLE

el/la periodista	*journalist*
el/la escritor/a	*writer*
el/la columnista	*columnist*
el/la reportero/a	*reporter*
el/la editor/a	*editor, publisher*
el/la editor/a de textos	*editor, copy editor*
el/la corrector/a	*proofreader*

NEWSPAPER AND MAGAZINE ADJECTIVES

parcial	*biased*
imparcial	*unbiased*
exclusivo	*exclusive*
sensacionalista	*sensationalist*
liberal	*liberal*
conservador	*conservative*
satinado	*glossy*

NEWSPAPER AND MAGAZINE VERBS

redactar	*to edit*
editar	*to edit*
corregir	*to proofread*
fotografiar	*to photograph*
recortar	*to crop*
justificar	*to justify*
publicar	*to publish*
imprimir	*to print*
distribuir	*to distribute*
suscribirse	*to subscribe*
suspender la subscripción	*to unsubscribe*
echarle una ojeada a una revista	*to flip through a magazine*

Words In Use

Cuando era pequeño me gustaba mucho leer el **periódico**. *I used to like to read the newspaper when I was a child.*

Me gusta mucho leer la **sección de arte**. *I like to read the arts section.*

Tengo que mirar la **sección de inmobiliaria**. *I have to look at the real estate section.*

La revista tiene muchos **artículos** interesantes. *The magazine has very interesting articles.*

Me interesaría **suscribirme** a la revista. *I would like to subscribe to the magazine.*

El periódico tiene una gran **tirada**. *The newspaper has a large circulation.*

El otro periódico tiene **titulares** sensacionalistas. *The other newspaper has sensationalist headlines.*

EXERCISES

I. Match the Spanish word on the left with the English word on the right.

1. el telón	A. *to print*
2. la crítica	B. *tickets*
3. rodar	C. *curtain*
4. el ensayo	D. *review*
5. la oración	E. *rehearsal*
6. imprimir	F. *sentence*
7. la película	G. *to film*
8. los billetes	H. *writer*
9. el párrafo	I. *movie*
10. el/la escritor/a	J. *paragraph*

II. Fill in the blanks with the appropriate Spanish word.

1. Fue el _____ (*concert*) más emocionante que he visto.

2. A mi tía siempre le gusta _____ (*to sing*) en las fiestas.

3. El _____ (*author*) de novelas de misterio ahora escribe novelas policíacas.

4. Voy a terminar de leer la _____ (*novel*) hoy.

5. El _____ (*museum*) tiene una colección europea muy importante.

ANSWERS: I. 1. C 2. D, 3. G, 4. E, 5. F, 6. A, 7. I, 8. B, 9. J, 10. H
II. 1. FUE EL **CONCIERTO** MÁS EMOCIONANTE QUE HE VISTO. 2. A MI TÍA SIEMPRE LE GUSTA **CANTAR** EN LAS FIESTAS. 3. EL **AUTOR** DE NOVELAS DE MISTERIO AHORA ESCRIBE NOVELAS POLICÍACAS. 4. VOY A TERMINAR DE LEER LA **NOVELA** HOY. 5. EL **MUSEO** TIENE UNA COLECCIÓN EUROPEA MUY IMPORTANTE.

Vacation

Vacaciones

GENERAL VACATION TERMS
Términos generales sobre las vacaciones

GENERAL VACATION NOUNS

la playa	*beach*
el autobús	*tour bus*
el autocar	*tour bus*
las ruinas	*ruins*
el museo	*museum*
el crucero	*cruise ship*
el acuario	*aquarium*

GENERAL VACATION VERBS

relajarse	*to relax*
descansar	*to rest*

NOTE: More words related to Vacation can be found in other categories of this book, such as Transportation and Sports and Leisure.

Words In Use

Visité muchas **ruinas** antiguas en mi viaje a Egipto. *I visited many ancient ruins on my trip to Egypt.*

Este verano quiero pasarme dos semanas en la **playa**. *This summer I want to spend two weeks on the beach.*

Mis padres tomaron un **crucero** por el Mediterráneo el año pasado. *My parents took a cruise ship on the Mediterranean last year.*

Lo único que quiero hacer estas **vacaciones** es **descansar**. *The only thing I want to do on my vacation is to rest.*

AT THE BEACH
En la playa

BEACH NOUNS—NATURAL

el sol	*sun*
la arena	*sand*
el castillo de arena	*sand castle*
la concha marina	*seashell*

Vacation Vacaciones

las olas	*waves*
el oleaje	*surf*
la resaca	*surf, undertow*

BEACH NOUNS—HUMAN-RELATED

el bañador	*swim suit*
el traje de baño	*swim suit*
el/la bikini	*bikini*
el bañador impermeable	*wet suit*
la toalla	*towel*
las gafas de sol	*sunglasses*
la (loción, crema) protectora	*sunscreen*
el filtro solar	*sunscreen*
la loción para broncearse	*suntan lotion*
el balón de playa	*beach ball*
la tabla para el surfing	*surfboard*
la tabla hawaiana	*surfboard*

BEACH NOUNS—PEOPLE

el/la socorrista	*lifeguard*
el/la salvavidas	*lifeguard*

BEACH ADJECTIVES

soleado	*sunny*
arenoso	*sandy*
mojado	*wet*
con mucho oleaje	*wavy*
profundo	*deep*
llano, poco profundo	*shallow*

BEACH VERBS

tomar el sol	*to sunbathe*
hacer un castillo de arena	*to build a sand castle*
vadear	*to wade*
nadar	*to swim*
bucear con tubo para respirar	*to snorkel*
hacer esnórkel	*to snorkel*
bucear, hacer submarinismo	*to scuba dive*
hacer surfing	*to surf*

| hacer surfing sin tabla | *to bodysurf* |
| navegar | *to sail* |

NOTE: More words related to the Beach appear in other sections of this book, such as Ocean and Swimming and Diving.

Words In Use

El **sol** está muy fuerte hoy. *The sun is very strong today.*

No dejes de usar **loción protectora**. *Don't forget to use sunscreen.*

Los **socorristas** se van a las seis de la tarde. *The lifeguards leave at 6 p.m..*

Voy a **nadar** un rato. *I'm going to swim for a while.*

Sí, pero ten cuidado; las **olas** están muy fuertes. *Yes, but be careful; there are strong waves today.*

Vamos a hacer un **castillo de arena** con los niños. *Let's make a sand castle with the kids.*

22

General Vacation Terms

At the Beach

Camping

City Vacation

Skiing

Holidays and Celebrations

CAMPING
Camping

CAMPING NOUNS

la tienda de campaña	*tent*
los patines	*stakes*
las sogas	*ropes*
el catre	*cot*
el saco de dormir	*sleeping bag*
la fogata	*campfire*
el farol	*lantern*
la linterna	*lantern*
el botiquín de primeros auxilios	*first aid kit*
el repelente contra insectos	*bug spray*
el mosquitero	*mosquito net*
las ollas y las sartenes	*pots and pans*
la cantimplora	*canteen*
el termo	*thermos*
las botas para alpinismo/ andinismo	*hiking boots*
el dulce de altea	*marshmallow*

CAMPING VERBS

acampar	*to camp*
hacer una excursión a pie	*to hike*
montar el campamento	*to pitch a tent*

cazar	*to hunt*
pescar	*to fish*
asar	*to roast*

Words In Use

La **tienda de campaña** era muy pequña para cuatro personas. *The tent was too small for four people.*

Pudimos **acampar** cerca del río. *We were able to camp near the river.*

Esa noche encendimos una **fogata**. *That night we lit up a campfire.*

La mañana siguiente fuimos a **pescar**. *The next morning we went fishing.*

Usamos bastante **repelente contra insectos**. *We used plenty of bug repellent.*

No tuvimos que usar el **mosquitero**. *We didn't have to use the mosquito net.*

CITY VACATION

Vacaciones en la ciudad

CITY VACATION NOUNS

el hotel	*hotel*
el restaurante	*restaurant*
el café	*café*
el teatro	*theater*
el concierto	*concert*
la ópera	*opera*
el subterráneo	*subway, underground*
el metro	*subway, metro*
el taxi	*taxi*

CITY VACATION VERBS

visitar atracciones	*to go sightseeing*
ir de compras	*to go shopping*

NOTE: More words related to City Vacation can be found in the Around the Town category.

Words In Use

Nos quedamos en un **hotel** muy céntrico. *We stayed at a centrally located hotel.*

Esta noche vamos al **teatro**. *We're going to the theater tonight.*

Mañana pensamos **ir de compras**. *We're planning on going shopping tomorrow.*

¿Podemos ir andando o debemos tomar un **taxi**? *Can we walk there or should we take a taxi?*

SKIING

Esquí

SKIING NOUNS—GENERAL

la nieve	*snow*
el eslálom	*slalom*
el montículo de nieve endurecida	*mogul*
el salto en esquí	*ski jump*
el telesquí	*chairlift, ski lift*
la telesilla	*chairlift, ski lift*
la clase	*class*
el/la instructor/a	*instructor*

SKIING NOUNS—EQUIPMENT

los esquís	*skis*
las botas	*boots*
los pantalones de esquiar	*ski pants*
el traje de esquiar	*ski suit*
las gafas protectoras	*goggles*
el sombrero	*hat*
la gorra	*hat*
los guantes	*gloves*
la bufanda	*scarf*
el abrigo de lana	*fleece*

SKIING NOUNS—PLACES

el curso	*course*
la pendiente	*slope, course*
la cumbre	*peak*
la cima	*peak*
la pista de esquiar	*ski run, trail*
la pendiente de principiantes	*bunny slope*
el alojamiento	*lodge*

SKIING NOUNS—OTHER SNOW-RELATED ACTIVITIES

el patinaje en tabla	*snowboard*
el snowboard	*snowboard*
la tabla de esquiar	*snowboard*

SKIING VERBS

esquiar	*to ski*

Words In Use

Hace años que no vamos a **esquiar**. *We haven't gone skiing in a few years.*

Debes esperar hasta enero, cuando hay más **nieve**. *You should wait until January when there's more snow.*

Tengo que comprarme un **traje de esquiar** nuevo. *I have to get a new ski suit.*

Sería buena idea tomar una **clase** para principiantes. *It might be a good idea to take a beginner's class.*

Este **telesquí** te lleva hasta la **cumbre** más alta. *This ski lift takes you to the highest peak.*

HOLIDAYS AND CELEBRATIONS

Feriados y celebraciones

HOLIDAY NOUNS—GENERAL

la fiesta	*party*
la tradición	*tradition*
el cumpleaños	*birthday*
el aniversario	*anniversary*
el globo	*balloon*
la serpentina	*streamer*
las velitas	*candle*
los fuegos artificiales	*fireworks*
el regalo	*gift*
el gorro de fiesta	*party hat*

HOLIDAY NOUNS—SPECIFIC DAYS

el día de Año Nuevo	*New Year's Day*
el Día de la Madre	*Mother's Day*
el Día del Padre	*Father's Day*
el pleno verano	*midsummer*
el Día de la Independencia	*Independence Day*
la noche de las brujas	*Halloween*
el día de Halloween	*Halloween*
la Nochebuena	*Christmas Eve*
las Navidades	*Christmas*
la Nochevieja	*New Year's Eve*
la víspera de Año Nuevo	*New Year's Eve*

HOLIDAY VERBS

celebrar	*to celebrate*
irse de fiesta	*to party*

irse de juerga	*to revel*
brindar por	*to toast*

NOTE: More words related to Vacations can be found in other categories in this book, such as Transportation and Sports & Leisure.

Words In Use

Vamos a pasar estas **Navidades** con mi suegra. *We're spending this Christmas with my mother-in-law.*

Pensamos volver para **Nochevieja**. *We're planning on being back for New Year's Eve.*

Esa noche vamos a **celebrar** con unos amigos. *We're going to celebrate with some friends.*

Vamos a ver los **fuegos artificiales** desde su apartamento. *We're going to see the fireworks from their apartment.*

Mi **cumpleaños** es en octubre. *My birthday is in October.*

Voy a dar una **fiesta** en mi casa. *I'm going to have a party in my house.*

EXERCISES

I. Match the Spanish word on the left with the English word on the right.

1. las gafas de sol	A. *deep*
2. navegar	B. *waves*
3. cazar	C. *gloves*
4. el cumpleaños	D. *balloon*
5. profundo	E. *sunglasses*
6. relajarse	F. *to sail*
7. las olas	G. *birthday*
8. el bañador	H. *to hunt*
9. los guantes	I. *to relax*
10. el globo	J. *swim suit*

II. Fill in the blanks with the appropriate Spanish word.

1. Visité la _____ (*beach*) más bonita de todas las islas de Hawai.

2. Mi primo y yo vamos a _____ (*to fish*) al lago.

3. El _____ (*restaurant*) es uno de los mejores de toda la ciudad.

4. Se me olvidó traer la _____ (*scarf*) cuando fui a esquiar.

5. La _____ (*towel*) es muy pequeña; necesito una más grande.

ANSWERS: I. 1. E, 2. F, 3. H, 4. G, 5. A, 6. I, 7. B, 8. J, 9. C, 10. D
II. 1. VISITÉ LA **PLAYA** MÁS BONITA DE TODAS LAS ISLAS DE HAWAI. 2. MI PRIMO Y YO VAMOS A **PESCAR** AL LAGO. 3. EL **RESTAURANTE** ES UNO DE LOS MEJORES DE TODA LA CIUDAD. 4. SE ME OLVIDÓ TRAER LA **BUFANDA** CUANDO FUI A ESQUIAR. 5. LA **TOALLA** ES MUY PEQUEÑA; NECESITO UNA MÁS GRANDE.

The Natural World

El mundo natural

PLANTS

Plantas

PARTS OF A PLANT

la semilla	*seed*
la raíz	*root*
el tallo	*stem*
la hoja	*leaf*
el pétalo	*petal*
la fruta	*fruit*
la espina	*thorn*
el tronco	*trunk*

TYPES OF PLANTS

el helecho	*fern*
la hierba	*grass*
el césped	*lawn, grass*
la enredadera	*vine*
la parra	*vine*
la mala hierba	*weed*
el ovillo de maleza	*tumbleweed*
el alga marina	*seaweed*

Words In Use

Me gusta desayunar con **frutas**. *I like to have fruit for breakfast.*

No pudimos nadar porque había mucha **alga marina**. *We couldn't swim because there was too much seaweed.*

Estos **helechos** necesitan más agua. *These ferns need more water.*

Ten cuidado; hay **espinas** en el **tallo**. *Careful, there are thorns on the stem.*

Es un árbol de **tronco** ancho. *That tree has a very thick trunk.*

TREES
Árboles

el abedul	*birch*
el abeto	*fir*
el álamo temblón	*aspen*
el álamo	*poplar*
el alcanforero	*camphor tree*
el aliso	*alder*
el almendro	*almond tree*
el árbol de hierro	*ironwood*
el árbol de hoja de caduca	*deciduous*
el arce	*maple*
el avellano	*hazelnut*
el canelo	*cinnamon tree*
el castaño	*chestnut*
el castaño de Indias	*horse chestnut*
el cerezo	*cherry*
el cidro	*citron tree*
la encina	*holm oak*
el fresno	*ash*
el gingko	*gingko*
el haya	*beech*
la madreselva	*honeysuckle*
la magnolia	*magnolia*
el manzano	*apple*
el nogal	*walnut*
el olmo	*elm*
la pícea	*spruce*
el pino	*pine*
el roble	*oak*
el sauce	*willow*
el tejo	*yew*
el tilo	*linden*

Words In Use

¿No sabías que la aspirina proviene del **sauce**? *Didn't you know that aspirin comes from the willow tree?*

Ese parque tiene unos **robles** muy bonitos. *That park has beautiful oak trees.*

Estas manzanas son del **manzano** del patio de mi madre. *These apples are from my mother's apple tree.*

¿Podemos coger cerezas de este **cerezo**? *Are we allowed to pick cherries from this cherry tree?*

No debes usar madera de **pino** para ese armario. *You should not use pine for that wardrobe.*

FLOWERS

Flores

la acenoria	*Queen Anne's lace*
la amarilis	*amaryllis*
el ave del paraíso	*bird of paradise*
la azucena	*lily*
el brezo	*heather*
la cala	*calla lily*
la caléndula	*marigold*
la campilla	*bluebell*
el clavel	*carnation*
el crisantemo	*mum*
el diente de león	*dandelion*
el dragón	*snap dragon*
las espuelas de caballero	*larkspur*
la flor de zanahoria	*Queen Anne's lace*
las gipsófilas	*baby's breath*
el girasol	*sunflower*
el gladiolo	*gladiola*
el lirio	*iris, lily*
el lirio americano	*tiger lily*
la maravilla	*marigold*
la margarita	*daisy*
el narciso	*daffodil*
la orquídea	*orchid*
la rosa	*rose*
el tulipán	*tulip*
la violeta	*violet*

Words In Use

¿Cuál es tu **flor** favorita? *What's your favorite flower?*

Me gustan mucho los **lirios** blancos. *I love white lilies.*

Mi flor tropical favorita es el **ave del paraíso**. *My favorite tropical flower is the bird of paradise.*

Le voy a regalar una docena de **rosas** para su cumpleaños. *I'm getting her a dozen roses for her birthday.*

Las **orquídeas** no necesitan tanta luz solar. *Orchids do not need so much sunlight.*

ANIMALS
Animales

ANIMAL NOUNS

el mamífero	*mammal*
el ave	*bird*
el reptil	*reptile*
el anfibio	*amphibian*
el pez	*fish*
el insecto	*insect*

ANIMAL ADJECTIVES

omnívoro	*omnivorous*
herbívoro	*herbivorous*
carnívoro	*carnivorous*
nocturno	*nocturnal*
salvaje	*wild*
domesticado	*domesticated, tame*
manso	*tame*
entrenado	*trained*
suave	*gentle*
dócil	*gentle, docile*
bestial	*beastly*
terco	*ornery*
rabioso	*rabid*

ANIMAL VERBS

criar	*to breed, to rear*
procrear	*to breed, to procreate*
domesticar	*to tame*
ronronear	*to purr*
gruñir	*to growl*
aparear	*to mate*
castrar	*to neuter*
esterilizar	*to spay*

Words In Use

La mordió un perro **rabioso**. *She was bitten by a rabid dog.*

Yo pensaba que era un perro **manso**. *I thought it was a tame dog.*

El perro estaba **gruñendo**. *The dog was growling.*

Los perros son animales **carnívoros**. *Dogs are carnivorous animals.*

Mi primo **cría** pastores alemanes. *My cousin breeds German shepherds.*

PETS

Mascotas

PET NOUNS—GENERAL

el perro	*dog*
el gato	*cat*
el pájaro	*bird*
el jerbo	*gerbil*
el hámster	*hamster*
el conejo	*rabbit*
la serpiente	*snake, serpent*
la culebra	*snake*

PET NOUNS—EQUIPMENT

la jaula	*cage*
el plato del perro	*dog bowl*
la correa	*leash*
la arena higiénica para animales	*litterbox*
el acuario	*fish tank*

PET VERBS

acariciar	*to pet*
alimentar	*to feed*
sacar a pasear	*to walk (the dog)*
ladrar	*to bark*
gruñir	*to growl*
aullar	*to howl*
ronronear	*to purr*
saltar	*to hop*
dar saltos	*to hop*
piar	*to chirp*
gorjear	*to chirp*
silbar	*to whistle*

Words In Use

Esa **jaula** es muy pequeña para ese pájaro. *That cage is too small for that bird.*

Ya era hora de que limpiaras el **acuario**. *It was about time that you cleaned your fish tank.*

Voy a **sacar a pasear al perro**. *I'm going to walk the dog now.*

No puedo encontrar la **correa**. *I can't find the dog's leash.*

Es muy fácil mantener un **gato** dentro de la casa. *Cats are easy to keep indoors.*

FARM ANIMALS
Animales de granja

FARM ANIMAL NOUNS—GENERAL

la vaca	*cow*
el caballo	*horse*
el cerdo	*pig*
el gallo	*rooster*
la gallina	*hen*
el pollo	*chicken*
la oveja	*sheep*
la cabra	*goat*

FARM ANIMAL NOUNS—PLACES AND EQUIPMENT

el granero	*barn*
la paja	*hay*
el establo	*stable*
el comedero	*trough*

FARM ANIMAL VERBS

ordeñar una vaca	*to milk (a cow)*
montar a caballo	*to ride (a horse)*
dar de comer gachas	*to slop (a pig)*

NOTE: More words related to Farm Animals can be found in the Agriculture section of this book.

Words In Use

Este fin de semana vamos a visitar una **granja**. *We're visiting a farm this weekend.*

Nunca he comido queso de **cabra**. *I've never had goat cheese.*

Los **establos** están en detrás de la gran mansión. *The stables are behind the great mansion.*

En el granero encontrarás muchas **gallinas**. *You will find many hens in the barn.*

Esta tarde vamos a **montar a caballo**. *We're going to ride the horses this afternoon.*

WILD ANIMALS

Animales salvajes

HOOVED ANIMALS

la llama	*llama*
el antílope	*antelope*
el camello	*camel*
la jirafa	*giraffe*
la gacela	*gazelle*
la cebra	*zebra*
el ciervo	*deer*

BEARS

el oso	*bear*
el oso panda	*panda bear*
el oso pardo	*brown bear*
el oso polar	*polar bear*

MARSUPIALS

el koala	*koala bear*
el canguro	*kangaroo*

CATS

el león	*lion*
el tigre	*tiger*
el lince	*bobcat*
el puma	*mountain lion*

PRIMATES

el mico	*monkey*
el mono	*monkey*
el chimpancé	*chimpanzee*
el gorila	*gorilla*
el mandril	*baboon*
el orangután	*orangutan*

RODENTS

la rata	*rat*
el ratón	*mouse*
la ardilla	*squirrel*
el topo	*mole*

CANINES

el coyote	*coyote*
el lobo	*wolf*
el zorro	*fox*

OTHER MAMMALS

el elefante	*elephant*
la foca	*seal*
el león marino	*sea lion*
el hipopótamo	*hippopotamus*
el rinoceronte	*rhinoceros*
el tejón	*badger*
la marmota	*groundhog*
el castor	*beaver*
la nutria	*otter*
el mapache	*raccoon*
el zorrillo	*skunk*
la mofeta	*skunk*

AMPHIBIANS AND REPTILES

la rana	*frog*
el sapo	*toad*
la tortuga	*tortoise*
la tortuga marina	*turtle*
la culebra	*snake*
el lagarto	*lizard*
la lagartija	*lizard*
el camaleón	*chameleon*
la iguana	*iguana*
el caimán	*alligator*
el cocodrilo	*crocodile*

WILD ANIMAL VERBS

cazar	*to hunt*
correr	*to run*

| saltar | *to pounce* |
| abalanzar | *to pounce* |

Words In Use

Mi sección favorita del zoológico es la de **animales salvajes**. *The wild animals section is my favorite area in the zoo.*

Tenían unos **monos** muy graciosos. *They had some very funny monkeys.*

¿Viste qué grande es ese **gorila**? *Did you see how big that gorilla is?*

No te acerques tanto a la jaula de los **tigres**. *Don't get so close to the tigers' cage.*

Ahora podemos ir a darles comida a las **focas**. *We can now feed the seals.*

BIRDS

Aves

BIRDS NOUNS

la urraca azul	*blue jay*
el cardenal	*cardinal*
el gorrión	*sparrow*
el pinzón	*finch*
el colibrí	*hummingbird*
la paloma blanca	*dove*
la paloma	*pigeon*
la gaviota	*seagull*
el pato	*duck*
el ganso	*goose*
el cisne	*swan*
la grulla	*crane*
la cigüeña	*stork*
el flamenco	*flamingo*
el tucán	*toucan*
el avestruz	*ostrich*
el pingüino	*penguin*
el águila	*eagle*
el halcón	*hawk*
el búho	*owl*
el buitre	*vulture*
el cuervo	*crow, raven*

BIRD VERBS

| volar | *to fly* |

Words In Use

El **avestruz** es incapaz de **volar**. *Ostriches are unable to fly.*

Todas las mañanas veo a los **cardenales** junto a mi ventana. *Every morning I see cardinals right outside my window.*

"La **gaviota**" es una obra famosa de Chejov. *"The Seagull" is a famous Chekhov play.*

"El **cuervo**" es un poema famoso de Edgar Allan Poe. *"The Raven" is a famous poem by Edgar Allan Poe.*

El **colibrí** bate sus alas un promedio de cincuenta veces por segundo. *Hummingbirds flap their wings an average of fifty times per second.*

AQUATIC ANIMALS
Animales acuáticos

FISH

el pez	*fish*
el pez de colores	*goldfish*
la carpa	*carp*
el salmón	*salmon*
el pez espada	*swordfish*
la trucha	*trout*
el atún	*tuna*
la piraña	*piranha*

MUSSELS

el mejillón	*mussels*
la almeja	*clam*
la ostra	*oyster*

CRUSTACEANS

el cangrejo	*crab*
la langosta	*lobster*

MAMMALS

el delfín	*dolphin*
la ballena	*whale*
el tiburón	*shark*

OTHER AQUATIC ANIMALS

el pulpo	*octopus*
el calamar	*squid*

| la medusa | *jellyfish* |
| la raya venenosa | *stingray* |

AQUATIC VERBS

nadar	*to swim*
sumergirse	*to dive*
salir a la superficie	*to surface*

Words In Use

En algunos ríos del Brasil hay muchas **pirañas**. *You can find piranhas in some rivers in Brazil.*

En mi crucero por Alaska pude ver varias **ballenas**. *I was able to see a few whales on my cruise around Alaska.*

Ten cuidado con las **medusas** cuando vayas al agua. *Watch out for jellyfish when you go in the water.*

Les tengo mucho miedo a los **tiburones**. *I'm terrified of sharks.*

Los **delfines** son animales muy nobles e inteligentes. *Dolphins are very noble and intelligent animals.*

INSECTS

Insectos

INSECTS—GENERAL

el insecto	*bug, insect*
el bicho	*bug*
la araña	*spider*
la cucaracha	*cockroach*
la lombriz	*worm*
la oruga	*caterpillar*

FLYING INSECTS

la mosca	*fly*
la abeja	*bee*
la avispa	*wasp*
la mariposa	*butterfly*
la mariposa nocturna	*moth*
el escarabajo	*beetle*
el mosquito	*mosquito, gnat*

OTHER INSECT NOUNS

| la pupa | *pupa* |
| la crisálida | *chrysallis, pupa* |

la larva	*larva*
la cresa	*maggot*
el gusano	*maggot*

INSECT VERBS

zumbar	*to buzz*
volar	*to fly*
picar	*to sting, to bite*
morder	*to bite*
retorcerse	*to squirm*

Words In Use

Cierra la ventana antes de que entren los **mosquitos**. *Close the windows before the mosquitoes get in.*

Había muchas **arañas** en el ático. *There were many spiders in the attic.*

Mi mamá les tiene pánico a las **cucarachas**. *My mother is terrified of cockroaches.*

No comas esa parte del pastel; se le posó una **mosca**. *Don't eat that part of the cake; there was a fly on it.*

No sé diferenciar las **avispas** de las **abejas**. *I can't tell wasps apart from bees.*

ANIMAL BODY PARTS
Partes del animal

el cuerno	*horn*
el hocico	*snout, muzzle*
las ancas	*haunches*
la pezuña	*hoof*
la garra	*claw*
el pelo	*fur, hair*
el pelaje	*fur*
la melena	*mane*
la cola	*tail*
el rabo	*tail*
el pico	*beak*
el ala	*wing*
la crin	*mane*
las plumas	*feathers*
las escamas	*scales*
la aleta	*fin*
las agallas	*gills*

el caparazón	shell
el exoesqueleto	exoskeleton
la antena	antenna
el tórax	thorax
el aguijón	sting

Words In Use

Parece que la paloma tiene una fractura en el **ala**. *It seems that the pigeon has a fractured wing.*

El toro tiene unos **cuernos** muy afilados. *The bull has very sharp horns.*

Los insectos están protegidos por un **exoesqueleto**. *Insects are protected by their exoskeleton.*

Tu perro tiene un **pelaje** muy bonito. *Your dog has beautiful fur.*

¿Has visto qué grandes son las **garras** del tigre? *Did you see how big the tiger's claws are?*

ANIMAL SOUNDS

Sonidos de animales

el ladrido	bark
el maullido	meow
el mugido	moo
el relincho	whinny, neigh
el gruñido	oink
el balido	baa
el gorjeo	chirp
el cacareo	cock-a-doodle-doo
el zumbido	buzz

Words In Use

Me despertó el **ladrido** de los perros. *The barking of dogs woke me.*

Se podía oír el **zumbido** de las abejas desde el árbol más cercano. *The buzzing of the bees could be heard from the next tree.*

Salí a la puerta al oír el **maullido** del gato. *I went out the door after hearing the cat's meow.*

GEOGRAPHY

Geografía

GEOGRAPHY NOUNS—GENERAL

la tierra	earth
el mapa	map

el globo	*globe*
el hemisferio	*hemisphere*
la latitud	*latitude*
la longitud	*longitude*
el ecuador	*equator*
el grado	*degree*
la elevación	*elevation*
la topografía	*topography*
el nivel del mar	*sea level*
el clima	*climate*
el continente	*continent*
la frontera	*boundary*
la península	*peninsula*
la isla	*island*
el archipiélago	*archipelago*
el estrecho	*strait*
la bahía	*bay*
el lago	*lake*
la ciénaga	*marsh*
el pantano	*marsh, swamp*
la ciénaga	*swamp*
la colina	*hill*
el cerro	*hill*
la montaña	*mountain*
la cordillera	*mountain range*
el valle	*valley*
el cañón	*canyon*
la cueva	*cave*
la caverna	*cavern*
la llanura	*plain*
el llano	*plain*
la sabana	*savanna*
el desierto	*desert*
la tundra	*tundra*
la roca	*rock*
la tierra	*soil*
la erosión	*erosion*

Words In Use

El **archipiélago** de las Antillas comienza en la boca del Golfo de México. *The Antilles archipelago starts at the mouth of the Gulf of Mexico.*

En el centro del país hay una importante **cordillera**. *There's an important mountain range in the middle of the country.*

Todavía no me he comprado el **mapa** para mi viaje. *I haven't bought the map that I need for my trip.*

Sudán es el país más grande del **continente** africano. *Sudan is the largest country in the African continent.*

FOREST

Bosque

FOREST NOUNS

el bosque pluvial	*rain forest*
la jungla	*jungle*
la selva	*jungle*
el árbol	*tree*
la maleza	*brush*
la vid	*vine*
la flor silvestre	*wildflower*
las hojas	*leaves*
el follaje	*foliage*
la tierra	*earth, dirt*
el barro	*mud, clay*
el maná	*manna*
el camino	*path*
el sendero	*trail*
la trocha	*trail*
el claro	*clearing, glade*

FOREST ADJECTIVES

exuberante	*lush*

Words In Use

La **selva** tropical cubre la mayor parte del país. *The tropical jungle covers most of the country.*

El **bosque pluvial** del Yunque recibe 120 pulgadas de lluvia al año. *The El Yunque rain forest receives 120 inches of rainfall annually.*

Este **sendero** te lleva hasta la cumbre de la montaña. *This trail will take you to the peak of the mountain.*

El área es famosa por su paisaje **exuberante**. *That area is known for its lush landscape.*

MOUNTAINS
Montañas

MOUNTAIN NOUNS

la cordillera	range
la cima	peak, heights
el pico	peak
la cumbre	heights
el risco	cliff
el precipicio	cliff, precipice
la cuesta	slope
la pendiente	slope
la trocha	trail, pass
el paso	pass
la meseta	plateau
la altitud	altitude
el volcán	volcano

MOUNTAIN ADJECTIVES

alto	high
rocoso	rocky
cubierto de nieve	snow-topped

MOUNTAIN VERBS

trepar	to climb
atravesar	to traverse

Words In Use

La erupción del **volcán** sorprendió a los habitantes del pueblo. *The eruption of the volcano surprised the town's inhabitants.*

La **altitud** de la montaña es de 3.533 pies. *The mountain has an altitude of 3,533 feet.*

Desde el **pico** más **alto** se puede ver la capital. *You'll be able to see the capital city from the highest peak.*

La parte occidental de la **cordillera** consiste en formaciones **rocosas**. *The western part of the range consists of rocky formations.*

OCEAN
Océano

OCEAN NOUNS

el agua salada	salt water
la ola	wave

la arena	sand
el banco de arena	sand bar
la playa	beach
el arrecife	reef
el alga marina	seaweed
el submarinismo	scuba diving
el pescador	fisherman
el crucero	cruise
la regata	regatta
el naufragio	shipwreck

OCEAN ADJECTIVES

profundo	deep
extenso	vast, extensive
marino	marine
vasto	vast

Words In Use

Vamos a nadar hasta el **banco de arena**. *Let's swim all the way to the sand bar.*

Tenemos que pasar esa área con **algas marinas**. *We have to go past that area with seaweed.*

Detrás del **banco de arena** hay un pequeño **arrecife**. *There's a small reef beyond the sand bar.*

El **pescador** sale a pescar de madrugada. *The fisherman goes fishing in the early morning.*

RIVERS AND LAKES
Ríos y lagos

el río	river
el lecho del río	riverbed
el delta	delta
el lago	lake
la cala	inlet, cove
la ensenada	inlet, cove
el arroyo	creek, stream, brook
el lecho del arroyo	creekbed
el riachuelo	creek, stream
el barranco	ravine
la curva	bend
la corriente	tide

los rápidos	*rapids*
el dique	*dam*
la cascada	*waterfall*
la isla	*island*

Words In Use

El **delta** del **río** es un área muy fértil. *The river delta is a very fertile area.*

Ten cuidado al llegar al área de los **rápidos**. *Be careful when you get to the rapids area.*

La **corriente** hoy está muy fuerte. *The tide is very strong today.*

En la carretera al pueblo encontrarás unas **cascadas** muy bonitas. *You'll find beautiful waterfalls on the road to town.*

Hay una **isla** en medio del **lago**. *There's an island in the middle of the lake.*

DESERT

Desierto

DESERT NOUNS

la arena	*sand*
la duna	*dune*
la tempestad de arena	*sandstorm*
el oasis	*oasis*
el espejismo	*mirage*
el cactus	*cactus*
la palmera	*palm tree*
los ovillos de maleza	*tumbleweed*

DESERT ADJECTIVES

seco	*dry*
árido	*arid, barren*
estéril	*barren*

Words In Use

Cuando estuvimos en Marruecos nos pasamos dos días en el **desierto**. *When we were in Morocco we spent two days in the desert.*

Solamente pudimos ver un **oasis** en la distancia. *We only saw one oasis in the distance.*

Descansamos debajo de unas **palmeras**. *We rested under some palm trees.*

De repente vino una **tempestad de arena** y tuvimos que parar. *We had to stop when suddenly a sandstorm came.*

WEATHER

Tiempo

WEATHER NOUNS

la temperatura	*temperature*
el grado	*degree*
el calor	*heat, warmth*
el frente	*front*
el frente frío	*cold front*
el frente cálido	*warm front*
la humedad	*humidity*
el sol	*sun*
la luz de sol	*sunshine*
la nube	*cloud*
la lluvia	*rain*
el aguacero	*rain shower*
el chubasco	*shower, squall*
el chaparrón	*downpour, rain shower*
la lluvia torrencial	*torrential downpour*
la tormenta de truenos	*thunderstorm*
el trueno	*thunder*
el rayo	*lightning, thunderbolt*
el relámpago	*lightning*
el aguanieve	*sleet*
el hielo	*ice*
el carámbano	*icicle*
la nieve	*snow*
la tempestad de nieve	*blizzard*
la niebla	*fog*
el smog	*smog*
la niebla tóxica	*smog*
el paraguas	*umbrella*
la sombrilla	*umbrella*

WEATHER ADJECTIVES

soleado	*sunny*
lluvioso	*rainy*
nevado	*snowy*
cálido	*hot*
caluroso	*warm*

frío	cold
húmedo	*humid*
Fahrenheit	*Fahrenheit*
Celsius	*Celsius*
centígrado	*Celsius, centigrade*

WEATHER VERBS

llover	*to rain*
nevar	*to snow*
templar	*to warm up*
abonanzarse	*to clear up*

Words In Use

Se espera mal **tiempo** para este fin de semana. *They expect bad weather for this weekend.*

Si sales, asegúrate de llevar el **paraguas**. *If you go out make sure you bring your umbrella.*

Tuvimos una primavera de mucha **lluvia**. *We had a very rainy Spring.*

La **temperatura** en abril fue muy agradable. *The temperature in April was very pleasant.*

El mes de mayo fue uno de los más **lluviosos**. *The month of May was one of the rainiest.*

NATURAL DISASTERS

Desastres naturales

NATURAL DISASTER NOUNS

el terremoto	*earthquake*
el temblor	*tremor*
la réplica	*aftershock*
el vendaval	*gale*
el tornado	*tornado*
el huracán	*hurricane*
el monzón	*monsoon*
el tsunami	*tsunami*
la inundación	*flood*
la sequía	*drought*
la avalancha	*avalanche*
la erupción de volcán	*volcanic eruption*
el fuego incontrolable	*wildfire*
las placas tectónicas	*tectonic plates*

NATURAL DISASTER ADJECTIVES

peligroso	*dangerous*
espantoso	*scary*
sísmico	*seismic*

NATURAL DISASTER VERBS

sacudir	*to shake*
temblar	*to tremble*
soplar	*to blow*
inundar	*to flood*
evacuar	*to evacuate*

Words In Use

La temporada de **huracanes** comienza en junio. *The hurricane season begins in June.*

El área central se ve afectada por muchos **tornados**. *The central region is being affected by many tornadoes.*

Hubo una **avalancha** en los Alpes suizos. *There was an avalanche in the Swiss Alps.*

El **temblor** duró unos veinte segundos. *The tremor lasted twenty seconds.*

El **terremoto** registró una magnitud de 7,2. *The earthquake registered a magnitude of 7.2.*

METALS, MINERALS, GEMS

Metales, minerales y piedras preciosas

METALS AND MINERALS

el acero	*steel*
el aluminio	*aluminum*
el bronce	*bronze*
el carbón	*coal*
el cinc	*zinc*
el cobre	*copper*
el estaño	*tin*
el hierro	*iron*
el oro	*gold*
la plata	*silver*
el plomo	*lead*
el uranio	*uranium*

GEMS AND STONES

la aguamarina	*aquamarine*
la amatista	*amethyst*
el citrino	*citrine*
el cristal	*crystal*
el diamante	*diamond*
la esmeralda	*emerald*
el granate	*garnet*
el jade	*jade*
el ópalo	*opal*
la perla	*pearl*
el rubí	*ruby*
el topacio	*topaz*
la turmalina	*tourmaline*
la turquesa	*turquoise*
el zafiro	*sapphire*

METALS, MINERALS AND GEMS VERBS

cavar	*to dig*
excavar	*to excavate*
extraer	*to extract, to mine*
minar	*to mine*

Words In Use

Le regalé a mi novia una sortija de **esmeraldas**. *I gave my girlfriend an emerald ring.*

Me gustan mucho tus aretes de **perlas**. *I love your pearl earrings.*

El precio del **oro** ha subido últimamente. *The price of gold has gone up lately.*

El **aluminio** es el segundo elemento más común en la corteza terrestre. *Aluminum is the second most common element in the Earth's crust.*

El **estaño** está en el grupo IV de la tabla periódica; su símbolo es el Sn. *Tin is a member of Group IV of the Periodic table; its symbol is Sn.*

FUEL AND ENERGY
Combustible y energía

FUEL AND ENERGY NOUNS

la electricidad	*electricity*
el cable de alta tensión	*power line*
el gas natural	*natural gas*

el petróleo	*oil*
el petróleo crudo	*petroleum, crude oil*
el aceite	*oil*
la gasolina	*gas*
el gasóleo	*diesel*

FUEL AND ENERGY ADJECTIVES

| solar | *solar* |
| nuclear | *nuclear* |

Words In Use

Los Estados Unidos es el segundo país en consumo de **electricidad**. *The USA ranks second in total electricity consumption.*

Es el país número veintitrés en consumo de **gas natural**. *It ranks number twenty-three in consumption of natural gas.*

Los países industrializados dependen mucho del **petróleo**. *Industrialized countries depend heavily on oil.*

El precio de la **gasolina** ha subido en los últimos meses. *The price of gas has gone up in the past few months.*

Los residentes del área se oponen a la construcción de una planta **nuclear**. *The area residents are opposed to the construction of a nuclear plant.*

COMMON ELEMENTS, COMPOUNDS, AND SUBSTANCES

Elementos comunes, compuestos y sustancias

COMMON ELEMENTS NOUNS

el átomo	*atom*
la molécula	*molecule*
el compuesto	*compound*
el núcleo	*nucleus*
el electron	*electron*
el protón	*proton*
el neutrón	*neutron*
el oxígeno	*oxygen*
el carbono	*carbon*
el dióxido de carbono	*carbon-dioxide*
el hidrógeno	*hydrogen*
el helio	*helium*
el nitrógeno	*nitrogen*
el neón	*neon*
el sodio	*sodium*

el aluminio	*aluminum*
el magnesio	*magnesium*
el fósforo	*phosphorus*
el azufre	*sulfur*
el cloro	*chlorine*
el calcio	*calcium*
el hierro	*iron*
el oro	*gold*
el mercurio	*mercury*
el cobre	*copper*
el plomo	*lead*
el uranio	*uranium*
el gas	*gas*
el ácido	*acid*

COMMON ELEMENTS ADJECTIVES

sólido	*solid*
líquido	*liquid*
gaseoso	*gaseous*
radiactivo	*radioactive*

Words In Use

El **aluminio** se usa en la fabricación de autos. *Aluminum is used in the manufacturing of cars.*

Sentimos la falta de **oxígeno** al subir a la cima de la montaña. *We felt the lack of oxygen when we reached the mountain top.*

El **carbono** se encuentra en muchos **compuestos**. *Carbon is found in many different compounds.*

El **cloro** puede ser un **gas** muy venenoso. *Chlorine can be a very poisonous gas.*

SOLAR SYSTEM
El sistema solar

SOLAR SYSTEM NOUNS

el planeta	*planet*
la Luna	*moon*
el Sol	*Sun*
Mercurio	*Mercury*
Venus	*Venus*
Tierra	*Earth*
Marte	*Mars*

Júpiter	Jupiter
Saturno	Saturn
Neptuno	Neptune
Urano	Uranus
Plutón	Pluto

SOLAR SYSTEM VERBS

orbitar	to orbit
eclipsar	to eclipse

Words In Use

A **Mercurio** le toma ochenta y ocho días darle la vuelta al Sol. *Mercury takes eighty-eight days to circle the Sun.*

Venus es el planeta más luminoso del **sistema solar**. *Venus is the brightest planet in the Solar System.*

Tres cuartas partes de la **Tierra** están cubiertas por agua. *Three-quarters of the Earth are covered by water.*

El día en **Júpiter** dura nueve horas y cincuenta y cinco minutos. *A day in Jupiter lasts nine hours and fifty-five minutes.*

UNIVERSE
El universo

la galaxia	galaxy
la Vía Láctea	Milky Way
la estrella	star
la estrella fugaz	shooting star
la constelación	constellation
la nova	nova
la supernova	supernova
el agujero negro	black hole
el vacío	vacuum
el meteoro	meteor
la lluvia de meteoros	meteor shower
el asteroide	asteroid
el cometa	comet

NOTE: More words related to the Universe can be found in the Space Travel section of this book.

Words In Use

El período orbital del **cometa** Halley es de setenta y seis años. *The average period of Halley's Comet's orbit is 76 years.*

Este mapa de las **constelaciones** te ayudará a identificar las estrellas. *This constellation map will help you identify stars.*

6000+ Essential Spanish Words

La Vía Láctea es una gran **galaxia** que contiene a nuestro sistema solar. *The Milky Way is a large galaxy that contains our solar system.*

Hay muchos **asteroides** entre las órbitas de Marte y Júpiter. *Asteroids are found mainly in the area between the orbits of Mars and Jupiter.*

Si te concentras en el cielo podrás ver una **estrella fugaz**. *If you focus on the sky, you'll see a shooting star.*

ENVIRONMENTAL ISSUES
Asuntos del medio ambiente

ENVIRONMENTAL ISSUES NOUNS

la contaminación	*pollution*
la fuga de petróleo	*oil spill*
la marea negra	*oil spill*
la contaminación del aire	*air pollution*
la contaminación del agua	*water pollution*
la deforestación	*deforestation*
la erosión	*erosion*
la reducción	*depletion*
la disminución	*depletion*
la extinción	*extinction*
la extensión urbana	*urban sprawl*
el calentamiento global	*global warming*
la reducción de la capa de ozono	*ozone depletion*
el reciclaje	*recycling*
el Día de la Tierra	*Earth Day*

ENVIRONMENTAL ISSUES VERBS

reciclar	*to recycle*
reutilizar	*to reuse*

Words In Use

Es muy importante **reciclar** metales, papeles y vidrios. *It's important to recycle metals, paper and glass.*

La **fuga de petróleo** creó el peor desastre ecológico del área. *The oil spill created the worst environmental disaster in the area.*

La **deforestación** es un problema global. *Deforestation is a global problem.*

La **contaminación del aire** es más alta este año. *The air pollution has increased this year.*

La **erosión** del mar afecta las casas de la playa. *The beach erosion is affecting the houses on the shore.*

EXERCISES

I. Match the Spanish word on the left with the English word on the right.

1. la hoja	A. *daisy*
2. el sauce	B. *monkey*
3. la niebla	C. *sand*
4. la arena	D. *fog*
5. la semilla	E. *willow*
6. la margarita	F. *seed*
7. la mariposa	G. *copper*
8. la cabra	H. *butterfly*
9. el cobre	I. *leaf*
10. el mono	J. *goat*

II. Fill in the blanks with the appropriate Spanish word.

1. El _____ (*bird*) tropical más bonito es el tucán.

2. Entre los mamíferos acuáticos, el _____ (*dolphin*) es un animal muy dócil.

3. Hay que llamar al fumigador; vi una _____ (*cockroach*) en la cocina.

4. El _____ (*equator*) divide los dos hemisferios.

5. El precio del _____ (*gold*) ha subido mucho en los últimos meses.

ANSWERS: I. 1. I, 2. E, 3. D, 4. C, 5. F, 6. A, 7. H, 8. J, 9. G, 10. B
II. 1. EL **PÁJARO** TROPICAL MÁS BONITO ES EL TUCÁN. 2. ENTRE
LOS MAMÍFEROS ACUÁTICOS, EL **DELFÍN** ES UN ANIMAL MUY DÓCIL.
3. HAY QUE LLAMAR AL FUMIGADOR; VI UNA **CUCARACHA** EN LA COCINA.
4. EL **ECUADOR** DIVIDE LOS DOS HEMISFERIOS. 5. EL PRECIO DEL ORO HA
SUBIDO MUCHO EN LOS ÚLTIMOS MESES.

Part II

Situations

1. Itinerario de viaje
Egipto en sus manos

10 días, incluye transporte aéreo

Incluye lo siguiente:

- Vuelos transatlánticos

- Traslados entre aeropuerto y hotel

- Guía experto en egiptología

- Habitaciones con baño, impuestos de hotel, servicio y propinas

- Crucero por el Nilo en cabina de lujo con vista al exterior

- Todas las excursiones desde el crucero

- Vuelos del Cairo a Asuán y de Luxor al Cairo, con traslados de aeropuertos

- Cóctel de bienvenida; 4 desayunos tipo bufé; 4 desayunos completos; 5 cenas; 4 almuerzos

- Transporte terrestre en autocar privado con aire acondicionado

Día 1, viernes 28 de marzo

Salida del vuelo transatlántico, en vuelo toda la noche

Día 2, sábado 29 de marzo

Llegada al Cairo

Un cóctel de bienvenida le espera en el hotel. Tarde libre para empezar a disfrutar la ciudad.

Día 3, domingo 30 de marzo

El Cairo y las pirámides

A las ocho de la mañana nos reunimos con el guía para comenzar el recorrido por una de las mayores metrópolis de África. Comenzamos en el Museo Egipcio con los famosos tesoros de Tutankamón y nuestro primer encuentro con el esplendor de los tres milenios de civilización egipcia. Luego continuamos hacia Menfis para admirar la estatua de Ramsés II y la Esfinge de Alabastro. Nuestro recorrido sigue hacia Sákkara para ver la pirámide escalonada, la más antigua de todas las pirámides. Luego llegamos a Giza para ver la enigmática Esfinge y las fantásticas Pirámides de Giza. La pirámide de Keóps es la más grande de todas.

Día 4, lunes 31 de marzo

El Cairo—Asuán

Mañana libre para una excursión opcional al antiguo Cairo. Se sugiere visitar la ciudadela de Saladino, la Mezquita de Alabastro y el bazar. En la tarde volamos quinientas millas al sur hasta el pueblo de Asuán.

Día 5, martes 1 de abril

Asuán. Abordamos el crucero

Mañana libre en Asuán. Excursión opcional para ver el grandioso templo de Abu Simbel. Volvemos al barco para el almuerzo. Por la tarde cruzamos las aguas del Nilo en una feluca para visitar la Isla Elefantina, los Jardines Botánicos en la Isla Kitchener y el espléndido Mausoleo del Aga Khan.

Día 6, miércoles 2 de abril

Crucero por el Nilo: Asuán, Kom Ombo

Excursión por la mañana a la Presa Antigua, la presa más ancha del mundo. Luego continuamos a la gigantesca Presa de Asuán, construida en 1970. Más tarde abordamos un barco para visitar el Templo de Isis, trasladado de la inundada isla de Philae. Volvemos al crucero para el almuerzo y zarpamos en dirección norte. Llegamos a Kom Ombo para una corta caminata por el templo al dios cocodrilo y al dios falcón.

Día 7, jueves 3 de abril

Crucero por el Nilo: Edfu, Esna

Por la mañana vamos en carruaje hasta el templo de Horus en Edfu. Este templo de 2.000 años ha sido restaurado recientemente. Después de la visita volvemos al barco para continuar nuestro viaje hasta Esna. En Esna visitamos el Templo Hundido dedicado a Khnum. Por la noche atracamos en Luxor.

Día 8, viernes 4 de abril

Crucero por el Nilo: Luxor

Por la mañana visitamos el Valle de los Reyes y el Valle de las Reinas en la ribera oeste del Nilo. En el valle se han encontrado sesenta y dos tumbas reales, incluyendo la de Tutankamón. Visitamos el fantástico Templo de la Reina Hatshepsut, en Bahari. Esta tarde se la dedicamos al Templo de Luxor en la ribera este del Nilo.

Día 9, sábado 5 de abril

Luxor—El Cairo

Por la mañana terminamos el recorrido por la ribera este del Nilo con nuestro recorrido por Karnak, la ciudad más grande del antiguo Egipto. Damos una caminata por el Templo de Amón Ra y la Avenida de las Esfinges. Por la tarde volamos de regreso al Cairo. Tarde libre en el Cairo.

Día 10, domingo 6 de abril

Vuelo de regreso

NOTE: Vocabulary words from Situation 1 can be found in the following categories: Human Society, Vacation, Transportation, and Food & Cooking.

Flight Itinerary Egypt at your fingertips

10 days, including air travel

All this is included:

- Transatlantic flights

- Airport and hotel transfers

- Services of an Egyptologist guide

- Rooms with private bath, hotel taxes, service charges and tips

- Nile cruise accommodation in luxury outside cabin

- All shore excursions

- Flights between Cairo and Aswan and between Luxor and Cairo, including airport transfers

- Welcome drink; 4 buffet breakfasts, 4 full breakfasts, 5 dinners, 4 lunches

- Transportation on land by private air-conditioned bus

Day 1, Friday, March 28

Board your overnight transatlantic flight

Day 2, Saturday, March 29

Arrival in Cairo
A welcome drink awaits you at the hotel. Afternoon at your leisure to start enjoying the city.

Day 3, Sunday, March 30

Cairo. The Pyramids
Meet your guide at 8 a.m. for your sightseeing trip in and around Africa's largest metropolis. Start at the Egyptian Museum with Tutankhamon's famous treasures and our first encounter with three millennia of Egyptian civilization. Then leave for Memphis to admire the statue of Ramses II and the Alabaster Sphinx. Our tour takes us now to Sakkara to see the "stairway to the sky," the oldest of all pyramids. We finally arrive at Giza to see the enigmatic Sphinx and the wonderful Pyramids of Giza. The Pyramid of Cheops is the largest of them.

Day 4, Monday, March 31

Cairo—Aswan
Time this morning for an optional excursion to Old Cairo. The visit includes Saladin's Citadel, the Alabaster Mosque and the bazaar. In the afternoon we fly south 500 miles to the town of Aswan.

Day 5, Tuesday, April 1

Aswan. Board Hotel Boat

Morning at your leisure in Aswan. You may want to take an optional excursion to see the magnificent temple of Abu Simbel. We return to the hotel boat for lunch. In the afternoon we board a felucca and sail across the Nile to see the Elephantine Island, Kitchener Island's Botanical Gardens and the Aga Khan Mausoleum.

Day 6, Wednesday, April 2

Nile Cruise: Aswan, Kom Ombo

Morning excursion to the Old Dam, the widest in the world, and the Aswan Dam, built in 1970. We board a motor launch to visit the Temple of Isis, transplanted from the submerged island of Philae. We return to the hotel boat for lunch and sail north. We arrive in Kom Ombo in the afternoon for a short walk in the temple dedicated to the crocodile and falcon gods.

Day 7, Thursday, April 3

Nile Cruise: Edfu, Esna

Board a horse-drawn carriage to the Temple of Horus. This 2,000 year old temple was restored recently. After our visit we return to our hotel boat and sail to Esna. In Esna we visit the Sunken Temple dedicated to Khnum. Tonight we arrive in Luxor.

Day 8, Friday, April 4

In the morning we visit the Valley of the Kings and the Valley of the Queens in the west bank of the Nile. Sixty-two royal tombs have been uncovered so far, including the tomb of Tutankhamon. Then we visit the magnificent Temple of Queen Hatshepsut in El Bahari. This afternoon is dedicated to Luxor Temple on the east bank of the Nile.

Day 9, Saturday, April 5

In the morning we finish the tour of the east bank of the Nile when we visit Karnak, the largest city in Ancient Egypt. We take a walk in the Temple of Amon Ra and the Avenue of the Sphinxes. Afternoon flight to Cairo. Afternoon at your leisure in Cairo.

Day 10, Sunday, April 6

Homebound Flight

2. Campamento de Verano: Programa Semanal
Guía para los padres

Lunes: Día en el zoológico

8:00	El autobús sale desde la puerta principal de la escuela intermedia Robert Wagner en la ciudad de Nueva York.
10:00	Llegada al zoológico.
10:30	Merienda ligera con frutas, jugos y emparedados.
11:00	Espectáculo con los delfines, los leones marinos y las focas.
12:00	Alimentar a los delfines.
12:30	Almuerzo tipo picnic (se servirán hamburguesas, papas fritas y jugos) seguido de un descanso.
14:00	Visita al mundo de los reptiles.
15:00	Espectáculo de las aves.
16:00	Salida del zoológico.
18:00	Llegada a la escuela.

Martes: Día en Wall Street

9:00	Salida de la escuela.
9:30	Viaje en metro hasta la zona financiera.
10:00	Desayuno en el parque Battery (la comida está incluida).
10:30	Visita a la Bolsa de Valores.
11:30	Recorrido por las calles del centro financiero.
12:30	Picnic en el parque (se ofrecerán quesos, embutidos, pan y fruta).
13:30	Paseo por el puerto de South Street.
14:30	Salida en metro.
15:30	Llegada a la escuela.

Miércoles: Visita al Museo Metropolitano

10:00	Salida de la escuela, vamos andando en dirección al museo.
10:30	Corta visita a la Colección Frick para ver la exposición permanente.
12:00	Llegada al Museo Metropolitano.
12:30	Almuerzo libre en la cafetería del museo. Lleven dinero para comprar la comida.
13:30	Visita independiente a la colección de pintura europea.
14:30	Descanso
15:00	Película sobre la pintura renacentista en el teatro del museo.

16:00	Presentación de la colección con un invitado especial.
17:00	Salida del museo.
17:30	Llegada a la escuela.

Jueves: Día de deportes en el Parque Central

10:00	Salida de la escuela; hoy también vamos andando.
10:30	Llegada al parque, vamos directamente al campo de béisbol donde tendremos equipo disponible. También ofreceremos una merienda para todos.
12:00	Las canchas de tenis han sido reservadas para nuestro uso.
13:30	Barbacoa con pollo, perros calientes y hamburguesas.
14:00	Visita a la piscina.
16:00	Las canchas de baloncesto han sido reservadas para nuestro uso.
17:00	Salida del parque.
17:30	Llegada a la escuela.

Viernes: Excursión al parque de diversiones de Coney Island

8:30	Salida de la escuela en autobús.
10:00	Llegada a Coney Island.
12:00	Almuerzo libre, traigan dinero para comprar comida.
14:00	Visita al acuario de Coney Island.
16:00	Salida de regreso.
17:30	Llegada a la escuela.

Avisos importantes:

○ Todas las llegadas son aproximadas. En caso de cualquier demora se puede comunicar con el coordinador del campamento, el Sr. Jonathan Smith, al 917-917-3737.

○ Necesitamos tener los permisos de los padres antes de comenzar nuestra primera excursión el lunes.

○ Es importante que llenen la ficha de números de teléfonos de emergencia en caso de que tengamos que comunicarnos con algún padre. No todos los números de teléfono están actualizados.

○ Los estudiantes no tienen que pagar por el transporte o las entradas. Algunas comidas están incluidas excepto cuando se indica. Es importante que los estudiantes traigan dinero suficiente para comprar comida y otros artículos.

○ Todos los padres están invitados a acompañarnos a cualquiera de las excursiones. Favor comunicarse con nosotros de antemano.

NOTE: Vocabulary words from Situation 2 can be found in the following categories: School, Sports & Leisure, Around Town, Entertainment & Media, The Natural World, Food & Cooking, and Transportation.

Summer Camp—Weekly Program Parents' Guide

Monday—A day at the zoo

8 a.m.	The bus departs from the main entrance at Robert Wagner Middle School in New York City.
10 a.m.	Arrival at the zoo
10:30 a.m.	Light snack with fruit, juice and sandwiches
11 a.m.	Live show with dolphins, sea lions and seals
12 p.m.	Dolphin feeding
12:30 p.m.	Picnic lunch (hamburgers, french fries and juice will be served) followed by a break
2 p.m.	World of Reptiles visit
3 p.m.	Bird show
4 p.m.	Departure from zoo
6 p.m.	Arrival at school

Tuesday—A Day in Wall Street

9 a.m.	Depart school
9:30 a.m.	Subway trip to the Financial District
10 a.m.	Breakfast in Battery Park (food will be supplied)
10:30 a.m.	Visit to the Stock Exchange
11:30 a.m.	Stroll around the Financial District
12:30 p.m.	Picnic in the park (cheese, cold cuts, bread and fruit will be supplied)
1:30 p.m.	Walk around South Street Seaport
2:30 p.m.	Departure from Financial District by subway
3:30 p.m.	Arrival at school

Wednesday—Visit to the Metropolitan Museum

10 a.m.	Departure from school, walk in the direction of the Museum
10:30 a.m.	Short visit to the Frick Collection to see the permanent exhibit.
12 p.m.	Arrival at the Metropolitan Museum
12:30 p.m.	Lunch in the museum cafeteria. Bring money to buy food.
1:30 p.m.	Independent visit to the European Collection
2:30 p.m.	Break
3 p.m.	Film about Renaissance painting in the theater
4 p.m.	Special presentation on the collection with guest speaker
5 p.m.	Departure from the museum
5:30 p.m.	Arrival at school

Thursday—Field Day in Central Park

10 a.m.	Departure from school, walk in the direction of Central Park
10:30 a.m.	Arrival at the park, we go directly to the baseball field where we will have baseball equipment available. We will also have a snack waiting for us.
12 p.m.	Tennis courts reserved for us
1:30 p.m.	Barbecue with chicken, hot dogs and hamburgers
2 p.m.	Visit to the swimming pool
4 p.m.	Basketball courts reserved for us
5 p.m.	Departure from park
5:30 p.m.	Arrival at school

Friday—Trip to Coney Island amusement park

8:30 a.m.	Departure from school by bus
10 a.m.	Arrival at Coney Island
12 p.m.	Lunch in the park, bring your own money to buy food.
2 p.m.	Visit to the Aquarium in Coney Island
4 p.m.	Return to school
5:30 p.m.	Arrival at school

Important announcements:

- All arrival times are approximate. In case of a delay, you may contact the coordinator of the camp, Mr. Jonathan Smith, at 917-917-3737.

- We need to have all parent's consent forms before we begin our first trip on Monday.

- It's important that you return the form with all emergency phone numbers in case we need to contact a parent. We don't have all numbers updated.

- Students don't have to pay for transportation or trips. Some meals are included except where indicated. It's important that students bring enough money to buy food or other items.

- Parents are welcome to join us on any of the excursions. Please let us know in advance.

3. El árbol genealógico de Javier

Javier es un hombre de 33 años que vive en la ciudad de Nueva York. Es profesor de literatura en la Universidad de Nueva York. El año pasado Javier se casó con Gretchen Kamps. Gretchen tiene 32 años y nació en Alemania. Ella trabaja en una compañía de sistemas computarizados en el distrito financiero de la ciudad de Nueva York. Javier y Gretchen no tienen hijos.

La hermana de Javier se llama Alina. Alina tiene 39 años y vive en Puerto Rico. Alina es vendedora ambulante para una compañía de artículos de oficina en la zona metropolitana de San Juan, capital de Puerto Rico. El marido de Alina es Juan García. Juan nació hace 42 años en Málaga, España. Juan es administrador de restaurantes. Juan y Alina tienen dos hijos, una niña y un niño. Mónica tiene seis años y Alejandro tiene cuatro años. Los dos estudian en el mismo lugar, en el colegio Baldwin, en Guaynabo.

Javier y Alina son hermanos. Sus padres son Enrique Montes y Lourdes Suárez. Enrique se jubiló hace poco. Trabajó muchos años como ejecutivo para una compañía en la industria farmacéutica. Lourdes siempre se dedicó a sus hijos y a su familia como ama de casa. Ahora que Enrique y Lourdes están disfrutando de su jubilación, les dedican mucho tiempo a sus nietos Mónica y Alejandro.

Enrique nació en La Habana, Cuba. Su madre se llamaba Celia Rodríguez y su padre se llamaba Roberto Montes. Celia y Roberto solamente tuvieron un hijo. Enrique no se quejó nunca de no tener hermanos porque para Navidades él recibía todos los regalos de la familia. Celia y Roberto fallecieron hace algunos años.

La nuera de Roberto y Celia es Lourdes. El padre de Lourdes es Ricardo Suárez. Ricardo era médico del ejército en Cuba antes de Castro. La madre de Lourdes es Olga Díaz. Olga Díaz fue secretaria ejecutiva para la compañía nacional de teléfonos de Cuba. Ricardo y Olga tuvieron otro hijo, Sergio. Sergio siempre era muy protector de su hermana Lourdes. Sergio se casó con Yolanda y tuvo dos hijos, María Cristina y Ernesto. Sergio, Yolanda, María Cristina y Ernesto viven en la Florida. Ernesto y María Cristina no están casados ni tienen hijos. María Cristina y Ernesto son los únicos primos de Javier y Alina.

¿Cómo se llaman los abuelos de Javier? Sus abuelos paternos son Celia y Roberto y sus abuelos maternos son Olga y Ricardo. ¿Tienen Javier y Alina primos? Sí, sus primos se llaman María Cristina y Ernesto. ¿Quién es la suegra de Enrique? La suegra de Enrique se llama Olga.

NOTE: Vocabulary words from Situation 3 can be found in the following categories: People, Family & Relationships, Work.

Javier's Family Tree

Javier is a 33 year old man who lives in New York City. He is a literature professor at New York University. Last year Javier married Gretchen Kamps. Gretchen is 32 years old and was born in Germany. She works in a computer software company in the financial district in New York City. Javier and Gretchen do not have any children.

Javier's sister is Alina. Alina is 39 years old and she lives in Puerto Rico. Alina is a traveling salesperson for a company of office equipment in the metropolitan area of San Juan, capital of Puerto Rico. Alina's husband is Juan García. Juan was born forty two years ago in Málaga, Spain. Juan is a restaurant administrator. Juan and Alina have two children, a girl and a boy. Mónica is six years old and Alejandro is four years old. Both study in the same school, the Baldwin Academy, in the town of Guaynabo.

Javier and Alina are siblings. Their parents are Enrique Montes and Lourdes Suárez. Enrique retired recently. He worked many years as an executive for a company in the pharmaceutical industry. Lourdes devoted her life to her children and her family as a housewife. Now that Enrique and Lourdes are enjoying his retirement, they spend a lot of time with their grandchildren Mónica and Alejandro.

Enrique was born in Havana, Cuba. His mother was Celia Rodríguez and his father was Roberto Montes. Celia and Roberto only had one child. Enrique never complained of not having any siblings because at Christmas he received all the gifts from the members of his family. Celia and Roberto passed away a few years ago.

Lourdes is Roberto's and Celia's daughter-in-law. Lourdes' father is Ricardo Suárez. Ricardo was a doctor for the Cuban Army before Castro. Lourdes' mother is Olga Díaz. Olga Díaz was an executive secretary for the Cuban National Telephone Company. Ricardo and Olga had another child, Sergio. Sergio was always very protective of his sister Lourdes. Sergio married Yolanda and had two children, María Cristina and Ernesto. Sergio, Yolanda, María Cristina and Ernesto live in Florida. Ernesto and María Cristina are not married and have no children. María Cristina and Ernesto are Javier's and Alina's only cousins.

Who were Javier's grandparents? His paternal grandparents were Celia and Roberto and his maternal grandparents are Olga and Ricardo. Do Javier and Alina have any cousins? Yes, their cousins are María Cristina and Ernesto. Who is Enrique's mother-in-law? Enrique's mother-in-law is Olga.

4. Una visita al médico

Susana se levantó hoy con un fuerte dolor en el cuello. El dolor era tan intenso que decidió no ir al trabajo. Después de tomar el café llamó a su jefe, Pablo Ramírez, y le dijo que no se sentía bien. Pablo le sugirió a Susana que volviera a llamar a su ortopedista porque probablemente necesitaba un tratamiento de fisioterapia. Susana decidió seguir el consejo de su jefe y llamó a su ortopedista, el doctor Fernando Morales. La secretaria del doctor Morales le dijo que podía pasar a las 11 a. m. porque había recibido una cancelación de última hora. Susana se vistió con mucho cuidado y como no había mucho tráfico, llegó a la oficina del Dr. Morales en media hora.

Susana llevaba meses teniendo dolores de cuello y espalda. Algunas veces también sentía fuertes dolores de cabeza. Susana es una persona que no hace mucho ejercicio. Ella se pasa la mayor parte del tiempo en su escritorio en la oficina o en el sofá de su casa mirando la televisión.

Al llegar a la oficina, la secretaria la admitió enseguida ya que no había nadie en la sala de espera. El Dr. Morales, siempre tan entusiasta, la saludó con su habitual energía.

Dr. Morales: ¡Qué bueno verla Susana! Hacía días que no la veía.

Susana: Gracias, doctor. El dolor que tengo es increíble. No he mejorado desde la última visita. Realmente se ha puesto peor.

Dr. Morales: ¿Pudo seguir las recomendaciones que le di?

Susana: No voy a mentirle, doctor. No, la verdad es que no he podido. Los ejercicios que me recomendó me toman mucho tiempo. Es casi imposible poder hacerlos. Cuando llego a la casa los niños tienen hambre, hay que preparles la cena y ayudarles con las tareas.

Dr. Morales: Susana, yo entiendo, pero debería intentar hacer los ejercicios por la mañana. ¿A qué hora se van a la escuela?

Susana: El autobús los viene a recoger a las 7.30 de la mañana.

Dr. Morales: ¿Y a qué hora sale usted para el trabajo?

Susana: A las 8.30.

Dr. Morales: ¿Y cuánto tiempo tarda en hacer los ejercicios . . . ?

Susana: Media hora como máximo.

Dr. Morales: Susana . . . ya tiene la solución.

Susana: Sí, doctor, realmente voy a hacer todo lo posible por hacer los ejercicios, realmente no tengo excusa.

Dr. Morales: Además le voy a recetar un analgésico más fuerte y la voy a referir a un fisioterapeuta que conozco que es estupendo. Ya verá que se va a sentir mucho mejor.

Susana: Gracias, doctor. Esta vez voy a seguir sus instrucciones.

Dr. Morales: De nada, Susana. Y también quiero que lea este folleto informativo acerca de la fisioterapia porque seguramente la va ayudar. ¡Hasta luego, Susana!

Susana se marchó de la oficina con su folleto en mano y con una nueva determinación de seguir las instrucciones de su médico. Aquí está el folleto informativo:

Recomendaciones fisioterapéuticas diarias de la Federación Internacional de Fisioterapia

1. Cuide la postura en el puesto de trabajo. Si pasa mucho tiempo sentado, mantenga la espalda contra el respaldo de la silla y tome descansos con regularidad para cambiar de postura y mover las articulaciones. Si trabaja frente a una computadora, procure que los antebrazos no estén encima del teclado para evitar la tendonitis.
2. Haga ejercicios por la mañana para mover las articulaciones.
3. Practique algún tipo de deporte. No importa la cantidad, sino la calidad de lo que se haga.
4. A la hora de levantar pesos, siempre flexione las rodillas y mantenga la espalda recta.
5. Al llevar las bolsas de la compra, reparta el peso entre los dos brazos.

NOTE: Vocabulary words from Situation 4 can be found in the following categories: People, Feelings & Thoughts, Health, Hygiene & Safety, Parts of the Body, Work, and Actions.

A Visit to the Doctor

Susana woke up today with a very strong neck ache. The pain was so intense that she decided not to go to work. After having her cup of coffee she called her boss, Pablo Ramírez, and told him that she was not feeling well. Pablo suggested that she call her orthopedist again because she probably needed a physical therapy treatment. Susana decided to follow her boss's advice and called her orthopedist, Dr. Fernando Morales. The secretary said that she could stop by at 11 a.m. since there was a last minute cancellation. Susana got dressed very carefully and since there was little traffic, she arrived at Dr. Morales' office in a half hour.

Susana had been having strong neck and back pain for months. Sometimes they were accompanied by strong headaches. Susana is someone who does not exercise much. She spends most of her time at her desk in the office or on the sofa in her house watching television.

When she arrived at the doctor's office, the secretary let her in immediately since there was nobody in the waiting room. Dr. Morales, always so enthusiastic, greeted her with his usual high level of energy.

Dr. Morales: It is so good to see you , Susana! I haven't seen you in days.

Susana: Thanks, doctor. The pain that I have now is incredible. I haven't gotten better since the last time I was here. To be truthful, it's gotten worse.

Dr. Morales: Were you able to follow the recommendations that I gave you?

Susana: I won't lie to you, doctor. No, the truth is that I haven't been able to. The exercises that you recommended take too much time. It's almost impossible for me to do them. When I get home the children are hungry, I have to prepare dinner and help them with homework.

Dr. Morales:	Susana, I understand, but you should try to do the exercises in the morning. What time do they leave for school?
Susana:	The bus arrives at 7:30 a.m.
Dr. Morales:	And what time do you leave for work?
Susana:	At 8:30 a.m..
Dr. Morales:	And how long does it take you to do the exercises . . . ?
Susana:	Half an hour, tops.
Dr. Morales:	Susana . . . you already have the solution.
Susana:	Yes, doctor, this time I will try my best to do the exercises, I have no excuse.
Dr. Morales:	Also, I will prescribe a stronger analgesic and I am going to refer you to a physical therapist I know who is great. You'll feel much better, you'll see.
Susana:	Thanks, doctor. This time I will follow your instructions.
Dr. Morales:	You're welcome, Susana. I also want you to read this informational brochure about physical therapy because I am sure you will find it helpful. See you later, Susana!

Susana left the office with brochure in hand and with a new determination to follow her doctor's directions. This is what the brochure looked like:

Daily Physical Therapy Recommendations by the International Physical Therapy Federation

1. Watch your posture at the workplace. If you spend a long time sitting, make sure you keep your back against the chair and stop periodically to change your posture and move your joints. For those who work in front of a computer, make sure that your forearms do not rest on the keyboard, to avoid tendonitis.
2. Exercise in the morning to move the joints.
3. Practice some kind of sport. The quantity is not as important as the quality of what you do.
4. If you have to do heavy lifting, make sure you flex your knees and keep your back straight.
5. When returning from the supermarket, make sure you divide the bags evenly between both arms.

5. Guía Informativa del Banco Atlántico Progreso

El producto del mes en el Banco Atlántico Progreso: Guía Financiera

Seguro que cuando emprende un largo viaje se asegura de llevar un mapa de carreteras. Entonces, ¿no cree que debe hacer lo mismo con sus ahorros?

En muchas ocasiones, cuando hablamos de dinero, resulta complicado elegir el camino a seguir. Entre tantas opciones uno se puede sentir confundido.

En el Banco Atlántico Progreso encontrará la respuesta.

Con nuestra Guía Financiera Banco Atlántico Progreso, podremos analizar su situación económica para ofrecerle diferentes opciones para alcanzar un equilibrio financiero entre el dinero que tiene disponible, el que ha ahorrado y el que ha pedido prestado.

○ Si ha invertido en depósitos todo el dinero reservado para su jubilación, puede estar perdiendo la oportunidad de un mejor futuro para diversificar su dinero.

○ Si tiene un objetivo definido, logrará diversificar su inversión mientras reduce el riesgo.

Tras hacer una cita, le llamaremos para discutir sus necesidades y objetivos financieros y elaborar el Plan de Inversión que le conviene.

Le ayudaremos a encontrar el camino financiero que más le convenga, como si tuviera en sus manos el mejor de los mapas.

Y nuestra ayuda no termina ahí. Continuaremos analizando su plan periódicamente para adaptarlo a sus necesidades. Para más información acuda a su oficina del Banco Atlántico Progreso más cercana.

Otras noticias:

Promoción especial de otoño

Este otoño, cuando use una de las tarjetas de crédito del Banco Atlántico Progreso tendrá la oportunidad de ganar un premio. Sólo tiene que realizar, durante los meses de septiembre y octubre, 3 compras por un importe mínimo de $150 con cualquiera de las tarjetas del Banco Atlántico Progreso. Tendrá la oportunidad de ganar un minirradio, un paraguas o una bufanda. Además, estaremos regalando certificados de compra para artículos de esquí y de baloncesto. Le notificaremos por correo para reclamar el premio.

Ahora nuestras cuentas corrientes son gratis

A partir de este mes, nuestras cuentas corrientes son gratis si decide usar nuestro servicio de depósito directo. Además, si decide usar este conveniente servicio, le daremos acceso a una gran variedad de opciones y productos financieros.

○ Consulta financiera gratis

○ Dos tarjetas de crédito: una para usted y otra para un miembro de su familia

○ Ningún cargo para garantizar la mínima tasa de interés hipotecario

○ El mejor interés en Certificados de Depósitos

○ Acceso a una variedad de fondos mutulistas, acciones y bonos del estado

○ Nuestro prestigioso servicio de calidad "Cliente Primero"

NOTE: Vocabulary words from Situation 5 can be found in the following categories: Money & Banking, Transportation, Around Town, and Clothing.

Banco Atlántico Progreso Informational Brochure — Newsletter

Product of the month at Banco Atlántico Progreso: Financial Guide

We're certain that when you start a long trip you make sure to bring a road map. Don't you think you should do the same with your savings?

Many times, when it comes to money, it's difficult to choose the right road. With so many options you might find yourself feeling confused.

You can find the right answer in Banco Atlántico Progreso.

With our unique Banco Atlántico Progreso Financial Guide, we will be able to analyze your financial situation to offer you the different options in order to reach the right balance between the money that you already have, the money you have saved and the money that you have borrowed.

- If you have all your retirement money invested in regular deposits, you might be losing out on the opportunity of a better future by diversifying your money.

- If you have a defined objective, you will be able to diversify your investments while reducing your risk level.

After you make an appointment with us, we will call you to discuss your financial situation and objectives and elaborate the Investment Plan that suits your needs.

We will help you find the financial road that is best for you, as if you had in your hands the best of road maps.

And our help doesn't end there. We will continue to analyze your plan periodically in order to adapt it to your needs. For more information, visit your nearest Banco Atlántico Progreso branch.

Other news:

Special Promotion for the Fall Season
This fall, when you use one of our Banco Atlántico Progreso credit cards, you will have the opportunity to win a prize. You only have to make three purchases of at least $150 during the months of September and October using any of the Banco Atlántico Progreso credit cards. You will have the opportunity to win a mini radio, an umbrella, or a scarf. In addition to that, we will give away gift certificates for skiing and basketball equipment. You will be notified by mail to claim the prizes.

Our checking accounts are now free

Starting this month, our checking accounts are free of service charge if you decide to use direct deposit. Also, if you decide to use this convenient service, we will give you access to a great variety of options and financial products.

- Free Financial Consultation

- Up to two credit cards for yourself and another family member

- No charge for locking a low mortgage interest rate

- The best rate on our Certificates of Deposit

- Access to all of our mutual funds, stocks and bonds

- Our prestigious quality service "Client First"

6. Buscando una casa nueva

Nancy y Benjamín son un matrimonio del estado de Ohio que está de visita por la costa mediterránea de España. Nancy y Benjamín están en el área de Barcelona buscando una casa o un apartamento. Desde hace años habían decidido comprar otra propiedad en la costa mediterránea cerca de Barcelona. Benjamín lleva seis meses jubilado. Ellos habían decidido que después de la jubilación se pasarían los meses del invierno cerca de la playa.

Nancy y Benjamín llegaron ayer a Barcelona. Después de un día de descanso, alquilaron un coche y fueron en dirección sur hasta llegar al pueblo costero de Sitges. El pueblo de Sitges siempre les había llamado la atención por estar muy cerca de la ciudad. En solamente media hora están en el centro de la ciudad de Barcelona, ya sea en tren o en coche. También les gustaba el hecho de que aunque era un pequeño pueblo pintoresco, mantenía una vitalidad muy grande.

Como son extranjeros y no saben mucho castellano, no sabían cómo comenzar la búsqueda del apartamento. Lo único que Nancy tenía por seguro era que en España (contrario a Latinoamérica) a los apartamentos se les conocía por el término "piso". Decidieron no preocuparse mucho y se fueron a tomar un descanso de mediodía para disfrutar de la típica paella española y una sangría.

Al salir del restaurante se encontraron un folleto informativo que les iba a resultar muy útil. Después de leer el folleto, Nancy y Benjamín se sintieron mucho mejor . . . la búsqueda del apartamento iba a ser mucho más fácil de lo que se imaginaban.

AGENCIA INMOBILIARIA SITGES MARINO INTERNACIONAL

- Nos especializamos en compras y ventas con personas en el extranjero.

- Asistencia legal con las leyes de inmobiliaria.

- Expertos en asuntos de impuestos internacionales.

- Servicio rápido, experto y conveniente.

- Se habla castellano, catalán, inglés, francés e italiano.

Nuestra directora Victoria Hutton comprende sus necesidades. Victoria se mudó de Londres a Sitges hace diez años y pronto se convirtió en experta en los asuntos inmobiliarios que les interesan a los extranjeros. Llámenos para concretar una cita.

Aquí tenemos algunas de nuestras últimas ofertas.

CASA EN UNA SOLA PLANTA

Con jardín, 2 salones, chimenea, 2 habitaciones, cocina, baño trasero. 123.000€

DÚPLEX SEMINUEVO Penthouse

3 habitaciones, estudio, comedor, cocina, 2 baños, 2 terrazas, calefacción central. 240.000€

PISO EN EL CENTRO

4 habitaciones, cocina, totalmente restaurado, dos balcones. 236.000€

CASA DE 200 m²

Cerca de la estación de tren, ideal para parejas, cocina y comedor. 117.000€

PISO ÁTICO DE 65 m²

2 habitaciones, comedor con cocina, suelo parquet, puertas de roble, ventanas de aluminio, balcón. Precioso. 199.000€

ZONA DE VILANOVA

Piso de 95 m², salón inmenso, baño con ducha, cocina grande, calefacción, ascensor, aparcadero. 237.900€

ESTUPENDA CASA NUEVA

Magnífica casa de 240 m², 4 plantas, 5 habitaciones, 3 baños, aseo, cocina, oficina, jardín, barbacoa, 2 terrazas, cerca del centro. 319.000€

MAGNÍFICA CASA NUEVA

Superficie de 300 m² y 133 m² de jardín. Garaje para dos coches, comedor con chimenea, tres habitaciones, estudio, mármol en escaleras, electrodomésticos en la cocina. 455.200€

ÁTICO NUEVO

Zona céntrica, amplio salón, cocina y baños restaurados, terraza, ascensor, cerca de la estación, vista a la ciudad y al mar. 154.400€

Llámenos . . .

- ◦ Si está interesado en comprar o vender su propiedad.

- ◦ Si quiere encontrar asesoramiento en la financiación de su compra, solucionar trámites legales.

- Si le interesa tener acceso a más de mil viviendas.

- Si desea tener la más baja comisión de venta en el mercado.

- Si quiere tener el mejor servicio con el mejor equipo de especialistas.

Visítenos en nuestra oficina en la Plaza Central; la casa de sus sueños le espera.

NOTE: Vocabulary words from Situation 6 can be found in the following categories: Around the House, Around Town, Vacation, Food & Cooking, and Transportation.

Looking for a New House

Nancy and Benjamin are a couple from Ohio visiting the Mediterranean coast of Spain. Nancy and Benjamin are in the Barcelona area looking for a house or an apartment. They had decided many years ago to buy another property on the Mediterranean coast near Barcelona. Benjamin retired six months ago. They had decided that after his retirement they would spend the winter months near the beach.

Nancy and Benjamin arrived yesterday in Barcelona. After a day of rest, they rented a car and drove to the south until they reached the coastal town of Sitges. The town of Sitges had always interested them because it was very close to the city. In only a half hour they could be in the center of Barcelona via train or car. They also liked the fact that even though it was a small picturesque town, it remained very vibrant.

Being foreigners and not having a good command of Spanish, they didn't know how to start searching for an apartment. The only thing that Nancy was certain of was that in Spain (unlike Latin America) the term used to refer to apartments was "piso" instead of "apartamento." They decided not to worry about it too much and take a mid-day break to have a traditional Spanish paella and some sangria.

As they were leaving the restaurant they found an informational brochure that would turn out to be very helpful. After reading the brochure Nancy and Benjamin felt much better . . . the search for the apartment was going to be much easier than they expected.

SITGES MARINO INTERNACIONAL REAL ESTATE AGENCY

- Our specialty is purchase and sales to foreigners.

- Assistance with international real estate law.

- We are experts in dealing with international taxes.

- Fast, expert and convenient service.

- Spanish, Catalonian, English, French, and Italian spoken.

Our director Victoria Hutton understands your needs. Victoria moved from London to Sitges ten years ago and soon became an expert in the real estate issues that concern foreigners. Call us to make an appointment.

Here are some of our latest offerings.

ONE LEVEL HOUSE

With garden, 2 living rooms, fireplace, 2 bedrooms, kitchen, bathroom in the back. 123,000€

SEMI NEW DUPLEX PENTHOUSE

3 bedrooms, studio, dining room, kitchen, 2 bathrooms, 2 terraces, central heating. 240,000€

APARTMENT IN THE CENTER OF TOWN SQUARE

4 bedrooms, kitchen, totally renovated, 2 balconies. 236,000€

200 m² HOUSE

Near the train station, ideal for couples, kitchen and living room. 117,000€

65 m² APARTMENT IN THE ATTIC

2 bedrooms, dining room with kitchen, parquet floors, oak doors, aluminum windows, balcony. Beautiful. 199,000€

AREA OF VILANOVA

95 m² apartment, huge living room, bathroom with shower, large kitchen, heating, elevator and parking. 237,900€

GREAT NEW HOUSE

Great house of 240 m², 4 levels, 5 bedrooms, 3 bathrooms, half bathroom, kitchen, office, garden, 2 terraces, near the center of town. 319,000€

MAGNIFICENT NEW HOUSE

Area of 300 m² plus a garden of 133 m². Garage for two cars, dining room with fireplace, three bedrooms, studio, marble staircase, all kitchen appliances. 455,200€

NEW ATTIC

Centrally located, large living room, renovated kitchen and bathrooms, terrace, elevator, near the station, view to the ocean and the city. 154,400€

Call us . . .

- If you are interested in buying or selling your home
- If you want to find help in financing your purchase and guide you with legal documentation

○ If you are interested in having access to over one thousand homes

○ If you want to have the lowest commission in the market

○ If you want the best service with the best team of specialists

Visit us in our office in the Town Square, the house of your dreams is waiting for you . . .

7. El fin de semana de Raúl

Raúl estaba muy cansado y tenía muchas ganas de que llegara el fin de semana. Llevaba dos semanas trabajando sin descansar. Lo que más le llamaba la atención era pasarse todo el sábado en la playa con sus amigos. Raúl miró el pronóstico del tiempo en el periódico. El pronóstico decía lo siguiente:

Nubes en el área norte que se irán desplazando hacia nuestra área esta noche. Para mañana sábado estará muy nublado, con tormentas esporádicas. Para el domingo continuará la nubosidad y habrá nubes bajas a primera hora de la mañana. Por la tarde del domingo continuarán las precipitaciones. Los vientos serán fuertes en el sureste de la costa. Neblina por la mañana del lunes. Las temperaturas continuarán bajas hasta principios de la semana. Las precipitaciones serán más fuertes en las áreas costeras.

Efectivamente, no iba a ser un buen fin de semana para ir a la playa. Raúl llamó a sus amigos y les informó que la idea de ir a la playa tenía que ser pospuesta. Se le ocurrió la idea de ir al cine. Miró la cartelera en el periódico para ver qué películas iban a exhibir en los cines de su pueblo. La descripción de las películas decía lo siguiente:

28 días después

Un extraño virus liberado de un laboratorio de investigación ha acabado con la población del planeta y la raza humana se enfrenta a su extinción.

Ciudad de Dios

Trayectoria de 20 años en la vida de dos niños que viven en la Ciudad de Dios, un suburbio de Río de Janeiro.

El libro de la selva 2

En su nueva vida en el poblado, Mowgli, aunque siente que lo quieren, echa de menos a sus amigos Baloo y Bagheera.

Boda del monzón

Relato de la sociedad actual de Nueva Delhi. La película usa la celebración de la boda entre Aditi y Hemant para narrar las contradicciones de tipo moral y social en la India actual.

Réquiem por un sueño

Una viuda adquiere una peligrosa adicción a píldoras para el adelgazamiento. Su hijo, junto con su novia y su mejor amigo, se lanzan con éxito a la venta de drogas.

Simbad, la leyenda de los siete mares

Simbad y Marina se unirán para salvar la vida de Proteus, derrocar a la diosa Eris y rescatar el Libro de la Paz.

Raúl llamó a todos sus amigos y les dijo qué películas estaban exhibiendo en los cines del pueblo. Pero nadie se puso de acuerdo. José había visto cuatro de las películas, a Carolina solamente le interesaba ver una, Roberto no quería ir al cine y Carmen solamente podía ir a la función de la tarde.

Raúl es un fanático de los deportes en la televisión. Volvió a mirar el periódico y encontró la mejor manera de pasar el fin de semana: frente al televisor.

Aquí está la guía de deportes por televisión:

Viernes

Atletismo	Campeonato del Mundo de Atletismo en París: Canal 2, 15 horas.
Tenis	Abierto de Estados Unidos en Nueva York, hasta el domingo: Canal 5, 20 horas.
Fútbol	Trofeo Villa de Madrid. Atlético de Madrid: Boca Juniors. Canal 4, 21 horas

Sábado

Golf	Circuito Europeo. Open: Canal Golf, 15 horas.
Fútbol	Supercopa de España: Campeonato del Mundo—Canal 2, 16 horas
Baloncesto	Torneo Europeo, Polonia contra Alemania: Canal 5, 21 horas

Domingo

Béisbol	Campeonato Internacional, Japón contra Estados Unidos: Canal 2, 15 horas
Gimnasia	Eliminatoria Europea (Noruega, Finlandia, Italia, Suiza, Suecia): Canal 5, 22 horas
Atletismo	Campeonato del Mundo (Canadá, México, Austria, Portugal): Canal 4, 22 horas

NOTE: Vocabulary words from Situation 7 can be found in the following categories: Sports & Leisure, Entertainment & Media, the Natural World, and Actions.

Raúl's Weekend

Raúl was very tired and was looking forward to the weekend. He had spent two weeks working nonstop. He was interested in spending Saturday on the beach with his friends. Raúl checked the weather forecast in the newspaper. The forecast read like this:

There will be clouds in the northern area that will move to our area overnight. It will be very cloudy tomorrow Saturday, with irregular storms. Sunday will continue to be cloudy and there will be low clouds in the first hours of the morning. Sunday afternoon will have more precipitation. The winds will be stronger in the south east of the coast. There will be fog on Monday morning. The temperatures will remain low until the beginning of the week. All precipitation will be higher near the coastal areas.

It was not going to be a good weekend for the beach. Raúl called his friends and told them that the plans to go to the beach had to be postponed. It occurred to him to go to the movies. He looked in the newspaper to see which movies were playing in his town. Here is the description of the movies playing near him:

28 Days Later

A strange virus that escaped from a laboratory has exterminated the human population in the planet and human race faces extinction.

City of God

The story of 20 years in the lives of two children who live in the City of God, a suburb of Rio de Janeiro.

The Jungle Book 2

In his new life in the new town, Mowgli feels loved but he misses his friends Baloo and Bagheera.

Monsoon Wedding

Tale of present day society in New Delhi. The movie uses the wedding between Adity and Hemant to expose the moral and social contradictions in present day India.

Requiem for a Dream

A widow becomes addicted to dangerous dieting pills. Her son, along with his girlfriend and best friend, become successful drug dealers.

Sinbad, the Legend of the Seven Seas

Sinbad and Marina unite to save the life of Proteus, defeat the goddess Eris and rescue the Book of Peace.

Raúl called all his friends and told them which movies were showing in the theaters in town. But nobody could agree on anything. José had seen four of the movies, Carolina only wanted to see one, Roberto didn't want to go to the movies, and Carmen could only go to the afternoon showing.

Raúl loves to watch sports on television. He looked in the newspaper again and found the best way to spend this weekend: in front of the television. Here is the TV sports schedule:

Friday

Track & Field	World Track and Field Championship from Paris—Channel 2, 3 p.m.
Tennis	U.S. Open from New York, until Sunday—Channel 5, 8 p.m.
Soccer	Trophy of the Madrid Region. Madrid's Atlético-Boca Juniors—Channel 4, 9 p.m.

Saturday

Golf	European Circuit. Open—Golf Channel, 3 p.m.
Soccer	Spain Supercup—World Championship—Channel 2, 4 p.m.
Basketball	European Tournament—Poland—Germany—Channel 5, 9 p.m.

Sunday

Baseball	International Championship—Japan—USA—Channel 2, 3 p.m.
Gymnastics	European tryouts—Norway—Finland—Switzerland—Sweden—Channel 5, 10 p.m.
Track & Field	World Championship—Canada—Mexico—Austria—Portugal—Channel 4, 10 p.m.

8. Nuevo trabajo, más estudios

Francisco había trabajado como periodista durante muchos años en un periódico. Solamente tenía una licenciatura en periodismo. Pero Francisco tenía muchos deseos de hacer un cambio profesional. Su sueño siempre había sido ser reportero de televisión. Además, desde muy pequeño había sido aficionado a las ciencias y a la salud. Cuando Francisco vio la siguiente oferta de trabajo, donde se combinaba el periodismo con las ciencias, se decidió a continuar con sus estudios. Todo lo que le faltaba era un máster en periodismo.

EMPLEADO DE TIEMPO COMPLETO
Industria: Radiodifusión y transmisión televisiva
Tipo de trabajo: Periodismo
Requisitos educativos: Máster en periodismo
Requisitos de experiencia: Al menos 3 años
Necesidad de viajar: Mínima
Compensación por mudanza: No

OTROS REQUISITOS
La estación de mayor audiencia en la ciudad de San Juan busca a un reportero de salud y medicina. Los candidatos deben poseer dominio absoluto para transmitir noticias en directo además de escribir y redactar reportajes. Es su responsabilidad desarrollar artículos médicos; desde la investigación hasta la escritura y transmisión en directo. Se espera que el candidato pueda manifestar la imagen y la cultura de profesionalismo de la emisora.

Francisco había obtenido un folleto de la Universidad Regional de Puerto Rico donde se anunciaba la posibilidad de terminar un máster en periodismo en el transcurso de un año. Francisco se dio cuenta de que si quería seguir adelante en su carrera profesional, tendría que continuar con sus estudios.

Escuela de periodismo Máster en periodismo

La escuela de periodismo de la Universidad Regional de Puerto Rico anuncia que su plazo de inscripción para las pruebas de admisión al próximo curso quedará abierto en el mes de octubre.

Los estudios seguidos en la escuela permiten optar al título de "Máster en periodismo".

El número de plazas es limitado y los aspirantes han de realizar una serie de pruebas selectivas. Se requiere ser licenciado por cualquier Facultad Universitaria o, en el caso de extranjeros, poseer un título equivalente.

Becas y financiación: La fundación de la escuela ofrece siete becas por el importe completo de la matrícula a aquellas personas que las hayan solicitado y obtengan las mejores calificaciones en las pruebas de selección. También, todos aquellos que lo deseen pueden acogerse al acuerdo de préstamos, de interés reducido y financiación hasta cinco años, que la escuela de periodismo ha venido manteniendo con el Banco Santillana de Puerto Rico.

Plan de estudio: Las enseñanzas del Máster son fundamentalmente prácticas, aplicadas al periodismo impreso, radiofónico y electrónico. El curso, de un año de duración, se imparte de lunes a viernes, de diez de la mañana a ocho y media de la noche, en unas instalaciones propias, situadas en el mismo edificio donde se publica el periódico La Vanguardia, lo que permite a los alumnos tener acceso a medios técnicos, fuentes informativas y los archivos del periódico.

La escuela tiene tres redacciones informatizadas, un estudio de radio, un aula de proyección y cubículos de estudio.

Es obligatorio que los alumnos realicen en los meses de verano prácticas remuneradas en medios informativos. Durante el presente curso, la totalidad de los alumnos ha podido realizar dichas prácticas en distintos medios y canales de televisión.

Más información: El folleto informativo y la solicitud de inscripción están disponibles en nuestra página web.

La oficina de admisiones dará más información a partir del día 4 de septiembre.

NOTE: Vocabulary words from Situation 8 can be found in the following categories: Work, School, and Entertainment & Media.

New Job, More Studying

Francisco had worked as a journalist in a newspaper for many years. His highest degree was a B.A in Journalism. But Francisco was very eager to make a career change. His dream had always been to be a television reporter. Also, as a child he had always shown great interest in science and health issues. When Francisco saw the following job offer, one that combined journalism with science, he decided that it was time to continue with his studies. What he needed now was to finish a Master's in Journalism.

FULL TIME EMPLOYEE
Industry: Broadcasting, Radio and Television
Job Type: Journalism
Required Education: Master's in Journalism
Required Experience: At least 3 years
Required Travel: Minimum
Relocation Covered: No

OTHER REQUIREMENTS
The station with the greatest audience in the city of San Juan is seeking a Health and Medicine Reporter. Candidates must possess an absolute command of live news delivery in addition to writing and editing news stories. It is the job's responsibility to develop medical stories; from researching to the writing and live broadcast. The candidate is expected to effectively project the station's professionalism and image.

Francisco had gotten a brochure from the Regional University of Puerto Rico where they announced the possibility of finishing a Master's Degree in Journalism in only one year. Francisco realized that if he was to go ahead with his professional career, he needed to continue with his studies.

Department of Journalism Master's Degree in Journalism

The School of Journalism of the Regional University of Puerto Rico announces that the enrollment period for the admission test for the new academic year will be offered during the month of October.

The course of study that the school offers will lead you to the title of "Master's in Journalism."

Enrollment is limited and all candidates must pass a series of enrollment tests. The minimum requirement is to hold a Bachelor's Degree from any accredited college; foreign students must have a similar type of degree.

Scholarships and Financial Aid: The school offers seven scholarships that cover all tuition to those students who request financial aid and achieve the highest scores in the enrollment tests. In addition to this, all students who are interested may request student loans; these loans of low interest rate and five-year financing period are handled by Banco Santillana of Puerto Rico, in conjunction with the School of Journalism.

Course Plan: The courses offered in the Master program have a practical approach, applied to print, radio, television and internet reporting. The course lasts one year; classes are held Monday to Friday, from 10 a.m. to 8:30 p.m., in our own facilities located in the same building where La Vanguardia newspaper is printed; this would allow students to have access to technical facilities, news sources and the archives of the newspaper.

The school has three computerized editorial offices, a broadcast studio, a screening room and classrooms.

It is mandatory that students spend the summer months doing paid work onsite. During the current year, all of our students have had the opportunity to work in different news outlets and news channels.

For more information: The informational brochure and the application are also available on our website.

The Admissions Office will release more information on September 4th.

9. Las nuevas ciudades españolas (artículo de La Gaceta de la Capital)
"Las nuevas ciudades españolas" de La Gaceta de la Capital, 3 de octubre

Ciudades como Amsterdam, Nueva York y Londres siempre han sido un verdadero crisol de culturas. Las ciudades españolas nunca vieron un gran flujo de inmigración, pero esto ha ido cambiando dramáticamente durante la última década. Hace unos años, cuando uno anunciaba que se iba de viaje a París o Londres, siempre se recibía el consejo de algún amigo que decía: "Cuando estés en el metro mantén abiertos los oídos y los ojos, vas a encontrar mucha gente de todo el mundo". Estas ciudades estaban marcadas por la mezcla de culturas, razas y costumbres.

Ahora, en la capital de Madrid ya estamos en esa fase. En el centro de la ciudad, en los metros y en las plazas podemos encontrar este crisol que ha hecho cambiar la dinámica social y cultural de la capital. Hay unos rasgos muy concretos en la evolución, situación y tendencias de la inmigración en Madrid. La provincia sigue siendo la de mayor número de extranjeros del territorio nacional. En el último censo del año 2002 se contabilizaban 291.866 extranjeros con permiso de residencia, el 22,4% del total de extranjeros residentes en España (1.301.342). Lo que más llama la atención es la increíble mezcla de culturas. No es solamente una inmigración latinoamericana que se beneficia del poder hablar la misma lengua. Además de los inmigrantes de las Américas existe un considerable número de extranjeros procedente de Africa, Asia y Europa Oriental. Los ecuatorianos representan el mayor grupo de extranjeros con un total de 126.000 habitantes. En segundo lugar se encuentran los colombianos con 58.000 habitantes, seguidos por marroquíes (53.000) y rumanos (31.000). Entre otros grupos considerables de extranjeros se encuentran peruanos, dominicanos, portugueses, argentinos, chinos, filipinos, polacos, cubanos, ucranianos y nigerianos.

Y Madrid no es la única ciudad que ha demostrado un gran crecimiento poblacional extranjero. Barcelona, la segunda ciudad española, ha seguido un patrón muy similar. Se calcula que hay un total de 163.898 extranjeros viviendo en la ciudad. Como en el caso de Madrid, el mayor número de extranjeros son procedentes del Ecuador, con un 16,5% del total de inmigrantes en la ciudad.

Donde mejor se puede ver este crisol es lógicamente en el metro. Sentado en el vagón de la línea uno del metro de Madrid llegando a la estación de la Puerta del Sol me encuentro con una chica alta y rubia leyendo una novela en ruso. A su lado tiene a dos jóvenes chinas que se están contando la vida con todo detalle. Al otro lado, una mujer argentina le grita a su hijo que se quite de la puerta. Me dirijo a hacer el trasbordo con el tren de la línea dos en dirección a Ventas. Mientras espero el tren, me encuentro a dos chicos ecuatorianos con sus camisetas de fútbol. Al otro lado hay una chica marroquí que mezcla árabe y castellano cuando le dice a su amiga que el tren está retrasado.

Y es que hemos cambiado mucho como ciudad. Ya no somos la misma ciudad provinciana de antes. Somos ahora una ciudad mucho más cosmopolita, internacional, que se siente orgullosa de mirar hacia adelante.

NOTE: Vocabulary words from Situation 9 can be found in the following categories: People, Family & Relationships, Human Society, Social Problems & Controversial Issues, Around Town, and Transportation.

The New Spanish Cities (article taken from La Gaceta de la Capital)
"The New Spanish Cities" from La Gaceta de la Capital, October 3

Cities like Amsterdam, New York and London have long been true melting pots. Spanish cities never saw a considerable influx of immigration, but this has been changing dramatically over the past decade. Only a few years ago, after telling a friend about an upcoming trip to Paris or London I always took their advice when they said: "When you are traveling by subway keep your ears and eyes open; you will find people from everywhere." These cities were known for the mixture of many cultures, races and customs.

Now Madrid is in that phase. In the center of the city, on the subways and town squares you can find that melting pot that has changed the social and cultural dynamics of the capital. There is a very concrete pattern to the evolution, stage and tendency of immigration to Madrid. The province of Madrid is still the one with the most immigrants in the whole country. The last census figures from 2002 show that there were 291,866 legal residents of foreign nationalities, 22.4% of all foreigners residing in Spain (1,301,342). What is more interesting is the incredible mixture of cultures.

The immigration trend is not confined to Latin American immigrants who benefit from being able to speak the language. In addition to migrants from the Americas, there is a considerable number of foreigners from Africa, Asia and Eastern Europe. Ecuadorians are the most numerous with a total of 126,000 inhabitants. Colombians are in second place with a total of 58,000, followed by Moroccans (53,000) and Romanians (31,000). Among the other large groups of foreigners there are Peruvians, Dominicans, Portuguese, Argentines, Chinese, Filipinos, Poles, Cubans, Ukrainians and Nigerians.

And Madrid is not the only city that has shown an increase in immigration. Barcelona, the second largest city in size, has followed a similar pattern. It is estimated that there are 163,898 foreigners living in Barcelona. As is the case with Madrid, most foreigners are from Ecuador, with a total of 16.5% of the city's immigrants.

Logically, the best place to notice this new melting pot is on the subway. Sitting on the subway car on the number one line as I approach the Puerta del Sol station in Madrid, I notice a tall blonde girl reading a novel in Russian. Next to her there are two Chinese girls telling each other about their lives in great detail. On the other side, an Argentine woman yells at her son asking him to stay away from the subway door. I walk over to make a transfer to the number two subway line in the direction of Ventas. As I wait for the train, I find two young Ecuadorian men wearing their national soccer jerseys. On the other side there is a Moroccan girl who mixes Arabic and Spanish as she tells her friend that the train is delayed.

The truth is that we have changed a great deal as a city. We are no longer the same provincial city of yesterday. We are now a much more cosmopolitan, international city that feels proud as it looks to the future.

10. Ordenando equipo para el trabajo

Pablo Ruiz había sido nombrado administrador de servicios de una pequeña firma de servicios de referencias de abogados. Una de sus primeras asignaciones es actualizar el equipo de la oficina que se ha quedado anticuado por la negligencia de muchos años. Está interesado en cambiar las computadoras de la oficina y en comprar una impresora que tenga un escáner integrado. También quiere conseguir un nuevo proveedor de servicios de Internet. Sus empleados están teniendo dificultades con la lenta conexión que tienen ahora; sienten que el equipo y la conexión no son adecuados para sus necesidades.

Pablo decidió buscar alguna oferta de servicios de Internet para pequeñas empresas. En la revista Mensual para Abogados encontró un anuncio publicitario que le llamó la atención. El anuncio era de una nueva compañía de telecomunicaciones llamada Colombia Online.

El anuncio decía:

¿Le gustaría que su empresa tuviera veinte horas gratis a la semana para navegar en Internet?
Colombia Online "El acceso rápido a Internet de calidad"

Visite www.colombiaonline.info y apúntese a la promoción. Obtenga veinte horas a la semana para navegar gratis. Ideal para su presupuesto porque pensamos en las necesidades de las pequeñas empresas. Además, no tendrá que perder más tiempo con las conexiones lentas. Nuestro servicio es el más rápido del mercado.

¡No pierda tiempo y apúntese ya!

La semana siguiente Pablo tenía ya instalada la conexión rápida de Internet en su oficina. El siguiente paso sería hacer una búsqueda por Internet para hacer un pedido de equipo informático de oficina. Decidió hacer las compras por la red porque no tenía mucho tiempo para citas y visitas de vendedores.

Lo que más le hacía falta era una impresora con escáner. Escribió la palabra *impresora* en el encasillado de búsqueda e hizo clic. Lo que encontró era exactamente lo que estaba buscando.

Impresora con escáner. Nuevo precio $129 Ahorra $45. Imprime, escanea y copia.
Impresora: Resolución de 2400 puntos por pulgada en color y 600x600 en blanco y negro, 10 páginas por minuto, bandeja para 100 hojas. Conexión USB.
Escáner: Resolución 600x600 por pulgada.
Copiadora: 8 páginas por minuto

También estaba interesado en comprar computadoras nuevas para la oficina. Su búsqueda le dio el siguiente resultado:

Computadora Titanio. Nuevo precio $1219. Ahorra $129.
Procesador: 2,4 GHz
Memoria de 512 MB
Disco duro 160 Gb
Tarjeta gráfica 128 MB
Reproductor DVD y CD
Módem de fax 56 KB
Teclado multimedia
Ratón
Altavoces
Monitor
Garantía de 1 año

Finalmente ordenó una computadora portátil que necesitaba para sus viajes.

Computadora Portátil Mercurio. Nuevo precio $1299. Ahorra $300.
Procesador 2,6 GHz
Memoria 512 MB
Disco duro 40 Gb
Disquetera interna
Sonido 3D y micrófono
Batería litio
Módem interno 56K
Impresora, sólo $119

NOTE: Vocabulary words from Situation 10 can be found in the following categories: Work and Computers & The Internet.

Ordering New Equipment at Work

Pablo Ruiz was recently hired as the service administrator in a small lawyer referral firm. One of his first assignments is to update the outdated office equipment due to years of neglect. He wants to focus on changing the computers being used in the office as well as buying a new printer with scanning capabilities. He is also determined to find a new high speed Internet service provider. His employees are struggling with the slow speed of the current slow connection; they feel that the equipment and the connection are no longer adequate for their needs.

Pablo decided to look for special deals designed for small emerging companies. He looked in the magazine Lawyers Monthly and found an advertisement that caught his eye. The ad was from a new telecommunications company called Colombia Online.

The ad read:

Would you like your small company to have twenty free hours of Internet access per week?
Colombia Online : The fastest and best Internet Provider

Go to www.colombiaonline.info and sign up for this offer. Get twenty free hours per week to surf the web. Ideal for your budget because we keep the needs of small businesses in mind. You will never have to waste time with slow connections. Our service is the fastest in the market.

Don't waste time and sign up now!

The following week Pablo had the service installed in all the computers and rooms of his office. The next step would be to search the web to find a good offer for office equipment. He decided to order online since he did not have much time for appointments and meetings with salespeople.

What he needed the most was a printer with scanner. He typed in the word printer on the search box and hit click. What he found was exactly what he needed.

Printer with scanner. New price $129. Save $45. Printer, scanner, and copier.
Printer: 2400 pixel per inch resolution in color and 600x600 in black and white, 10 pages per minute, 100 page paper tray. USB connection.

Scanner: 600x600 pixel per inch resolution

Copier: 8 pages per minute

He was also interested in buying new computers for his office. His search yielded this model:

Titanium Computer. New price $1219. Save $129.

Processor: 2.4 GHz

512 MB Memory

160 Gb Hard drive

128 MB Graphics Card

DVD and CD recorder

56 KB Fax Modem

Multimedia Keyboard

Mouse

Speakers

Monitor

One year warranty

Finally he ordered a laptop computer which he needed for his business trips.

Mercury Laptop Computer. New Price $1299. Save $300.

2.6 GHz Processor

512 MB Memory

40 Gb Hard drive

Internal Disk Drive

3D sound with microphone

Lithium Battery

56Kb Internal Modem

Printer only $119

Part III

Guide to
Spanish Prefixes

Familiarizing yourself with the meanings of various prefixes in Spanish can help you recognize the meanings of other words you may not have come across yet in your studies. You will find that many prefixes are very similar in Spanish and English, as in both languages, most of them come from Greek and Latin.

ante—*before*

antemano—*beforehand*
(mano—*hand*)
Él me había dado la noticia de antemano. *He had given me the news beforehand.*

antebrazo—*forearm*
(brazo—*arm*)
Me lastimé el antebrazo jugando tenis. *I injured my forearm playing tennis.*

Other cases:
anteojos—*glasses*
(ojos—*eyes*)

anteanoche—*the night before last*
(noche—*night*)

anteayer—*the day before yesterday*
(ayer—*yesterday*)

anteponer—*to place in front of*
(poner—*to place, to put*)

anti—*against*

anticuerpo—*antibody*
(cuerpo—*body*)
Los anticuerpos ayudan a defender el cuerpo contra las infecciones. *Antibodies help the body fight infections.*

antihistamínico—*antihistamine*
(histamínico—*histamine*)
El médico me recetó un antihistamínico para el resfriado. *The doctor prescribed an antihistamine for my cold.*

auto—*self*

autodeterminación—*self-determination*
(determinación—*determination*, determinar—*to determine*)
En las Naciones Unidas se discute la autodeterminación política del país. *The political self determination of the country is being discussed now at the United Nations.*

autógrafo—*autograph*
(grafía—*graphic*, autografiar—*to autograph*)
Ella estaba muy cansada para firmar autógrafos. *She was too tired to sign autographs.*

Other cases:
autocrítica—*self-criticism*
(crítica—*criticism*, criticar—*to criticize*)

autobiografía—*autobiography*
(biografía—*biography*, biográfico—*biographical*)

---

bi—*two*

bicicleta—*bicycle*
(ciclo—*cycle*)
Ella va al trabajo en bicicleta. *She takes her bicycle to work.*

bilingüe—*bilingual*
(lengua—*tongue, language*)
Cuando tenga niños, quiero que sean bilingües. *When I have children, I want them to be bilingual.*

Other cases:
bifocal—*bifocal*
(foco—*focus*)

bimensual—*twice, monthly*
(mensual—*monthly*)

binocular—*binocular*
(ocular—*eye, ocular*)

---

cent—*hundred*

centígrado—*centigrade*
(grado—*degree*)
¿Cuánto es 65 Fahrenheit en centígrados? *How much is 65 F in centigrade?*

centímetro—*centimeter*
(metro—*meter*)
Hay cien centímetros en un metro. *There are one hundred centimeters in one meter.*

---

contra—*against*

contraataque—*counterattack*
(ataque—*attack*, atacar—*to attack*)
Después de la primera batalla vino el contraataque. *After the first battle came the counterattack.*

contraceptivo—*contraceptive*
(concepción—*conception*)
Los contraceptivos orales revolucionaron la década de los sesenta.
Oral contraceptives were revolutionary in the sixties.

Other cases:
contradecir—*contradict*
(decir—*to tell*)

contraluz—*back light*
(luz—*light*)

contrabando—*contraband*
(bando—*law, party*)

contraportada—*back page*
(portada—*cover*)

contraproducente—*counterproductive*
(producente—*productive*, producir—*to produce*)

contrarrestar—*counteract*
(arrestar—*to arrest*, arresto—*arrest*)

contratiempo—*setback*
(tiempo—*time*)

---

de, des—*undo, diminish*

deformar—*to deform*
(formar—*to form*, deforme—*deformed*)
Ese espejo es muy malo; parece deformar la imagen. *That is a bad mirror, it deforms the figure.*

descortés—*discourteous*
(cortés—*courteous*, cortesía—*courtesy*)
El dependiente de la tienda fue muy descortés conmigo. *The clerk in that store was very discourteous to me.*

Other cases:
desacreditar—*to discredit*
(acreditar—*to give credit*, crédito—*credit*)

desacuerdo—*disagreement*
(acuerdo— *accord*, acordar—*to accord*)

desafortunado—*unfortunate*
(afortunado—*fortunate*, fortuna—*fortune*)

desaparecer—*to disappear*
(aparecer—*to appear*, desaparecido—*disappeared*)

desarmar—*to disarm*
(arma—*arm*, armar—*to arm*)

desechar—*to discard*
(echar—*to throw*, desecho—*waste*)

desembarcar—*to disembark*
(barco—*ship*, embarcar—*to embark*)

desempacar—*to unpack*
(empacar—*to pack*, empaque—*package*)

desgastar—*to wear out*
(gastar—*to waste*, gasto—*expense*)

desgracia—*disgrace*
(gracia—*grace*, desgraciado—*unfortunate*)

desenmascarar—*to unmask*
(máscara—*mask*, enmascarar—*to mask*)

---

entre—*between, among*

entrelazar—*to intertwin*e
(lazo—*ribbon*)
Un equipo de científicos estadounidenses logró entrelazar partículas atómicas. *A team of US scientists managed to intertwine atomic particles.*

entremeter—*to place between*
(meter—*to put*)
Tienes que entremeter esta pieza entre las dos barras. *You have to place this piece between the two bars.*

Other cases:
entreplanta—*mezzanine*
(planta— *plant, floor*)

entreabierto—*ajar*
(abierto—*open*, abrir—*to open*)

---

ex—*former, outside*

excéntrico—*eccentric*
(céntrico—*central*, excentricidad—*eccentricity*)
Él no es un personaje nada común; es muy excéntrico. *He is not a very normal character, he is very eccentric.*

exportar—*to export*
(puerto—*port*, exportación—*export*)
Francia exporta vino a muchos países. *France exports wine to many countries.*

Other cases:
ex marido—*ex-husband*
(marido—*husband*)

ex mujer—*ex-wife*
(mujer—*wife*)

homo—*same*

homófono—*homophone*
(fono—*Greek for sound*)
Los homófonos son las palabras que suenan de la misma manera. *Homophones are words that sound the same way.*

homologar—*to approve*
(logos—*Latin for word*)
Me pidieron que le escriba a mi universidad para poder homologar mi diploma extranjero. *They asked me to write my university in order to approve my foreign diploma.*

Other cases:
homónimo—*homonym*
(onoma—*Latin for name*)

homosexual—*homosexual*
(sexo—*sex*)

i, im, in—*opposite*

inquieto—*restless*
(quieto—*quiet*)
Pedrito siempre está muy inquieto por las mañanas. *Pedrito is always so restless in the morning.*

inmaduro—*immature*
(maduro—*mature*, madurez—*maturity*)
Para su corta edad, es una muchacha muy madura. *For her young age, she is a very mature girl.*

Other cases:
inoportuno—*untimely*
(oportuno—*timely, opportune*)

inmoral—*immoral*
(moral—*moral*, inmoralidad—*immorality*)

inhumano—*inhuman, cruel*
(humano—*human*)

irresistible—*irresistible*
(resistir—*to resist*, resistencia—*resistance*)

irresponsable—*irresponsible*
(responsable—*responsible*, responsabilidad—*responsibility*)

ilegal—*illegal*
(legal—*legal*, ley—*law*)

inter—*between, among*

intercambio—*exchange*
(cambiar—*to change,* cambio—*change*)
En el programa de intercambio hay estudiantes de Australia, Vietnam y
Rusia. *There are students from Australia, Vietnam and Russia in the exchange
program.*

intermedio—*intermediate*
(medio—*middle,* intermediario—*intermediary*)
El curso intermedio es bastante difícil. *The intermediate course is very
difficult.*

Other cases:
interlocutor—*speaker*
(locutor—*announcer*)

intermitente—*intermittent*
(emitir—*to emit*)

internacional—*international*
(nación—*nation*)

mal—*bad*

malentendido—*misunderstanding*
(entendido—*understood,* entender—*to understand*)
Hubo un terrible malentendido entre los dos. *There was a terrible
misunderstanding between the two of us.*

malhablado—*foul-mouthed*
(hablado—*spoken,* hablar—*to speak*)
Es muy malhablado; siempre dice groserías. *He is so foul-mouthed, he's
always cursing.*

Other cases:
malgastar—*to waste*
(gastar—*to spend*)

maltratar—*to mistreat*
(tratar—*to treat, to try,* trato—*treatment*)

mono—*on*

monógamo—*monogamous*
(gamo—*Latin for matrimony*)
Los habitantes de la tribu son monógamos. *The inhabitants of the tribe are
monogamous.*

monografía—*monograph*
(graph—*Greek for to write*)
La monografía que tuve que escribir tenía 60 páginas. *The monograph that
I had to write ended up being 60 pages long.*

Other cases:

monólogo—*monologue*
(logo—*Greek for discourse*)

monopolio—*monopoly*
(poleo—*Latin for to sell*)

monoteísmo—*monotheism*
(zeos—*Greek for god*)

monótono—*monotonous*
(tono—*tone*)

---

para—*for*

paracaídas—*parachute*
(caer—*to fall*, paracaidista—*parachutist*)
El paracaídas abrió más tarde de lo esperado. *The parachute opened later than what was expected.*

parabrisas—*wipers*
(brisa—*breeze*)
Tengo que mandar a arreglar los parabrisas. *I have to have the wipers repaired.*

Other cases:

parachoques—*bumper*
(choque—*crash*, chocar—*to crash*)

paramédico—*paramedic*
(médico—*medic*, medicina—*medicine*)

---

poli—*many*

policlínica—*general hospital*
(clínica—*clinic*)
En ese policlínico tienen muchos médicos especialistas. *They have many specialists in that hospital.*

polideportivo—*sports center*
(deportes—*sports*)
Están construyendo un nuevo polideportivo en mi barrio. *They are building a new sports center in my neighborhood.*

Other cases:

polifacético—*versatile*
(faceta—*facet*)

poligamia—*polygamy*
(gamo—*Greek for matrimony*)

polígono—*polygon*
(gonia—*Greek for angles*)

polígloto—*polyglot*
(glotta—*Greek for language, tongue*)

pre—*before*

prehistoria—*prehistory*
(historia—*history*, prehistórico—*prehistoric*)
La prehistoria termina con la creación de la escritura. *Prehistory ends with the appearance of writing.*

preposición—*preposition*
(posición—*position*)
Las preposiciones sirven para unir diferentes aspectos de una oración. *Prepositions unite different aspects of a sentence.*

Other cases:
predominio—*predominance*
(dominio—*domain*, dominar—*to dominate*)

predecir—*to predict*
(decir—*to tell*)

prejuicio—*prejudice*
(juicio—*judgement*, juzgar—*to judge*)

---

re—*again*

rehacer—*to redo*
(hacer—*to do*)
La maestra le dijo al estudiante que tenía que rehacer el trabajo.
The teacher told the student that he needed to redo his work.

reciclar—*to recycle*
(ciclo—*cycle*, reciclaje—*recycling*)
Todavía existe gente que no hace el intento de reciclar en sus hogares.
There are still people who do not make the effort to recycle in their homes.

Other cases:
recrear—*to recreate*
(crear—*to create*, creación—*creation*)

reforzar—*to reinforce*
(forzar—*to force*, fuerza—*force*)

---

sub—*under*

subestimar—*to underestimate*
(estimar—*to estimate*)
Nunca subestimes las cualidades de otros. *Never underestimate the qualities of others.*

suburbano—*suburban*
(urbano—*urban*)
El tren suburbano tiene una parada cerca de aquí. *The suburban train stops near here.*

Other cases:

subdirector—*subdirector*
(director—*director*, dirigir—*to direct*)

subclase—*subclass*
(clase—*class*, clasificar—*to classify*)

submarino—*submarine*
(marino—*marine*)

subcultura—*subculture*
(cultura—*culture*, cultural—*cultural*)

---

tele—*at a distance*

telegrama—*telegram*
(grama—*Greek for written*)
Hace varias décadas los telegramas eran muy populares. *Telegrams were very popular a few decades ago.*

teléfono—*telephone*
(fone—*Greek for voice*)
Mi teléfono móvil me permite enviar mensajes escritos. *My mobile telephone allows me to send text messages.*

Other cases:

telepatía—*telepathy*
(patía—*Greek for feeling*)

telescopio—*telescope*
(skopeo—*Greek for to observe*)

---

uni—*one*

unificar—*to unify*
(facere—*Latin for to do*)
Hay que unificar los esfuerzos por la paz mundial. *We have to unify our efforts for world peace.*

unilateral—*unilateral*
(lateral—*lateral*, lado—*side*)
La decisión de atacar se tomó de forma unilateral. *The decision to attack was unilateral.*

Other cases:

unisex—*unisex*
(sexo—*sex*)

uniforme—*uniform*
(forma—*form*)

6000+ *Essential Spanish Words* is the perfect supplement
to any **Living Language course including . . .**

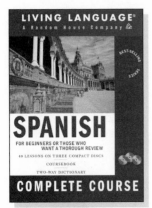

ISBN: 1-4000-2031-X

ISBN: 0-609-81063-4

ISBN: 0-609-81130-4

ISBN: 1-4000-2054-9

ISBN: 1-4000-2119-7

ISBN: 1-4000-2075-1

Available at your local bookseller or
for a complete list of Living Language titles,
please visit our Web site at www.livinglanguage.com